Study Guide

for use with

Principles of Auditing and Other Assurance Services

Fourteenth Edition

O. Ray Whittington
DePaul University

Kurt Pany
Arizona State University

Boston   Burr Ridge, IL   Dubuque, IA   Madison, WI   New York   San Francisco   St. Louis
Bangkok   Bogotá   Caracas   Kuala Lumpur   Lisbon   London   Madrid   Mexico City
Milan   Montreal   New Delhi   Santiago   Seoul   Singapore   Sydney   Taipei   Toronto

Study Guide for use with
PRINCIPLES OF AUDITING AND OTHER ASSURANCE SERVICES
O. Ray Whittington and Kurt Pany

Published by McGraw-Hill, an imprint of The McGraw-Hill Companies, Inc., 1221 Avenue of the Americas, New York, NY 10020. Copyright © 2004, 2001, 1998, 1995, 1992, 1989, 1985, 1982, 1977, 1973, 1969, 1964, 1959, 1953 by The McGraw-Hill Companies, Inc. All rights reserved.

1 2 3 4 5 6 7 8 9 0 BKM/BKM 0 9 8 7 6 5 4 3

ISBN 0-07-283504-4

www.mhhe.com

To the Student

This Study Guide was prepared to accompany *Principles of Auditing and Other Assurance Services, fourteenth edition*, by Whittington & Pany. However, it can be used effectively with other introductory auditing texts. The key purpose of this study guide is to help you in mastering the text material by providing a summary of the essential points in each chapter and testing your knowledge with a series of objective questions and exercises.

The manner in which individual students use this study guide will differ. However, we recommend the following approach:

1. Study the chapter in your textbook.
2. Read the Highlights of the Chapter section of the study guide, referring back to the text for a review of any statements that you do not understand.
3. Work the questions and exercises in the Test Yourself section of the study guide and check your answers against the solutions included at the end of the guide. Again, if you encounter items you do not understand, refer to your textbook for a thorough discussion of the subject.
4. Work the homework assignments made by your instructor.

Once you have mastered the material in this manner, rereading the Highlights of the Chapter section of the study guide will assist you in quickly reviewing the material before examinations.

O. Ray Whittington
Kurt Pany

Contents

CHAPTER 1

The Role of the Public Accountant in the American Economy

Highlights of the Chapter

1. The key people in virtually every part of our economy rely upon financial information as a basis for their decision making. Often the goals of the providers of financial information run counter to the interests of the users of this information. The conflict of interest between the users and providers of financial information suggests a social need for independent auditors. For example, consider the case of a business that is applying for a bank loan and submitting financial statements to support its application. Management may have an incentive to overstate the financial statements to increase the likelihood of obtaining the loan. The banker can reach a sound decision if the reliability of the financial statements has been established by an independent audit. Effective independent auditing relies upon CPA firms composed of individuals of professional competence and integrity who accurately report on whether the financial information on which we rely constitutes a fair picture of what is really going on.

2. CPAs endeavor to provide a broad range of assurance services that (1) enhance the reliability of information, or (2) put information in a form or context that facilitates decision making. An audit of financial statements is an example of the first type of assurance services, an attest service. To attest to information is to provide assurance as to its fairness and dependability. In an attest engagement, a CPA issues a written communication with a conclusion on the reliability of information (subject matter) or an assertion about information. CPAs attest to a host of other types of information, including financial forecasts, internal control, and compliance with laws and regulations.

3. The term audit is generally used to mean a CPA firm's examination of the financial statements of a client. The audit includes evaluating the accounting records and supporting evidence, both within and outside the client's business. The end product of the audit process is an audit report in which the CPA firm expresses its professional opinion on the fairness of the financial statements. A CPA firm never issues an audit opinion without first completing an audit.

4. When making an investment decision, users of financial statements face two types of risk: business risk and information risk. Audits have only a limited effect on business risk, which is the risk that a company will not be able to meet its financial obligations because of economic conditions or poor management decisions. Audits, however, can significantly reduce information risk--the risk that the information used to assess business risk is not accurate.

5. In formulating plans for an audit, the auditors obtain an understanding of the client's internal control. A client's **internal control consists** of all measures used by an organization to provide assurance that specific objectives of the company will be achieved, including efficient and effective operations, compliance with laws and regulations, and reliable financial reporting. Strong controls tend to screen out accidental errors and to make difficult the concealment of any intentional falsification of the accounting records or financial statements. The stronger the internal control, the less testing required by the auditors in completing their audit. If weakness in controls exists, the auditors try to compensate by expanding the scope and intensity of their tests.

6.   Throughout the 20th century the audit function continually evolved. Among the most significant developments are:

    a.   A shift in emphasis to the determination of fairness of financial statements.
    b.   Increased responsibility of the auditors to third parties, such as governmental agencies, stock exchanges, and an investing public numbered in the millions.

    c.   The change of auditing method from detailed examination of individual transactions to the use of sampling techniques, including statistical sampling.

    d.   Recognition of the need to consider internal control as a guide to the direction, and amount of testing and sampling to be performed.

    e.   Development of new auditing procedures applicable to information technology (IT)—based systems, and use of the computer as an auditing tool.

    f.   Recognition of the need for auditors to find means of protecting themselves from litigation.

    g.   An increased demand for prompt disclosure of both favorable and unfavorable information concerning any publicly owned company.

    h.   Increased responsibility to assess the risk of material fraud.

    i.   Increased demand for attestation by CPAs to management's assertions about compliance with laws and regulations and the effectiveness of internal control.

Many of these ideas will be analyzed in detail in later sections of this Study Guide.

7.   The changes in audit function brought about by the 21st century have already been profound, and include:

    a.   The Panel on Audit Effectiveness recommended changes in the function relating to the detection of fraud, documentation of audit evidence and judgments, risk assessments, and the linkage of audit procedures to audit risks.

    b.   The Enron Corporation and WorldCom bankruptcies, followed by a record number of public companies restating prior-period financial statements, led to investor uncertainty about the reliability of financial statements and losses in an already weak financial market in the latter half of 2001.

    c.   The conviction of Andersen LLP on charges of destruction of documents related to the Enron case led to the bankruptcy of that firm and to questions about the ethical principles of the accounting profession.

    d.   Passage of the Sarbanes-Oxley Act of 2002 resulted in tougher penalties for corporate fraud, restriction of consulting services that CPAs may perform for public audit clients, and the creation of the Public Company Accounting Oversight Board to oversee the accounting profession.

8.   In addition to audits of financial statements auditors often perform compliance audits. Performance of a compliance audit is dependent upon the existence of verifiable data and recognized criteria or standards established by an authoritative body. An example is the audit of an income tax return by an auditor of the Internal Revenue Service (IRS). Another example is the periodic examination of a bank by a bank examiner of a state government. The goal is to determine compliance with existing laws, regulations, and standards.

9.   An operational audit is a review of a department or other unit of a business, governmental or nonprofit organization to measure the efficiency and effectiveness of operations. Auditors of the General Accounting Office (GAO) perform many operational audits; the end product is usually a report to management containing recommendations for improvements in operations.

10.   Types of auditors include CPAs, internal auditors, GAO auditors, and internal revenue agents. Of these four types, CPAs are the longest established and best known. Each state recognizes public accounting as a profession and issues CPA certificates. To be licensed as CPAs, individuals must demonstrate through a written examination and the satisfaction of educational and experience requirements their qualifications for entry to the public accounting profession.

11.   A staff of internal auditors is found in every large corporation. Internal auditors investigate and appraise the effectiveness with which various organizational units of the company carry out their assigned functions. Often the internal auditing staff reports to a committee of the board of directors or to a top-level executive, thus assuring that the internal auditors will have access to all units of the organization and that their recommendations will receive prompt attention from department heads.

12.   Congress has its own auditing staff, known as the General Accounting Office, or GAO. These auditors determine whether spending programs follow the intent of Congress and evaluate the effectiveness and efficiency of selected government programs. The GAO is noted for its development of statistical sampling plans and computer auditing techniques.

13.   IRS agents conduct compliance audits of the income tax returns of individuals and corporations.

14.   At the very heart of the public accounting profession is the **American Institute of Certified Public Accountants** (AICPA), a voluntary, national organization of more the 350,000 CPAs. The AICPA historically has played a key role in establishing auditing standards and rules to guide CPAs in the conduct of audits. The extensive program of research and publication carried on by the AICPA has been a major factor in the growth and increasing stature of the public accounting profession. Examples of important AICPA publications are the *Statements on Auditing Standards* (SASs), *Statements on Standards for Attestation Engagements* (SSAEs), *Statements on Standards for Accounting and Review Services* (SSARS), *Industry Audit and Accounting Guides,* and the *Journal of Accountancy.*

15.   A CPA firm needs quality controls to assure that every audit it performs meets at least a minimum level of quality. A single substandard audit could create a financial liability sufficient to destroy a CPA firm. While historically, most of the regulation of accounting firms was through the AICPA, passage of the Sarbanes-Oxley Act of 2002 resulted in creation of the Public Company Accounting Oversight Board that now regulates all accounting firms that audit public companies. A section of the AICPA (*PCPS/Partnering for CPA Practice Success/the AICPA Alliance for Public Accounting Firms Section*) attempts to improve the quality of accounting firms that audit nonpublic companies, in part through peer reviews. A peer review occurs when a CPA firm arranges for a critical review of its practices by other CPAs. The purpose is to encourage adherence to the AICPA's quality control standards (presented in detail in Chapter 2).

16.   The AICPA has also adopted regulations that apply to individual members, including a goal oriented *Code of Professional Conduct* (a code of ethics), continuing education requirements for all members, and a requirement that all members in practice work with a firm that engages in a peer review or inspection program.

17.   The CPA examination is a uniform national examination prepared and graded by the AICPA. The computerized examination extends over two days and has four parts: Auditing & Attestation; Financial Accounting & Reporting; Regulation; and Business Environment & Concepts.

18.   Auditors must determine whether financial statements are prepared in conformity with generally accepted accounting principles (GAAP). The AICPA has designated the **Financial Accounting Standards Board** (FASB) as the body with the power to set forth these principles for entities other than state and local governments. The **Governmental Accounting Standards Board** (GASB) and the **Federal Accounting Standards Advisory Board** (FASAB) have the authority to issue accounting principles to be followed by state and local government organizations and the federal government, respectively.

19.   **The Public Company Accounting Oversight Board** (PCAOB) was created in 2002 to oversee and discipline CPAs and public accounting firms that audit public companies. The five member PCAOB has the responsibility to establish or adopt auditing, quality control, ethics, independence and other standards relating to the preparation of audit reports for SEC registrants. In addition, it has responsibilities relating to registering public accounting firms that audit public companies, performing various inspections and investigations of those firms, and when appropriate, sanctioning those firms. Much of the self regulation authority of the AICPA has been taken over by this board.

20.   The **Securities and Exchange Commission** (SEC) is an agency of the federal government. Its function is to protect the investing public by requiring full disclosure by corporations offering securities for sale to the public. A registration statement containing audited financial statements must be submitted for the review of the SEC before a new issue of securities is placed on the market. Publicly-traded companies also must provide the SEC with their annual audited financial statements; thus the SEC exercises an ongoing influence on accounting practice and auditing standards. The SEC does not pass on the merits of securities; its role is only to make sure that the investor has available all pertinent information needed in deciding whether to buy a given security.

21.   In addition to auditing, CPA firms offer other types of services, including tax services, consulting services, accounting and review services, litigation support services, fraud investigation services, and personal financial planning.

22.   Audits are costly, but essential for large publicly-owned corporations. For a small business, the principal reason for an audit may be a request by a banker for audited financial statements of a borrower before making a loan. An alternative to an audit for a small business is to retain a CPA firm to perform accounting and review services, including the compilation or review of financial statements.

23.   Public accountants practice as sole practitioners as members of a partnership, as a professional corporation or as a limited liability company.

24.   The partnership and professional corporation form of organizations offer several advantages, including the opportunity for specialization by the owners, the ability to reward staff by granting an ownership interest, and an opportunity for exchange of ideas between the owners. The limited liability company form offers these advantages but also protects the personal assets of any shareholders or partners not directly involved in engagements resulting in litigation.

25.   CPA firms range in size from one person to thousands on the professional staff. In terms of size, CPA firms are often considered to fall into four groups: local firms, regional firms, national firms, and the Big Four. Small CPA firms usually focus on income tax work, consulting services, and accounting services, rather than auditing. Large CPA firms devote a major part of their time to auditing. The Big Four accounting firms audit most of the largest American corporations.

26   The organizational structure of a typical public accounting firm includes partners, managers, senior auditors, and staff assistants.

    a.   The responsibilities of partners include maintaining contacts with existing clients, obtaining new clients, recruiting staff members, supervising the professional staff, reviewing the audit working papers, and signing the auditors' report. The audit partner assumes ultimate responsibility for adequate performance of the audit.

    b.   Audit managers assume the responsibility of supervising two or more concurrent audit engagements. Often, managers perform the administrative duties of billing for services and collecting fees.

    c.   The senior auditor is responsible for conducting the audit engagement in the field. Audit planning, supervising and reviewing the work of assistants, and drafting the audit report are among the senior auditor's major tasks.

    d.   Staff assistants are responsible for performing the audit work assigned to them by the senior auditor.

27.   Large CPA firms have professional development sections that assist the firm's personnel in keeping up-to-date on technical issues. These sections distribute summaries of new professional pronouncements, research technical issues, and offer a wide range of seminars and educational programs to firm personnel.

Test Yourself on this Introductory Chapter

TRUE OR FALSE

For each of the following statements, circle the T or the F to indicate whether the statement is true or false.

T   F   1.   An independent audit of a small business by a CPA firm usually results in an unconditional guarantee of the accuracy of the financial statements.

T   F   2.   If the independent auditors satisfy themselves that a client's accounting records are up-to-date and reliable, and that internal control is strong, they will not need to gather evidence from banks or other outside sources.

T   F   3.   CPA firms sometimes compile or review financial statements for small companies not having trained accountants in their employ. Under these circumstances the CPA firm issues a report, but a report that differs from that issued as a result of an audit.

T   F   4.   Because of the prospective nature of financial forecasts, auditors never are involved with attesting to reasonableness of this type of data.

T   F   5.   Attest services are one form of assurance services.

T   F   6.   The AICPA issues CPA certificates to candidates that pass the CPA examination.

T   F   7.   The Sarbanes-Oxley Act of 2002 restricted the types of consulting services that may be performed by CPA firms for public audit clients.

T   F   8.   The final step in most audits is a consideration of internal control. This tells the auditors whether the scope of their investigation has been adequate.

T   F   9.   The internal auditing staff of a large corporation usually reports to a committee of the board of directors or to a member of the top management group.

T   F   10.   As compared to smaller CPA firms, large CPA firms generally spend a greater percentage of the time performing audits.

T   F   11.   A registration statement containing audited financial statements generally must be filed with the SEC before a new issue of securities is offered for sale to the public.

T   F   12.   The term "peer review" refers to the process of evaluating CPA staff members for promotion to partnership in the firm.

T   F   13.   The primary purpose of an audit is the detection or prevention of fraud.

T   F   14.   An independent audit on an annual basis is required by the AICPA for all corporations.

T   F   15.   The economic interests of the providers of financial information and the users of the information are the same, and this common interest creates the demand for an annual independent audit.

T   F   16.   Since corporations have limited liability, CPA firms must be organized as sole proprietorships or partnerships.

T   F   17.   The Public Company Accounting Oversight Board was established to issue accounting standards for publicly traded companies.

T   F   18.   Managers are often assigned to supervise several concurrent audit engagements.

T   F   19.   A senior auditor may plan and conduct an audit, in which case that auditor takes ultimate responsibility for the engagement.

T   F   20.   Associations of CPA firms provide their members with many of the benefits of having their own professional development departments.

COMPLETION

Fill in the necessary words to complete the following statements.

1.   The two most essential qualities for a CPA to perform the attest function properly are professional competence and _____.

2.   To _____ to information means to provide assurance as to its fairness and dependability.

3.   "Accounting and review services" is the term used by CPA firms to describe work done for small businesses that do not want audits, but periodically need the services of professional accountants. Such services often consist of the _____ or _____ of financial statements.

4.   Primary responsibility for audited financial statements rests with _____ even though the statements may be drafted and typed in the auditors' office.

5.   The _____ _____ _____ _____ is a governmental organization that regulates the sale of securities, while the _____ _____ _____ is a governmental organization that serves the audit function for the U. S. Congress.

6.   The _____ _____ _____ _____ _____ regulates all accounting firms that audit public companies. *PCPS/Partnering for CPA Practice Success/the AICPA Alliance for Public Accounting Firms Section*) attempts to improve the quality of accounting firms that audit nonpublic companies, in part through _____ _____ which involve a critical review of a firm's practices.

7. Public accounting firms are organized as sole _____, partnerships, or professional _____,

    or _____ _____ _____.

8. The professional staff of a typical public accounting firm includes partners, _____, _____

    _____, and _____ _____.

9. The AICPA requires members in public practice to obtain 120 hours of _____ _____

    every three years.

10. An operational audit is a study of a unit of an organization to evaluate the _____ and

    _____ of the unit. The usual user of an operational audit report is the organization's _____.

MULTIPLE CHOICE

Choose the best answer for each of the following questions and enter the identifying letter in the space provided.

_____ 1.   The risk that a company will not be able to meet its commitments is referred to as:

        a. business risk.
        b. information risk.
        c. inherent risk.
        d. risk of collapse.

_____ 2.   The CPA examination:

        a. requires a peer review prior to a candidate admittance to the exam.
        b. is administered and graded by the individual states.
        c. has four sections.
        d. must be taken by all who wish to work for a CPA firm.

_____ 3.   Which of the following is not an example of an assurance service?

        a. Attesting to the reliability of a financial forecast.
        b. Audit of financial statements.
        c. Preparation of a tax return.
        d. Review of internal control over operations.

_____ 4.   Which of the following is not a type of attest engagement?

        a. Agreed-upon procedures
        b. Compilation
        c. Examination
        d. Review

_____ 5.   The audit of an income tax return by an auditor of the Internal Revenue Service is considered a (an):

   a.   compliance audit.
   b.   financial statement audit.
   c.   internal audit.
   d.   operational audit.

_____ 6.   Some of the following criteria are essential to satisfactory performance in several professions. Which one is unique to audit work by CPAs?

   a.   Due professional care.
   b.   Independence.
   c.   General competence.
   d.   Familiarity with a complex body of technical knowledge.

_____ 7.   An effect of the Sarbanes-Oxley Act of 2002 was to:

   a.   eliminate SEC involvement with sales of securities.
   b.   reduce the accounting profession's level of self regulation.
   c.   require periodic peer reviews of large CPA firms performed by the General Accounting Office.
   d.   reduce the circumstances in which one may file securities with the SEC.

_____ 8.   Which of the following is an area in which the Public Company Accounting Oversight Board is **not** empowered to establish or adopt standards?

   a.   Accounting.
   b.   Auditing.
   c.   Ethics.
   d.   Quality Control.

_____ 9.   Independent auditors of the year 1900 differed from the auditors of today in that auditors in 1900 were more concerned with:

   a.   minimizing income taxes.
   b.   the validity of the income statement.
   c.   internal control.
   d.   the accuracy of the balance sheet.

_____ 10. Senior auditors typically perform all of the following tasks, except:

   a.   supervise staff assistants.
   b.   draft the audit report.
   c.   sign the audit report.
   d.   review the working papers prepared by staff assistants.

_____ 11. An audit designed to detect violations of laws and regulations would be referred to as:

   a.   a financial statement audit.
   b.   a compliance audit.
   c.   a performance audit.
   d.   an operational audit.

_____   12.   To improve the quality of financial statements filed with it, the SEC has adopted

      a.   Industry Audit and Accounting Guides.
      b.   Statements on Financial Accounting Standards.
      c.   Accounting Research Bulletins.
      d.   Regulation S-X.

EXERCISES

1.   Each auditing term, phrase, or organizational name in the first list below is closely related to a term or phrase in the second list. You are to enter each term in the second list opposite the related item in the first list.

     a.   SASs   _____

     b.   Internal Revenue Service   _____

     c.   Internal auditor   _____

     d.   Attest function   _____

     e.   Audited financial statements   _____

     f.   Quality control   _____

     g.   SEC   _____

     h.   Accounting services by CPA   _____

     i.   Consideration of internal control   _____

     j.   Independence   _____

     1.   Guide to amount of testing and sampling

     2.   Providing credibility

     3.   Protection of investors

     4.   Peer review

     5.   Operational audits

     6.   Compilation of financial statements

     7.   Interpretations of generally accepted auditing standards

     8.   Essential element for the attest function

9.   Compliance audits

10.   Dependable financial information

2.   Match the following organizations with the related descriptions.

_____   a.   SEC

_____   b.   FASB

_____   c.   GAO

_____   d.   IIA

_____   e.   FASAB

_____   f.   PCAOB

_____   g.   AICPA

_____   h.   GASB

1.   National organization of CPAs.

2.   International organization of internal auditors.

3.   Body designated to establish accounting standards for entities other than state and local governments.

4.   The audit arm of Congress.

5.   Administers the Securities Acts.

6.   Group created to oversee and discipline CPAs and public accounting firms that audit public companies.

7.   Body designated to establish accounting standards for state and local governments.

8.   Body designated to establish accounting standards for the federal government.

CHAPTER 2

Professional Standards

Highlights of the Chapter

1. This chapter describes the generally accepted auditing standards, attestation standards, and quality control standards. It also explains the nature of international auditing standards and describes the international auditing report.

2. The stature of any profession is largely dependent upon the quality of the daily work performed by its members. A uniformly high quality of work can be achieved only if the members of the profession accept and adhere to specific standards of professional performance. The American Institute of Certified Public Accountants has set forth the ten **generally accepted auditing standards** presented on page 32 of the textbook. These auditing standards have been of officially adopted by the membership of the AICPA. The expression "generally accepted auditing standards" as used in the auditors' report refers to these ten standards.

3. How do auditors acquire the "adequate technical training and proficiency" required by the first general standard? To meet this requirement one needs college or university education in accounting and auditing, public accounting experience, the ability to use procedures suitable for information technology–based systems, participation in continuing education programs, and a technical knowledge of the industry in which the client operates.

4. The independence of the auditor is perhaps the most important concept underlying public accounting. For example, if auditors were permitted to own shares of stock issued by audit clients, or if their spouses were allowed to serve as directors for client companies, they might subconsciously be biased in performing the attest function. Auditors must not only be independent, but must also appear to be independent. Auditors, therefore, should avoid any relationship with a client that would cause an outsider who had knowledge of all the facts to doubt their independence. Independence is more readily maintained when a CPA firm is large enough that no one client represents a significant portion of the CPA firm's income.

5. **Statement on Auditing Standards** (referred to as SASs) are serially numbered pronouncements issued by the Auditing Standards Board of the AICPA. The SASs are considered to be interpretations of the ten generally accepted auditing standards, and CPAs are required to follow them. Compliance with the SASs does not represent an ideal of audit performance, but rather a minimum standard for all audit engagements.

6. Auditing standards require auditors to assess the risk that material misstatements (due to errors or fraud) have occurred affecting the financial statements. Based on that assessment, they design their audit to provide **reasonable assurance** of detecting the misstatements. Auditing standards defines **errors** as unintentional mistakes or omissions in the financial statements. **Fraud** is a term used to describe intentional misstatements of financial statements (fraudulent financial reporting) and misappropriation of assets (defalcations).

7. The auditors also have a responsibility to design their audits to provide reasonable assurance of detecting violations of laws and regulations (illegal acts) that have a **direct** and **material** effect on line-item financial statement amounts. An audit cannot be relied upon to detect illegal acts that have an **indirect** effect on the financial statements. When the auditors discover evidence of an illegal act by the

client, they should attempt to assess its effect on the financial statements. The auditors should also discuss the situation with top management and notify the audit committee of the board of directors. If the client fails to take appropriate corrective action, the auditors should withdraw from the engagement.

8.   The auditors' standard unqualified report consists of three paragraphs. The first, or introductory paragraph, clarifies the responsibilities of management and the auditors; the second, or scope paragraph, describes the nature of an audit; and the final paragraph, the opinion paragraph, is a concise statement of the auditors' opinion based on the examination. The wording of the report usually follows quite closely the pattern recommended by the AICPA, as shown on page 38 of the textbook.

9.   The report is addressed to the person or persons who retained the auditors. The report is signed by the auditors and dated with the date on which all significant auditing procedures were completed (termed the last day of significant field work).

10.   The primary purpose of an audit is to provide assurance to the users of financial statements that the statements are reliable. The auditors do not express an opinion on the client's accounting records. In fact, the auditors' use of the accounting records is only a means to an end and merely one part of the audit. The audit of financial statements includes getting evidence from outsiders (such as banks, customers and suppliers), and the first-hand observation of inventories and plant assets, as well as analysis of the client's accounting records.

11.   In the opinion paragraph of an audit report, the auditors provide an opinion as to whether the financial statements **present fairly**, in all material respects, the financial position of the company as of the balance sheets date and the result of its operations and its cash flows for the period then ended in **conformity with accounting principles generally accepted in the United States of America**. Implicit are the implications that comparability between periods has not been materially affected by changes in accounting principles, including their method of application (second standard of reporting) and that disclosure is adequate (third standard of reporting).

12.   The auditors do not and cannot guarantee the correctness of the financial statements, because the statements include many estimates of future events (e.g., estimates of future uncollectible accounts, asset lives, and warranty reserves). Furthermore, the auditors do not make a complete and detailed examination of all transactions. In the auditors' report, the expression "present fairly" means that the financial statements are not misleading and that there is adequate disclosure of all essential information.

13.   Auditors cannot issue an unqualified opinion on financial statements that contain material deficiencies. Materiality depends on both the amount and the nature of an item.

14.   In evaluating whether financial statements are in accordance with generally accepted auditing principles (GAAP), the auditors must look to several sources. To be acceptable a particular principle should have **substantial authoritative support**. Figure 2-2 on page 42 of the textbook illustrates the relative authority of GAAP from the category with the highest authority to that with the least. Notice that the sources of GAAP are different for governments (state, local and federal) than they are for other types of organizations.

15.   We have discussed an unqualified audit report, but this type of report cannot be issued for every audit. Alternative forms of reports include a qualified opinion, an adverse opinion, and a disclaimer of opinion. The auditors issue a **qualified opinion** when there is a limitation on the scope of their examination, or when the financial statements contain a material departure from generally accepted accounting principles. The limitation or exception must be significant but not so material to overshadow an overall opinion on the financial statements.

16.   An **adverse opinion** is appropriate when there is a "very material" departure from generally accepted accounting principles. That opinion states that the financial statements are not fairly presented.

17.   The auditors issue a **disclaimer of opinion** when, because of a scope limitation, they are not able to determine the overall fairness of the financial statements. The auditors may also issue a disclaimer based on substantial doubt about an entity's ability to continue as a going-concern.

18.   The expansion of the attest function to other forms of information has led to the development of the **attestation standards** that are presented on page 43 of the textbook. These standards serve as a general framework for attesting to such information as financial forecasts and internal controls in computer software.

19.   It is important for CPA firms to establish quality control policies and procedures to insure that all engagements are performed in accordance with professional and firm standards.

20.   To guide CPA firms in establishing quality control policies and procedures, the AICPA has established a series of **Statements on Quality Control Standards.** These statements provide that a CPA firm should establish policies and procedures in the following areas:

   a.   **Independence, Integrity, and Objectivity**—policies and procedures should provide assurance that all personnel meet the ethics requirements regarding independence, perform services with integrity, and maintain their objectivity.

   b.   **Personnel Management**—policies and procedures should provide assurance that (1) those hired possess characteristics to perform competently, (2) work is assigned to those with appropriate training and proficiency, (3) personnel participate in appropriate continuing education and professional development activities, and (4) personnel selected for advancement have necessary qualifications.

   c.   **Acceptance and Continuance of Clients and Engagements**—policies and procedures should provide assurance that the firm will not accept, or continue to serve, clients whose management lack integrity.

   d.   **Engagement Performance**--policies and procedures should provide assurance that work performed meets applicable professional standards, regulatory requirements, and the firm's standards of quality.

   e.   **Monitoring**—policies and procedures should provide assurance that the procedures relating to other elements of quality control are suitably designed and effectively applied.

21.   All accounting firms that audit SEC registrants must register with the Public Company Accounting Oversight Board (PCAOB). The PCAOB currently uses the quality control standards established by the AICPA to perform annual inspections of each registered firm. Each inspection results in a written report transmitted to the SEC and appropriate regulatory agencies, as well as a letter of comments by the PCAOB, and any letter of response from the CPA firm.

22.   CPAs in firms that are not subject to oversight by the PCAOB undergo a peer review performed by another CPA firm, or a team of CPAs. A peer review involves a study of the adequacy of the firm's established quality control policies and tests to determine the extent of the firm's compliance with those policies. Even CPA firms that are subject to inspections by the PCAOB must have their nonpublic audits and reviews peer reviewed by another CPA firm.

23.   The **International Federation of Accountants** (IFAC) is a worldwide organization of national accounting bodies, established to harmonize standards throughout the world. The auditing pronouncements of IFAC do not override the national standards of its members. Rather, members are encouraged to adopt similar guidance in their countries.

24.   The international audit report (illustrated on page 47 of the textbook) differs in several ways from the U.S. report. The report may substitute the phrase "give a true and fair view" for "present fairly, in all material respects," may indicate that the financial statement comply with the country's relevant statutes and law, and may be signed using the name of the auditor, the firm, or both.

Test Yourself on Chapter 2

TRUE OR FALSE

For each of the following statements, circle T or F to indicate whether the statement is true or false

T   F   1.   In a repeat engagement in which a CPA firm relies heavily upon the investigative work done in prior years, the scope paragraph of the auditors' standard report is ordinarily omitted.

T   F   2.   Internal control is not specifically mentioned in the auditors' report.

T   F   3.   Compliance with generally accepted auditing standards is considered by the AICPA as ideal audit performance rather than as an attainable level for most audits.

T   F   4.   The pronouncements of the AICPA do not specify the percentage of purchase invoices to be examined or other quantitative measures, but leave to the auditor's judgment the determination of what constitutes sufficient competent evidential matter.

T   F   5.   Every audit of financial statements by a CPA includes obtaining evidence from sources outside the client company as well as from internal sources.

T   F   6.   All audits result in unqualified opinions.

T   F   7.   Professional standards permit a CPA firm to own shares of stock in corporations that they audit if such stock holdings are not material.

T   F   8.   The Public Company Accounting Oversight Board performs inspections of CPA Firms that audit SEC registrants.

T   F   9.   The Public Company Accounting Oversight Board establishes auditing standards for the audits of all companies.

T   F   10.   Quality control policies and procedures are necessary for large CPA firms, but not for small CPA firms.

T   F   11.   A peer review may be expected to analyze, to varying degrees, working papers for each attest engagement performed by the CPA firm.

T   F   12.   Fraud is a term that is used to refer to intentional misstatements of financial statements.

T   F   13.   The auditors have a responsibility to design their audit to obtain reasonable assurance of detecting material misstatements in the financial statements due to fraud or errors.

T   F   14.   An audit can be relied on to provide reasonable assurance of detecting "direct-effect" illegal acts that are material in amount.

T   F   15.   The highest category of generally accepted accounting principles include authoritative body pronouncements.

T   F   16.   When the scope of the audit is restricted by the client, the auditors should issue an adverse opinion.

T   F   17.   The Attestation Standards are primarily designed to provide guidance on the audit of financial statements.

T   F   18.   *Statement on Quality Control Standards* applies to all aspects of a CPA firm's practice-- auditing, tax work, and consulting services.

T   F   19.   International auditing standards have been developed by the AICPA.

T   F   20.   The international audit report may be signed using the name of the auditor, the firm, or both.

COMPLETION

Fill in the necessary words to complete the following statements.

1.   The three paragraphs of the auditors' unqualified report are known as the _____ paragraph,

the _____ paragraph, and the _____ paragraph.

2.   The serially numbered pronouncements issued by the Auditing Standards Board of the AICPA as

interpretations of the ten generally accepted auditing standards are known as _____ _____

_____ _____.

3.   Investors need to compare financial statements of different companies. The standards most frequently

followed to prepare financial statements are _____ _____ _____ _____.

4.   The ten generally accepted auditing standards are classified into three groups: (a) _____

_____, (b) _____ _____ _____ _____, and (c) _____

_____.

5.   Into which group of generally accepted auditing standards does the following standard fall? "The work

is to be adequately planned and assistants, if any, are to be properly supervised." _____

_____.

6.   Four financial statements are usually referred to in the introductory paragraph of the auditors' report upon completion of the examination of a corporate client. The four financial statements are: (a) _____ _____ _____, (b) _____ _____ _____ _____, (c) _____ _____ _____ _____ _____, and (d) _____ _____ _____ _____ _____.

7.   The highest category within the "GAAP Hierarchy is referred to as _____ _____ pronouncements.

8.   CPA firms should establish _____ _____ policies and procedures to provide assurance that their services adhere to firm and professional standards.

9.   An attestation engagement includes a report on subject matter, or on an _____ about subject matter.

10.   International auditing standards are issued by the _____ _____ _____ Committee of the _____ _____ _____ _____ .

MULTIPLE CHOICE

Choose the best answer for each of the following questions and enter the identifying letter in the space provided.

_____   1.   Which of the following statements concerning illegal acts by clients is correct?

   a.   An auditor's responsibility to detect illegal acts that have an indirect and material effect on the financial statements differs from that for errors and fraud that have a direct effect.
   b.   An audit in accordance with generally accepted auditing standards normally includes audit procedures specially designed to detect illegal acts that have an indirect but immaterial effect on the financial statements.
   c.   An auditor considers illegal acts from the perspective of the reliability of management's representations rather than their relation to audit objectives derived from financial statement assertions.
   d.   An auditor has no responsibility to detect illegal acts by clients that have a direct effect on the financial statements.

_____ 2.   Assume that there are only two sources of guidance on proper accounting for a transaction-- (a) an accounting principle supported by a pronouncement of a body of expert accountants not exposed for public comment and (b) a widely recognized accounting practice. If those sources conflict with one another which standard prevails?

a.   The pronouncement of a body of expert accountants not exposed for public comment.
b.   The widely recognized accounting practice.
c.   Both are of equal authority and the form of the transaction prevails over its substance.
d.   Neither, other accounting literature must be consulted to determine the appropriate accounting.

_____ 3.   Which of the following statement is most accurate in describing an auditor's responsibility to detect errors and fraud?

a.   The auditor should consider the client's internal control, and design the audit to provide reasonable assurance of detecting all errors and fraud.
b.   The auditor should assess the risk that errors and fraud may cause the financial statements to contain material misstatements, and determine whether the necessary controls are prescribed and are being followed.
c.   The auditor should consider the types of errors and fraud that could occur, and determine whether the necessary controls are prescribed and are being followed.
d.   The auditor should assess the risk that errors and fraud may cause the financial statements to contain material misstatements, and design the audit to provide reasonable assurance of detecting material errors and fraud.

_____ 4.   When the auditors discover an illegal act they will ordinarily report it to the:

a.   audit committee of the company being audited.
b.   Securities and Exchange Commission on Form 8-M.
c.   Justice Department of the United States government.
d.   American Institute of Certified Public Accountants Division of Professional Ethics.

_____ 5.   Which of the following is an element of quality control for a CPA firm?

a.   Independence and freedom from bias.
b.   Acceptance and continuance of personnel.
c.   Engagement performance.
d.   Supervision.

_____ 6.   The generally accepted auditing standards of field work include a requirement that the:

a.   auditors exercise due professional care.
b.   auditors obtain an understanding of internal control.
c.   financial statements be presented in accordance with generally accepted accounti
      principles.
d.   auditors maintain an independent mental attitude.

_____   7.   The first general standard requires that a person or persons have adequate technical training and proficiency as an auditor. This standard is met by:

     a.   an understanding of the field of business and finance.
     b.   education and experience in the field of auditing.
     c.   continuing professional education.
     d.   a thorough knowledge of the Statements on Auditing Standards.

_____   8.   In the event of an unresolvable difference of opinion between the client company and the CPA firm as to the valuation of an asset in the financial statements:

     a.   the final decision rests with the client's management and the auditors can express their disapproval in the audit report if they deem it appropriate to do so.
     b.   the auditors should change the financial statements to show the valuation they consider proper.
     c.   the difference of opinion should be submitted to arbitration by the FASB.
     d.   the auditors should withdraw from the engagement.

_____   9.   An auditors' unqualified standard report:

     a.   explicitly states that disclosure is adequate in the financial statements.
     b.   implies that disclosure is adequate in the financial statements.
     c.   explicitly states that all material facts have been disclosed in conformity with generally accepted accounting principles.
     d.   takes no position, explicit or implicit, with respect to the adequacy of disclosures.

_____   10.   The auditors cannot guarantee the correctness of audited financial statements because:

     a.   much of the audit work is performed by staff members with limited experience.
     b.   new accounting principles and practices may have been approved by the FASB during the year under audit.
     c.   the value of assets may change while the audit is in process.
     d.   financial statements are largely a matter of estimate and opinion rather than of precise facts.

_____   11.   A CPA is most likely to refer to one or more of the three general auditing standards in determining:

     a.   the nature of the CPA's report qualification.
     b.   the scope of the CPA's auditing procedures.
     c.   requirements for the consideration of internal control.
     d.   whether the CPA should undertake an audit engagement.

_____   12.   What is the nature of the three generally accepted auditing standards classified as standards of field work?

     a.   The competence, independence, and professional care of persons performing the audit.
     b.   Criteria for the content of the auditor's report on financial statements and related footnote disclosures.
     c.   The criteria of audit planning and evidence-gathering.
     d.   The need to maintain an independence in mental attitude in all matters relating to the audit.

EXERCISES

1.   Match each of the following terms with the appropriate description.

	Term		**Description**
_____	1. Annual inspection.	a.	Established by the Sarbanes-Oxley Act of 2002.
_____	2. Quality control policies	b.	The subject of a peer review.
_____	3. IFAC	c.	Issues international standards on auditing.
_____	4. PCAOB	d.	Requirement for all CPA firms with SEC reporting clients.
_____	5. IAASB	e.	A worldwide organization of national accounting bodies.
_____	6. Partnering for CPA Practice Success/the AICPA Alliance for CPA firms.	f.	Designed for CPA firms that audit nonpublic companies.

2.   Listed below are three areas of quality control for a CPA firm. For each area describe the objective of establishing quality control policies and procedures in the area, and provide an example policy that will help achieve that objective.

    a.   **Independence, Integrity, and Objectivity**

        (1)   Objective:

        (2)   Policy:

    b.   **Personnel Management**

        (1)   Objective:

        (2)   Policy:

    c.   **Engagement Performance**

        (1)   Objective:

        (2)   Policy:

3. The ten generally accepted auditing standards adopted by the AICPA consist of three general standards (Gl, G2, and G3), three standards of field work (FWl, FW2, and FW3), and four standards of reporting (Rl, R2, R3, and R4). For each of the following cases, indicate the standard or standards violated by writing one or more of the above symbols in the space provided.

Case A

_____ A CPA conducts an audit and expresses an opinion on the financial statements of a company in which he or she owns shares of stock.

Case B

_____ A CPA firm sends an assistant to a client's office to begin an audit without providing the assistant with any instructions or background information.

Case C

_____ A CPA firm conducted an audit of the financial statements of Y Co. Because of the incomplete scope of the work, the CPA firm declined to issue an audit report but at the client's request, provided financial statements on letterhead stationery of the CPA firm. The CPAs issued no report.

Case D

_____ When Davis and Lear, CPAs, began their first audit of Laser, Inc., they were informed by John Henry, the company's chief accountant, that several changes were being made or considered for the company's internal control. Henry suggested the CPAs postpone any consideration of internal control until the changes were completed. Davis and Lear agreed and did not consider internal control until the final day of field work.

Case E

_____ The CPA firm of Day, Mark & Co., was very short of help during the busy season when a flu epidemic incapacitated several members of its audit staff. To cope with this emergency, the firm eliminated all field work for one of its oldest clients and based the audit report on telephone inquiries of the officers of the client and on the CPAs' knowledge gained in prior examinations. The audit report was issued as usual, but the audit fee was cut in half.

Case F

_____ The CPA firm of Kay & Co. had informed a client that the audit would begin January 5, but found it had no staff members available at that time. To avoid criticism from the client, Kay instructed a newly employed secretary to go to the client's office, ask to see the general ledger, and to give the impression of being busy until an auditor could be assigned to the engagement.

CHAPTER 3

Professional Ethics

Highlights of the Chapter

1.   Professions have several characteristics in common, including (a) responsibility to serve the public, (b) a complex body of knowledge, (c) standards of admission to the profession, and (d) a need for public confidence. To guide the conduct of their members and demonstrate a dedication to serve the public's interest all recognized professions have established codes of professional ethics.

2.   The AICPA *Code of Professional Conduct* consists of the following two sections:

    a.   **Principles**—a goal-oriented, positively stated discussion of the profession's responsibilities to the public, clients, and fellow practitioners.

    b.   **Rules**—enforceable applications of the Principles.

To provide guidelines for applying the Principles and Rules, the AICPA also issues interpretations and ethics rulings.

3.   The conduct of a CPA is embodied in the six articles of the Principles:

    a.   **Responsibilities.** In carrying out their responsibilities as professionals, members should exercise sensitive professional and moral judgments in all their activities.

    b.   **The public interest.** Members should accept the obligation to act in a way that will serve the public interest, honor the public trust, and demonstrate commitment to professionalism.

    c.   **Integrity.** To maintain and broaden public confidence, members should perform all professional responsibilities with the highest sense of integrity.

    d.   **Objectivity and independence.** A member should maintain objectivity and be free of conflicts of interest in discharging professional responsibilities. A member in public practice should be independent in fact and appearance when providing auditing and other attestation services.

    e.   **Due care.** A member should observe the profession's technical and ethical standards, strive continually to improve competence and the quality of services, and discharge professional responsibility to the best of the member's ability.

    f.   **Scope and nature of services.** A member in public practice should observe the Principles of the *Code of Professional Conduct* in determining the scope and nature of services to be provided.

4.   The bylaws of the AICPA require that members adhere to the Rules of the *Code of Professional Conduct.* Members must be prepared to justify departures from these Rules.

5.   **Rule 101—Independence.** Requires that members be independent in the performance of professional services as required by professional standards. Professional standards require CPAs to be independent whenever they provide assurance to third parties.

6.   A CPA is not considered to be independent of any client in which the CPA has a direct or material indirect financial interest. Independence is also impaired by certain business relationships, such as serving as director or officer of the company.

7.   Two distinct ideas are involved in the rule of independence. First, auditors must **in fact** be independent of any enterprise, which they audit; and, second, the relationships of auditors with clients must be such that the auditors will **appear** independent to third parties.

8.   Financial interests (direct and material indirect) are prohibited during the performance of the audit and at the time the audit opinion is issued. Since a person cannot act independently in evaluating his or her own work, the restriction regarding business relationships also extends to the entire period covered by the auditors' report.

9.   To understand how the independence of an auditor affects the independence of a CPA firm you must have an understanding of the term covered members. The independence rule applies to all **covered members**. The term covered members includes (1) attest team members, (2) individuals who can influence the engagements (e.g., superior of the engagement partner), (3) other partners in the engagement office, and (4) certain others; the term is formally defined on page 67 of the textbook. Rule 101 also limits ownership interests and employment positions in the client by other professionals with the firm. Figure 3-3 on page 68 of the textbook summarizes the requirements.

10.   Independence of a CPA may be impaired by a direct interest of the CPA's spouse or dependents. It may also be impaired by a material interest by the CPA's close kin. Figure 3–4 on page 71 of the textbook summarizes the effects of interests of a CPA's relatives on the independence of the CPA.

11.   Although the AICPA has not opposed the performance of bookkeeping services for audit clients, the SEC does not consider a CPA firm to be independent if it performs such services for an SEC client.

12.   Consulting services for audit clients should be advisory in nature; if auditors were to assume **decision making roles** in the clients' affairs, independence would be impaired. The Sarbanes-Oxley Act of 2002 prohibits a performance of a variety of nonattest services when a CPA firm audits that company, including: bookkeeping, financial information systems design, appraisal or valuation services, actuarial services, internal audit outsourcing, management functions or human resources, certain investment services, and legal services..

13. **Rule 102—Integrity and objectivity.** A member should maintain objectivity and integrity, be free of conflicts of interest, and shall not misrepresent facts or subordinate his or her judgment to others.

14. **Rule 201—General standards.** A member shall comply with the following general standards:

    a.   Undertake only those engagements which the CPA can reasonably expect to complete with professional competence.

    b.   Exercise due professional care in the performance of an engagement.

    c.   Adequately plan and supervise an engagement.

    d.   Obtain sufficient relevant data to afford a reasonable basis for conclusions or recommendations in relation to an engagement.

15. **Rule 202—Compliance with standards.** A member who performs auditing, review, compilation, consulting, tax, or other professional services shall comply with standards promulgated by bodies designated by Council. The professional standards enforced by this rule are summarized on page 75 of the textbook.

16. **Rule 203—Accounting principles.** A member shall not express an opinion or provide limited assurance that financial statements or other financial data are in accordance with generally accepted accounting principles if the statements or data contain a material departure from a principle issued by the body designated by Council to establish such principles (i.e., the FASB and the GASB), unless the member can demonstrate that due to unusual circumstances the financial statements or data would be otherwise misleading.

17. **Rule 301—Confidential client information.** A member in public practice should not disclose any confidential information without consent of the client. However, this rule does not (a) relieve a member from his or her obligation to observe Rules 202 and 203, (b) affect compliance with a validly issued subpoena or summons enforceable by order of a court, (c) prohibit review of a member's professional practice as a part of a peer review, or (d) preclude a member from responding to any ethics investigation proceedings.

18. **Rule 302—Contingent fees.** Prohibits a member from making a fee contingent on a specified finding or attained result from any client for which the member also performs audits, reviews or certain compilations of financial statements, or examination of prospective financial statements. The member is also prohibited from preparing an original or amended tax return or claim for refund for a contingent fee.

19. **Rule 501—Acts discreditable.** A member shall not commit an act discreditable to the profession, such as signing a false opinion or statement, committing a felony, engaging in discriminatory employment practices, or improperly retaining a client's records.

20. **Rule 502—Advertising and other forms of solicitation.** A member in public practice shall not seek to obtain clients by advertising or other forms of solicitation that is false, misleading, or deceptive. Examples of unethical advertising include advertising that creates unjustified expectations of favorable results, or indicates an ability to influence a court or other official body.

21. **Rule 503—Commissions and Referral Fees.** A member in public practice should not pay or receive a commission or referral fee from any client for which the member also performs audits, reviews or certain compilations of financial statements, or examination of prospective financial information. Also, the member must disclose to the client any acceptable commissions or referral fees paid or received.

22.   **Rule 505—Form of practice and name.** A member may practice public accounting in any form of organization permitted by state law or regulation whose characteristics conform to AICPA requirements. The first name should not be misleading as to the type of organization.

23.   In addition to providing for adequate professional liability insurance, a CPA practice organized as a professional corporation should allow two-thirds ownership, voting rights and control over professional matters to rest only with individuals authorized to practice public accounting. Most states also allow CPAs to practice as a limited liability partnership (company) and, thereby, protect personal assets of those not involved in an engagement resulting in litigation.

24.   The Institute of Internal Auditors, Inc., has developed ethical standards for the practice of internal auditing. The ethics provisions primarily address internal auditors' obligations to their employers, but they also include provisions that prescribe integrity, objectivity, and competence in the practice of the internal auditing profession.

Test Yourself on Chapter 3

TRUE OR FALSE

For each of the following statements, circle T of F to indicate whether the statement is true or false.

T   F   1.   The Principles section of the Code consists of six articles.

T   F   2.   In most states, violation of Rules of the AICPA *Code of Professional Conduct* may result in suspension or revocation of a CPA's license to practice.

T   F   3.   High moral conduct in support of one's country is a basic ethical rule explicitly set forth in the AICPA *Code of Professional Conduct.*

T   F   4.   Not all sections of the AICPA *Code of Professional Conduct* are binding on all CPAs.

T   F   5.   An auditor may have a direct financial interest in an audit client as long as the investment is not material to the auditor's net worth.

T   F   6.   The AICPA rules regarding independence allow CPAs to perform bookkeeping services for audit clients.

T   F   7.   A CPA would not be considered independent of a savings and loan association where the CPA has a savings account.

T   F   8.   Utilizing outside computer services to process tax returns would be a violation of the ethics rule concerning confidential information.

T   F   9.   A CPA who previously was employed by a client may never be involved in an audit of the financial statements of that client.

T   F   10.   *Statements on Auditing Standards* are enforceable under the AICPA *Code of Professional Conduct.*

T   F   11.   A member of the AICPA may be held responsible for compliance with the ethics rules by persons under his or her supervision.

T   F   12.   Training a client's employees in the operation of a computer system is a consulting service that would not necessarily impair the auditor's independence with respect to the client.

T   F   13.   *Statements of Financial Accounting Standards* issued by the FASB are enforceable under the AICPA *Code of Professional Conduct.*

T   F   14.   Auditors may not allow their working papers to be reviewed in conjunction with a peer review unless their clients agree to the review.

T   F   15.   The *Code of Professional Conduct* prohibits CPAs from establishing fixed fees for an engagement.

T   F   16.   Advertising fees for services is an acceptable form of advertising under the AICPA *Code of Professional Conduct.*

T   F   17.   Engaging in discriminatory employment practices is considered to be an act discreditable to the profession.

T   F   18.   CPAs are prohibited from practicing in the form of a limited liability corporation.

T   F   19.   The *Code of Ethics of the Institute of Internal Auditors, Inc.,* requires that members report to the audit committee of the board of directors.

T   F   20.   The AICPA Code of Professional Conduct prohibits direct solicitation of clients by CPAs.

COMPLETION

Fill in the necessary words to complete the following statements.

1.   The AICPA *Code of Professional Conduct is* made up of two parts: the _____ and the _____.

2.   Auditors must be independent of any enterprise which they audit _____ _____ , and the auditors must also _____ independent to third parties.

3.   A CPA's independence with respect to an enterprise will be impaired if the CPA has any _____ _____ _____ or material _____ financial interest in the enterprise.

4.   In evaluating independence, financial interests of a CPA's _____ and _____ relatives are ascribed directly to the CPA.

5.   CPAs in public practice should not accept a fee from an audit client that is _____ upon a specified finding.

6.   Consulting services for audit clients should be _____ in nature; CPAs should not assume the role of _____ _____ for these clients.

7.   Rule of Conduct 203 requires the CPA to recognize the pronouncements of the _____ _____ _____ _____ and the _____ _____ _____ _____ .

8.   Retaining a client's accounting records for nonpayment of fees is an act _____ to the profession.

9.   CPAs should not seek to obtain clients by advertising that is _____ , _____ , or _____ .

10.   Violation of the AICPA *Code of Professional Conduct* may result in _____ , _____ ,or _____ of the offending member.

MULTIPLE CHOICE

Choose the best answer for each of the following questions and enter the identifying letter in the space provided.

_____ 1. A CPA ethically could:

    a. perform an audit of Tombstone for less than 1/2 of normal audit billing rates.
    b. base her audit fee on the proceeds of her client's stock issue.
    c. own preferred stock in a corporation which is an audit client.
    d. perform a review on a contingent fee basis.

_____ 2. The *Code of Professional Conduct* requires independence for all:

    a. audit and other accounting engagements.
    b. financial statement audits.
    c. services performed.
    d. services performed except tax engagements.

_____ 3. Which of the following is (are) required when a CPA is performing only consulting services for a client?

	Independence	Objectivity
a.	Yes	Yes
b.	Yes	No
c.	No	Yes
d.	No	No

_____ 4. Current auditing standards do not allow which of the following types of loans from a financial institution audit client?

    a. Credit card loans up to a specified limit.
    b. Borrowings collateralized by cash deposits
    c. Home mortgage loans.
    d. Loans of surrender value of an insurance policy.

_____ 5. A professional corporation form of organization:

    a. may ultimately decrease liability of all partners of a CPA firm.
    b. offers certain tax advantages as compared to partnerships.
    c. eliminates personal liability for selected partners.
    d. has similar liability requirements to that of a limited liability company form.

_____ 6. In which of the following circumstances is it most likely that a CPA has violated the Code of Professional Conduct?

    a. He has placed an ad in a newspaper in which he compares his audit firm personnel's experience with that of the personnel of several competing firms.
    b. He has started an audit of a nonpublic company for which last year's fees have not yet been received.
    c. He audits a company in which he previously owned stock.
    d. He serves as trustee of an audit client's profit-sharing trust.

_____   7.   The AICPA Code of Professional Conduct:

a.   does not apply to CPAs who function as tax advisors only.
b.   does not apply to CPAs whose work is limited to consulting services.
c.   does not apply to CPAs who hold positions below the rank of partner, manager, or senior in a national CPA firm.
d.   applies to all of the above categories.

_____   8.   Mavis, CPA, has audited the financial statements of South Bay Sales Incorporated for several years and had always been paid promptly for services rendered. Last year's audit invoices have not been paid because South Bay is experiencing cash flow difficulties, and the current year's audit is scheduled to commence in one week. With respect to the past–due audit fees, Mavis should:

a.   perform the scheduled audit and allow South Bay to pay when the cash flow difficulties are alleviated.
b.   perform the scheduled audit only after arranging a definite payment schedule and securing notes signed by South Bay.
c.   inform South Bay's management that the past–due audit fees are considered an impairment of auditor independence; therefore, it must be paid prior to the issuance of the auditors' report.
d.   inform South Bay's management that the past-due audit fees may be considered a loan on which interest must be imputed for financial statement purposes.

_____   9.   Which of the following individuals is least likely to be considered a covered member by the independence standard?

a.   Staff assistant who works on the audit.
b.   Manager who does not work on the audit.
c.   Tax partner whose only connection to the audit is assistance with the deferred tax liability.
d.   Partner in charge of the office.

_____   10.   Which of the following individuals is most likely to impair a CPA firm's independence with respect to an audit client?

a.   A partner owns 50 shares of stock in the client (the total value is immaterial to both the partner and to the audit client).
b.   A manager on the audit has a cousin who has a summer internship with the audit client.
c.   The partner in charge of the firm does not work on the audit client, but does provide input into remuneration decisions for all partners and professionals involved with the audit.
d.   A friend of a staff member who does not work on the audit owns approximately 10 percent of the client's outstanding stock.

_____ 11. In which of the following circumstances would a CPA be bound by ethics to refrain from disclosing any confidential information obtained during the course of a professional engagement?

   a. The CPA is issued a summons enforceable by a court order which orders the CPA to present confidential information.
   b. A major stockholder of a client company seeks accounting information from the CPA after management declined to disclose the requested information.
   c. Confidential client information is made available as part of a quality review of the CPA's practice by a review team authorized by the AICPA.
   d. An inquiry by a disciplinary body of a state CPA society requests confidential client information.

_____ 12. Mary Troutt, CPA, has been asked by an audit client to prepare income tax returns and serve as a tax advisor.

   a. She is obliged to maintain the same standards of objectivity and freedom from bias in tax work as in auditing.
   b. She may accept a fee for her tax services in the form of shares of common stock in the client company without impairing her independence as an auditor.
   c. She could properly agree to a combined fee for her audit and tax work based on a percentage of the client's after tax income.
   d. She would be free to resolve questionable issues in favor of the client in preparing the tax return.

_____ 13. Which of the following fee arrangements for an audit would constitute a violation of the AICPA *Code of Professional Conduct?*

   a. A fixed fee.
   b. A fee that is based on the number of hours spent on the engagement.
   c. A fee that is computed as a percentage of audited net income.
   d. A fee that is based on the difficulty of the engagement.

_____ 14. Advertising by CPAs:

   a. is presently prohibited by the Code of Professional Conduct.
   b. is permissible as long as it is not false, misleading, or deceptive.
   c. may include statements that the CPA is able to influence decisions by tax courts and other official bodies as long as names of officials are not used.
   d. must not mention fees for services.

EXERCISES

1. For each of the following situations, indicate whether the CPA is "independent" with respect to the client, by circling "yes" or "no."

		Independent?	
a.	The CPA's nondependent child owns an immaterial direct financial interest in the client.	Yes	No
b.	The CPA's spouse owns an immaterial direct financial interest in the client.	Yes	No
c.	The CPA's brother is a controller of the client.	Yes	No
d.	The CPA's father is a salesman for the client.	Yes	No
e.	The CPA's mother owns an immaterial direct financial interest in the client.	Yes	No

2. Listed below are selected Rules of Conduct and ethical problems. Match the rule with the problem to which it applies.

Rules

A	Rule 101	"Independence"
B	Rule 102	"Integrity and objectivity"
C	Rule 201	"General standards"
D	Rule 202	"Compliance with standards"
E	Rule 203	"Accounting principles"
F	Rule 302	"Contingent fees"
G	Rule 501	"Acts discreditable"
H	Rule 502	"Advertising and other forms of solicitation"
I	Rule 503	"Commissions and referral fees"
J	Rule 505	"Form or practice and name"

Problems

_____ a. An audit client owes the CPA past-due audit fees.

_____ b. The auditors fail to qualify their opinion on financial statements that do not properly apply a particular FASB *Statement*.

_____ c. A CPA who is the controller for a company knowingly issues misleading financial statements.

_____ d. A CPA performs tax services that the CPA is not competent to perform.

_____ e. A sole practitioner practices in a partnership name.

_____ f. A member violates rules issued by the Accounting and Review Services Committee.

_____ g. A CPA robs a service station.

_____ h. A CPA accepts a percentage of the client's loan as an audit fee.

CHAPTER 4

Legal Liability of CPAs

Highlights of the Chapter

1. The potential liability of CPAs for negligence is much greater than that of other professionals. If a CPA is negligent in expressing an opinion on financial statements, literally hundreds of thousands of investors may sustain losses.

2. The area of legal liability has a number of important terms, including:

   a. **Ordinary negligence**—failure on the part of the CPA to exercise "due professional care. "
   b. **Gross negligence**—failure on the part of the CPA to exercise even slight care; many jurisdictions consider gross negligence equivalent to constructive fraud.
   c. **Fraud**—intentional misrepresentation by one person that results in damages to another party.
   d. **Constructive fraud**—similar to fraud except that the misrepresentation is not be intentional. Gross negligence is sometimes considered to be constructive fraud.
   e. **Privity**—the relationship between parties to a contract.
   f. **Engagement letter**—the written contract between the client and the CPA.
   g. **Breach of contract**—failure of one or both parties to a contract to perform in accordance with the contract's provisions.
   h. **Third–party beneficiaries**—parties who have been identified as directly benefiting from the contracted services and, thus, become in privity with the auditors and their client.
   i. **Proximate cause**—damage to another directly attributable to a wrongdoer's act.
   j. **Plaintiff**—the party claiming damages and bringing suit against the defendant.
   k. **Contributory negligence**—negligence on the part of the plaintiff contributing to his or her loss.
   l. **Comparative negligence**—a concept used by the courts to allocate damages among negligent parties.
   m. **Common law**—unwritten law that has been developed by court decisions.
   n. **Statutory law**—law adopted by a governmental unit; of primary concern to auditors are the federal securities acts and the state blue–sky laws.

3. The CPAs' relationship with a client is that of an independent contractor. In undertaking a professional engagement, the CPAs are obliged to exercise due professional care, including adherence to professional standards and ethics.

4. CPAs' liability to clients most often arises from the CPAs' failure to detect fraud on the part of an employee of the client. To obtain a judgment against its auditors under common law, an injured client must prove that it sustained a loss as a result of the auditors' negligence. As defendants, the auditors can refute the charges by showing that (1) they were not negligent, or (2) their negligence was not the proximate cause of the client's loss (e.g., there was contributory negligence on the part of the client).

5. Auditors' liability to other third parties varies from one jurisdiction (state court) to the next. Some jurisdictions adhere to the legal precedent set by the *Ultramares* (Known User) Approach. This approach, established in *Ultramares v. Touche & Co.*, and upheld in *Credit Alliance Corp. v. Arthur Andersen & Co* holds auditors liable to unidentified (unforeseen) third parties for only gross negligence or fraud. Only third party beneficiaries can hold the auditor liable for ordinary negligence.

6.   Other state courts follow the Restatement of Torts (Foreseen User) Approach established by the *Second Restatement of the Law of Torts.* This principle expands the auditors' liability for ordinary negligence to include any limited class of known or intended users of the financial statements.

7.   Still other state courts follow the *Rosenblum* ((Foreseeable User) Approach, and hold auditors liable for ordinary negligence to all foreseeable third parties.

8.   Under common law, the plaintiffs seeking damages from a CPA firm must prove that they sustained a **loss**, the CPA accepted a **duty** of care, **breached that duty**, and the CPA's negligence performance **caused** (was the "proximate cause") the loss.

9.   Auditors also have liability under statutory law. Of primary concern is auditors' liability under the Securities Act of 1933 and the Securities Exchange Act of 1934. Auditors must also be concerned with the Racketeer Influenced and Corrupt Organizations (RICO) Act.

10.   The Securities Act of 1933 (1933 Act) deals with the initial issuance of securities to the public, and requires the company issuing the securities to file a registration statement (often Form S-1) with the SEC. The 1933 Act provides that accountants who express an opinion in a registration statement concerning a proposed offering of corporate securities may be held liable to third parties for their losses if the statements are later shown to include untrue statements of material fact or to omit material facts necessary to prevent the statements from being misleading.

11.   Under the 1933 Act, purchasers of the securities who sustained losses may sue the auditors, and need not prove that they relied upon the statements or that the auditors were negligent. The burden of proof is on the auditors to show that their examination was conducted with "due diligence," or that the losses of the plaintiff were not the result of errors or omissions in the audited statements.

12.   A significant case involving auditors' liability under the 1933 Act was the *BarChris* case. In that case the auditors were found to be negligent in their required investigation of subsequent events to the effective date of the company's registration statement.

13.   The Securities Exchange Act of 1934 (1934 Act) contains requirements for periodic reporting by public companies, including requirements for filing audited annual financial statements in the Form 10-K. Lawsuits against CPAs have been filed under Section 18(a) and Rule 10b-5 of the 1934 Act. The wording of these provisions implies that the act was written to create liability for fraudulent misrepresentations. However, some lower court decisions have broadly interpreted the provisions to hold auditors liable for ordinary negligence. Recently, the U.S. Supreme Court ruled in favor of the auditors in a landmark case (the *Hochfelder* case) regarding auditor liability under Rule 10b–5 of the 1934 Act.

14.   Historically, defendants in actions under the 1934 Act were jointly and severally liable for all losses by plaintiffs. The Private Securities Litigation Reform Act of 1995 amended the 1934 Act to place limits on the extent to which the auditors are liable for losses caused by other defendants, such as management.

15.   In the *Hochfelder* case, investors in fictitious escrow accounts filed suit against the auditors for losses resulting from failure to detect fraudulent use of their funds by the president of a small brokerage firm. The suit claimed that the fraud was made possible by the auditors' negligence in the study and evaluation of internal control. The U.S. Supreme Court ruled that the wording of the 1934 Act indicates that an action for damages is not warranted in the absence of knowing or intentional misconduct. Thus, this case may mark the end of auditors' liability for ordinary negligence under the 1934 Act, but they still may be held liable for gross negligence.

16.   Both the 1933 Act and the 1934 Act include provisions for criminal charges against persons, including auditors, violating provisions of the acts.

17.   The SEC, in administering the Securities Acts, can take punitive action against public accounting firms when it has found the audit work deficient with regard to financial statements filed with the Commission. Rule of Practice 2(e) gives the SEC the power of suspension and disbarment. Recently, the SEC has taken action against CPA firms by the use of consent decrees in which the CPAs have agreed to certain penalties or restrictions. As discussed in Chapter 2, the Public Company Accounting Oversight Board also may conduct investigations and disciplinary proceedings of both CPAs firms and their professional employees (including owners).

18.   In the *Continental Vending* case, three CPAs were convicted of criminal fraud when there was no proven intent to defraud; the fraud charges were based on gross negligence. The U.S. government's case of fraud hinged upon a note to the financial statements that omitted significant details of transactions between Continental Vending Machine Corporation and certain related parties.

19.   CPAs and public accounting firms may be subject to prosecution under various other criminal statutes. For example, in 2002 Arthur Andersen became the first major accounting firm to be convicted of a felony based on "wholesale destruction of documents" relating to the Enron Corporation collapse. Loss of the case effectively put the firm out of business.

20.   CPAs also may be involved with unaudited financial statements. For example, CPAs may compile or review the financial statements of nonpublic companies. A compilation refers to the preparation of financial statements from information provided by management, without providing any assurance on the statements. A **review** consists of performing inquiry and analytical procedures designed to provide the CPAs with a basis for providing limited assurance regarding the fairness of the financial statements.

21.   CPAs may also be held liable for negligence when performing services involving unaudited financial statements. The 1136 *Tenants' Corporation* case was a landmark case involving auditors' liability when associated with unaudited financial statements. This case contains many lessons for CPAs, including:

    a.   A CPA should adhere closely to Rules 102 and 202 of the AICPA *Code of Professional Conduct.*

    b.   Engagement letters are essential for accounting and review services, where the client might misunderstand the nature and scope of the CPAs' services.

    c.   A CPA performing accounting and review services should be alert for, and follow up on, matters that indicate the information provided to them is inaccurate.

    d.   CPAs should report on financial statements clearly and concisely, using the standardized language set forth in *Statements on Auditing Standards* and *Statements on Standards for Accounting and Review Services.*

22.   In light of the auditors' extensive exposure to litigation, public accounting firms must take positive action to withstand the threat of legal liability, including careful compliance with various professional standards, retaining legal counsel that is familiar with CPAs' legal liability, and consideration of the need to purchase liability insurance.

Test Yourself on Chapter 4

TRUE OR FALSE

For each of the following statements, circle the T or the F to indicate whether the statement is true or false.

T F 1. Laws and court interpretations concerning a CPA's liability vary from one jurisdiction to another.

T F 2. One reason that liability insurance rates are high for CPAs is that the number of persons who might be injured as a result of improper professional practice is large.

T F 3. CPAs who are found negligent will not be able to recover on a liability insurance policy covering the practice of public accounting.

T F 4. A violation of the AICPA *Code of Professional Conduct* may result in the CPA being found legally negligent.

T F 5. Under both common law and statutory law, CPA liability may arise from improper performance of audits or tax services, but not consulting services.

T F 6. In the event the auditors are negligent but no party suffers a financial loss, the auditors ordinarily have no civil liability.

T F 7. In the *Rosenblum v. Adler* case, the state supreme court ruled that auditors could not be held liable to unidentified third parties for ordinary negligence.

T F 8. Legal actions under common law require the plaintiffs to bear most of the burden of affirmative proof.

T F 9. Assuming that a registration statement omits a material fact and that the auditors were negligent, they can reduce their liability to initial investors if the auditors can demonstrate that the investors' losses were caused partially by other factors.

T F 10. The Securities Act of 1933 requires the auditors to prove that they acted in good faith," whereas the Securities Exchange Act of 1934 requires the auditors to prove "due diligence" to protect themselves from legal liability.

T F 11. In the *Continental Vending* case there was no proven intent to defraud on the part of the CPAs; they were convicted of criminal fraud on the basis of gross negligence.

T F 12. The auditors will always be considered to be negligent if material misstatements in audited financial statements due to errors or fraud go undetected.

T F 13. If the auditors are competent and thorough, there will be no possibility of audited financial statements being misleading.

T F 14. CPAs are not liable to any party if they can successfully prove that they performed their services with due professional care.

T F 15. Privity does not generally exist between the auditors and a securities analyst who relies upon audited financial statements.

T   F   16.   Audits are not designed to detect fraud, and auditors are never liable for losses to clients resulting from undetected fraud.

T   F   17.   Due standard care is a complete defense against a charge of negligence on the part of the auditors.

T   F   18.   The Public Company Accounting Oversight Board has dramatically increased the number of actions brought against CPAs under the Racketeer Influenced and Corrupt Organizations Act.

T   F   19.   CPAs may be held liable for losses sustained because of their association with unaudited financial statements.

T   F   20.   Compilations prepared by CPAs are intended to provide interested parties with a limited degree of assurance regarding the fairness of the financial statements.

COMPLETION

Fill in the necessary words to complete the following statements.

1.   When damage to another is directly attributable to a wrongdoer's act, _____ _____ is said to exist.

2.   Unwritten law that has developed through court decisions is referred to as _____ _____.

3.   Gross negligence is also referred to as _____ _____.

4.   Under the Securities Act of 1933, initial purchasers of securities may sue the auditors for misleading audited financial statements and need not prove that they _____ on the financial statements. The burden of proof is on the auditors to prove that they were _____ _____ in the performance of their work.

5.   A document including audited financial statements that must be filed with the SEC by any company intending to sell its securities to the public through the mails or interstate commerce is called a _____ _____.

6.   The _____ case, a landmark case of liability under the Securities Act of 1933, involved criticism of the auditors' review for subsequent events.

7.   An _____ _____ is the written contract summarizing the relationship between the auditors and the client.

8.   When CPAs are associated with _____ _____ _____, a possibility exists that the client may misinterpret the extent of the CPAs' services and believe that the accountants are acting as auditors.

9.   A _____ of financial statements involves the performance of limited investigative procedures that provide a basis for the expression of limited assurance that there are no material departures from generally accepted accounting principles.

10.   The _____ _____ _____ case was a landmark case regarding the accountant's liability for unaudited financial statements.

MULTIPLE CHOICE

Choose the best answer for each of the following questions and enter the identifying letter in the space provided.

_____ 1.   In connection with a lawsuit, a third party attempts to gain access to the auditor's working papers. The client's defense of privileged communication will be successful only to the extent it is protected by the:

        a.   auditor's agreement in the use of this defense.
        b.   common law.
        c.   AICPA *Code of Professional Conduct.*
        d.   state law.

_____ 2.   Under common law, auditors are generally liable to the client for:

        a.   lack of due diligence.
        b.   ordinary negligence, but not gross negligence.
        c.   ordinary negligence or gross negligence.
        d.   gross negligence, but not ordinary negligence.

_____ 3.   Under the 1934 Securities Exchange Act auditors are liable to ordinary trade creditors for:

        a.   lack of due diligence.
        b.   lack of good faith.
        c.   gross negligence
        d.   none of the above.

_____ 4. Valid statements concerning gross negligence include all but which one of the following?

     a. Gross negligence is the lack of even slight care.
     b. Gross negligence may be viewed as "failure to exercise due professional care."
     c. Gross negligence is indicative of a reckless disregard for one's professional responsibilities.
     d. Substantial failures to comply with generally accepted auditing standards might be interpreted as gross negligence.

_____ 5. As a consequence of their failure to adhere to generally accepted auditing standards in the course of their audit of Frost Corp., Jones & Telling, CPAs, did not detect the embezzlement of a material amount of money by the company's controller. As a matter of common law, to what extent would the CPAs be liable to Frost Corp. for losses attributable to the theft?

     a. They would have no liability, since the ordinary examination cannot be relied upon to detect fraud.
     b. They would have no liability because privity is lacking.
     c. They would be liable only if it could be proven that they were grossly negligent.
     d. They would be liable for all losses attributable to their negligence.

_____ 6. The Securities Act of 1934 applies to:

     a. all for–profit business corporations within the United States.
     b. all companies under the jurisdiction of the Securities and Exchange Commission.
     c. all companies within the United States with $1 million or more total assets.
     d. all companies within the United States with $10 million or more total assets and five or more shareholders.

_____ 7. According to *Statements on Auditing Standards,* the auditor's responsibility for failure to detect fraud arises:

     a. when such failure clearly results from failure to comply with generally accepted auditing standards.
     b. whenever the amounts involved are material.
     c. only when the examination was specifically designed to detect fraud.
     d. only when such failure clearly results from negligence so gross as to sustain an inference of fraud on the part of the auditor.

_____ 8. According to court decisions, the generally accepted auditing standards established by the AICPA apply:

     a. only to the AICPA membership.
     b. to all CPAs in public practice.
     c. only to those who choose to follow them.
     d. only when conducting audits subject to AICPA jurisdiction.

_____ 9. The *1136 Tenants Association* case was chiefly important because of its emphasis upon the legal liability of the CPA when associated with:

     a. a review on interim statements.
     b. unaudited financial statements.
     c. an audit resulting in a disclaimer of opinion.
     d. letters for underwriters.

_____ 10. Lessons to be learned from the *1136 Tenants Corporation* case include all but which of the following?

    a.   A CPA firm should never imply that it acted as an independent auditor unless it complied with GAAS.

    b.   Engagement letters are essential for accounting and review services.

    c.   Oral arrangements are necessary for supplementing items set forth in the engagement letter.

    d.   A CPA engaged to perform accounting or review services should follow up on unusual items such as missing invoices.

_____ 11. In the event that a CPA issues an unqualified audit report on financial statements which he or she knows to be misleading, that CPA is:

    a.   subject to criminal as well as civil liability.

    b.   subject to civil liability.

    c.   not subject to liability if the client also knows the financial statements to be misleading.

    d.   not subject to liability if he performed no audit procedures relating to the misleading portions of the statements.

_____ 12. For a CPA firm considering the acceptance of new clients, which of the following characteristics would be a deterrent?

    a.   The prospective client is long established but has shown little growth in recent years.

    b.   The prospective client is in the same line of business as two present clients and is in direct competition with one of them.

    c.   The prospective client is in a new much-publicized industry offering the possibility of rapid growth but is under financed and possibly on the brink of bankruptcy.

    d.   The prospective client is a defendant in an antitrust suit brought by the U.S. Department of Justice.

EXERCISES

1. Define the following common terms of business law.

    a.   Privity_____

    b.   Third–party beneficiary_____

           _____

    c.   Fraud_____

           _____

    d.   Negligence_____

           _____

    e.   Gross negligence_____

---

f.   Foreseen third party_____

---

2.   Listed below are sources of law and legal situations. For each of the situations indicate the letter corresponding to the law that applies.

SOURCES OF LAW

A   Common law
B   The Securities Act of 1933
C   The Securities Exchange Act of 1934

LEGAL SITUATIONS

___A___ a.   The client files a lawsuit against the CPAs for negligence in the performance of tax services.

___C___ b.   A stockholder sustains a loss when he purchases 100 shares of stock in a public company from another stockholder in reliance upon audited financial statements included in Form 10-K.

___A___ c.   A bank loses money that it loaned to a public company in reliance upon financial statements filed with the SEC.

___B___ d.   An initial purchaser of bonds of a public company sustains a loss.

___B___ e.   A CPA is criminally prosecuted for gross negligence in auditing financial statements contained in a registration statement.

CHAPTER 5

Audit Evidence and Documentation

Highlights of the Chapter

1. An audit may be regarded as the process of gathering and evaluating sufficient evidence to provide an adequate basis for expressing an opinion on financial statements. The third standard of field work states:

    > Sufficient competent evidential matter is to be obtained through inspection, observation, inquiries, and confirmations to afford a reasonable basis for an opinion regarding the financial statements under audit.

2. Audit procedures are designed to obtain evidence about the assertions that are contained in the financial statements. These assertions are representations of management that are set forth, implicitly or explicitly, in the financial statements. Broadly speaking, financial statements contain the following management assertions:

    a. **Existence or occurrence**—Assets, liabilities, and owners' equity reflected in the financial statements exist; the recorded transactions have occurred.

    b. **Completeness**—All transactions, assets, liabilities, and owners' equity that should be presented in the financial statements are included.

    c. **Rights and obligations**—The client has rights to assets and obligations to pay liabilities that are included in the financial statements.

    d. **Valuation or allocation**—Assets, liabilities, owners' equity, revenues, and expenses are presented at amounts that are determined in accordance with generally accepted accounting principles.

    e. **Presentation and disclosure**—Accounts are described and classified in the financial statements in accordance with generally accepted accounting principles, and all significant and material disclosures are provided.

3. In performing an audit, auditors seek to restrict **audit risk**—the possibility of issuing an unqualified opinion on financial statements that are materially misstated. Audit risk has three components: **inherent risk**—the possibility of a material misstatement occurring in an assertion, assuming no internal control; **control risk**—the possibility that the internal control over an assertion will not prevent or detect a material misstatement; and **detection risk**—the possibility that the auditors' procedures will not detect the material misstatement. The audit process involves assessing inherent and control risk for each assertion and designing tests to appropriately limit the level of detection risk.

4. The relationships among inherent risk, control risk, and detection risk may be described by the following formula:

    Audit risk = Inherent Risk x Control Risk x Detection Risk

5.   The major types of audit evidence may be summarized as:

    a.   **Accounting information system.**

        Comparison—agreeing or contrasting two different sources of information, such as by tracing or vouching (see below).

    b.   **Documentary evidence.**

        Tracing—following a transaction from the source document to the journals and ledgers.

        Vouching—establishing the authenticity and accuracy of entries in accounting records by examining source documents.

        Inspection—the process of reviewing a document or record.

        Reconciliation—the process of establishing agreement between two sets of independently maintained records of the same transactions.

    c.   **Third party representations.**

        Confirmation—the process proving the authenticity and accuracy of an account balance or entry by direct written communication with the debtor, creditor, or other party.

    d.   **Physical evidence.**

        Physical examination—means to view physical evidence of an asset. For example, the auditors may physically examine inventory.

        Observation—the process of viewing a client activity. For example the auditors may observe the client's taking of physical inventory.

    e.   **Computations.**

        Reperformance—the process of repeating a client activity. For example the auditors might reperform a bank reconciliation.

    f.   **Data interrelationships.**

        Analytical procedures—evaluations of financial information made by a study of expected relationships among financial and nonfinancial data.

    g.   **Client representations.**

        Inquiries—questions directed toward appropriate individuals.

6.   The term "competent" in the third standard of field work refers to the validity and relevance of evidence. The quality of a given piece of evidence varies based on its nature and the circumstances.

7.   Although there are sometimes exceptions, the following generalizations can be made about the validity of evidence:

   a.   When auditors obtain evidence from independent sources outside the client company, the reliability is increased.

   b.   Strong internal control contributes to the quality of accounting records and evidence created within the client organization.

   c.   The quality of evidence is enhanced when the auditors obtain the information directly-that is, by firsthand observation, correspondence, or computation rather than by obtaining the information secondhand.

8.   Auditors must gather sufficient evidence to serve as the basis for an opinion. While auditors must be reasonably certain before expressing an opinion, they are never completely certain. The extent of the evidence needed to support the auditors' opinion for a given audit is a matter of professional judgment, requiring the consideration of both materiality and audit risk.

9.   The need for evidential matter is closely related to the concept of materiality; the smaller an auditor's preliminary estimate of materiality for the engagement, the greater the scope of evidence that is needed. In addition, the more material a particular financial statement amount is to the financial statements, the greater the need for valid evidential matter.

10.   Every engagement involves a different level of risk that the financial statements contain material errors or fraud, including violations of generally accepted accounting principles. When the risk is higher, the auditors should demand more and better evidence than would normally be required as a basis for an opinion.

11.   Auditors must also assess the inherent risk of material misstatements of individual accounts. The very nature of some accounts makes the inherent risk of misstatement of those accounts greater than for others.

12.   The auditors' opinion that financial statements are free from material misstatement is based on a combination of their reliance upon (a) the effectiveness of the client's internal control in preventing the occurrence of such misstatement, and (b) the auditors' substantive procedures to detect any material misstatement that may have occurred.

13.   The evidence that the auditors obtain about a client's internal control (which determines the auditors' assessment of control risk) is a major factor in determining how much evidence the auditors will gather to restrict detection risk.

14.   Physical evidence is extremely reliable evidence of existence of certain assets, such as inventories and property, plant, and equipment. However, physical evidence often must be supplemented by other types of evidence to determine rights, completeness, and proper valuation of the assets.

15.   Documentary evidence is strongest when it is created outside the organization and transmitted directly to the auditors. An example of this type of documentary evidence is a bank cutoff statement.

16.   Documentary evidence created outside the client organization and held by the client generally is the next most reliable type of documentary evidence. Examples include bank statements, vendors' invoices, and property tax bills.

17.   Documentary evidence created within the organization, such as sales invoices and purchase orders, is generally considered less reliable than either category of externally created documentary evidence. The degree of reliance to be placed on such evidence depends on the adequacy of the client's internal control.

18.   Analytical procedures involve evaluations of financial information by the study of the relationships among financial and nonfinancial data. For example, financial balances for the current year may be compared to those of prior years, to budgeted levels, or to relevant nonfinancial data, such as units produced or hours of direct labor.

19.   If an audit client's operations are comparable to other firms in the same industry, industry averages obtained from financial reporting services provide a valuable source of information for analytical procedures.

20.   The process of performing analytical procedures involves: (1) developing an expectation of an account balance, (2) determining the amount of difference from the expectation that can be accepted without investigation, (3) comparing the company's account balance with the expected account balance, and (4) investigating significant deviations from the expected account balance.

21.   Analytical procedures must be performed during the planning stage of the audit to direct the auditors' attention to areas requiring special investigation, and in the final review stage of the audit. Also, they may be applied during the audit as substantive procedures to provide evidence about the reasonableness of specific account balances.

22.   The quality of the evidence obtained from analytical procedures varies based on the relevance and reliability of the data used for the comparisons, and the plausibility of the relationships.

23.   The evaluation of certain assertions in financial statements may require expertise not possessed by the auditors. In such cases, the auditors will rely on the work of a specialist in the appropriate field. In evaluating the competence of the evidence provided by a specialist, the auditors should investigate the professional qualifications and reputation of the specialist, and assess the risk that the independence of the specialist might be impaired. They also must obtain an understanding of the methods or assumptions used by the specialist.

24.   The purposes of client representation letters are to have officials of the client acknowledge their primary responsibility for the representations made in the financial statements and to get in writing the important oral representations made by these individuals during the course of the audit.

25.   The representation letter should be dated as of the last day of field work, and signed by officers that are knowledgeable of, and responsible for, the representations made (e.g., the chief financial officer and the chief executive officer). Management's refusal to furnish written representations constitutes a scope limitation that should preclude the issuance of an unqualified opinion.

26.   Gathering evidence in the areas of accounting estimates, fair market values, and related party transactions is difficult because judgments need to be made by both management and the auditors. The three basic approaches for **accounting estimates** are (a) review and test management's process of developing the estimates; (b) independently develop an estimate to compare to management's estimate; and (c) review subsequent events or transactions bearing on the estimate. A combination of the three approaches is often used.

27.   **Fair market values** are used for a variety of accounts (e.g., investments, intangible assets, derivates, impaired assets). When there are no organized market for the assets, management must develop models to estimate their fair values. In these cases, the approaches used to audit estimates (above) are often used to establish the reasonableness of the estimated fair values.

28.   **Related party transactions** are exchanges in which one of the parties has the ability to significantly influence the actions of the other party. Examples of related party transactions include transactions between a company and its officers, directors, major stockholders, or unconsolidated subsidiaries.

29.   The primary concern of the auditors is that related party transactions are adequately disclosed in the client's financial statements, including a description of the transactions, the relationship between the parties, and the dollar amounts involved.

30.   In auditing for related party transactions, the auditors should make inquiries of management as to the policies and procedures for identifying and accounting for such transactions. They should identify related parties early in the engagement and be alert throughout the audit for evidence of transactions with these parties. The auditors should also investigate any unusual transactions for indications of involvement by related parties.

31.   An audit is coordinated and documented with audit documentation (working papers). The information in the working papers constitutes the principal evidence of the auditors' work and their resulting conclusions.

32.   The auditors encounter different business organizations and internal control. Therefore, the auditors must tailor the form and content of their working papers to fit the circumstances of each engagement.

33.   Proper audit documentation (working papers) must be sufficient to enable members of the audit team to (1) understand who performed and reviewed the work, (2) to understand what work was performed, and (3) to show that the accounting records agree or reconcile with the financial statements.

34.   Audit working papers are the property of the auditors. However, much of the information in working papers is confidential, and generally must not be made available to outsiders without the consent of the client.

35.   Working papers must be safeguarded from employees of the client during the audit. Safeguarding working papers means keeping them locked in a briefcase during lunch and after working hours.

36.   If the auditors are charged with negligence, their working papers will be a major factor in refuting or substantiating the charge. Working papers including conflicting evidence or conclusions make it more difficult for the auditors to protect themselves in court. The Sarbanes-Oxley Act of 2002 requires that auditors retain working papers for a period of not less than seven years.

37.   The ultimate responsibility for decisions regarding complex accounting or auditing rests with the engagement partner. However, if other members of the audit team disagree with the resolution of a problem, they should document their disagreement in the working papers.

38.   The major types of audit working papers include (1) audit administrative working papers, (2) working trial balance and lead schedules, (3) adjusting journal entries and reclassification entries, (4) supporting schedules, analyses, reconciliations, and computational working papers, and (5) corroborating documents.

39.   **Audit administrative working papers** aid the auditors in the planning and administration of engagements, and include audit plans, programs, time budgets, internal control questionnaires and flowcharts, and engagement letters.

40.   The **working trial balance** is a schedule listing the balances of accounts in the general ledger for the current and previous year, with columns for adjusting entries, reclassification entries, and the financial statement amounts.

41.   A **lead schedule** is used to combine several amounts which total to an amount on the trial balance.

42.   The auditors usually maintain two files of working papers for each client: (1) **current files** for each year's engagement, and (2) the **permanent file** of relatively unchanging data. The current file pertains solely to that year's examination, while the permanent file contains such things as copies of the articles of incorporation which are of continuing audit interest.

43.   Working papers should meet the basic objectives of being complete but free of nonessential data and organized in a manner that makes them readily understandable to others. Also, working papers should usually possess the following characteristics:

a.   Every working paper must be identified as to client, audit date, and title.
b.   A separate working paper should be prepared for each topic.
c.   Every working paper should contain the name or initials of the auditor preparing it, the date prepared, and the initials of the auditors reviewing the working paper.
d.   All working papers should be indexed to permit systematic cross-referencing within the working papers.
e.   The source of all data should be clearly indicated.
f.   The nature and extent of the audit procedures performed should be indicated on the working papers.
g.   Whenever tick marks are used, they must be accompanied with a legend explaining their significance.
h.   When appropriate, the auditors should write a conclusion on individual working papers indicating how the results will affect the audit report.

44.   Many CPA firms prepare electronic working papers. Electronic working papers have the advantage of automatic adjustment of other working papers when a related working paper is changed.

7.   In relying upon the work of a specialist, the auditors must ascertain the professional _____ and reputation of the specialist and review the reasonableness of the underlying _____ made by the specialist.

8.   A letter signed by officers of the client company at the auditors' request which sets forth certain assertions about the company's financial position and operations is known as a _____ _____.

9.   Audit working papers provide evidence that the auditors complied with generally accepted auditing standards, especially the _____ _____ _____ _____.

10.   The _____ _____ _____ is a schedule listing the balances of accounts in the client's general ledger.

11.   Separate _____ _____ are used to combine similar general ledger accounts into the total that appears on the working trial balance.

12.   Working papers of audit interest over an extended period of time should be filed in the _____ _____.

13.   The auditors develop _____ _____ to correct the effects of errors or fraud in the client's accounting records.

14.   The purpose of an analysis of an account is to illustrate all _____ in the account for the period under audit.

15.   Symbols used to indicate the audit work performed on an item are referred to as _____ _____.

MULTIPLE CHOICE

Choose the best answer for each of the following questions and enter the identifying letter in the space provided.

_____   1.   The major reason auditors gather evidence is to:

   a.   form an opinion on the financial statements.
   b.   detect fraud.
   c.   evaluate management.
   d.   assess control risk.

_____ 2. In connection with the third generally accepted auditing standard of field work, auditors examine corroborating evidential matter which includes all of the following except:

    a. client accounting manuals.
    b. written client representations.
    c. vendor invoices.
    d. minutes of board meetings.

_____ 3. Which of the following statements relating to the competence of evidential matter is always true?

    a. Evidential matter gathered by the auditors from outside an enterprise is reliable.
    b. Accounting data developed under satisfactory conditions of internal control are more relevant than data developed under unsatisfactory internal control conditions.
    c. Oral representations made by management are not valid evidence.
    d. Evidence gathered by auditors must be both valid and relevant to be considered competent.

_____ 4. Evidence is generally considered sufficient when:

    a. it is competent.
    b. there is enough of it to afford a reasonable basis for an opinion on the financial statements.
    c. it has the qualities of being relevant, objective, and free from bias.
    d. it has been obtained by random selection.

_____ 5. The most reliable type of documentary evidence that auditors can obtain is:

    a physical examination by the auditors.
    b. documentary evidence calculated by the auditors from company records.
    c. confirmations received directly from third parties.
    d. internal documents.

_____ 6. Analytical procedures are:

    a. statistical tests of financial information designed to identify areas requiring intensive investigation.
    b. analytical tests of financial information made by a computer.
    c. tests that involve evaluations of financial statement information by a study of relationships among financial and nonfinancial data.
    d. diagnostic tests of financial information which may not be classified as evidential matter.

_____ 7. A principal purpose of a representation letter from management is to:

    a. serve as an introduction to company personnel and authorize the auditors to examine the records.
    b. remind management of its primary responsibility for the financial statements.
    c. substitute for other evidence-gathering audit procedures.
    d. confirm management's approval of the work performed by the auditors.

_____ 8. When an examination is made in accordance with generally accepted auditing standards, the independent auditors must:

   a. use statistical sampling.
   b. employ analytical procedures.
   c. test internal control.
   d. observe the taking of physical inventory on the balance sheet date.

_____ 9. Which of the following procedures is not customarily used by the auditors in determining the existence of related parties?

   a. Inquire of customers, suppliers, and employees as to their knowledge of related-party transactions.
   b. Review prior years' work papers for the names of known related parties.
   c. Evaluate the company's procedures for identifying and properly accounting for related-party transactions.
   d. Inquire of appropriate management personnel as to the names of all related parties and whether there were any transactions with these parties during the period.

_____ 10. Which of the following eliminates voluminous details from the auditors' working trial balance by classifying and summarizing similar or related items?

   a. Account analyses.
   b. Supporting schedules.
   c. Control accounts.
   d. Lead schedules.

_____ 11. Which of the following is not a factor that affects the independent auditors' judgment as to the quantity, type, and content of working papers?

   a. The timing and the number of personnel to be assigned to the engagement.
   b. The nature of the financial statements, schedules, or other information upon which the auditors are reporting.
   c. The need for supervision of the engagement.
   d. The nature of the audit report.

_____ 12. The auditors' working papers will generally be _least_ likely to include documentation showing how the:
   a. client's schedules were prepared.
   b. engagement had been planned.
   c. client's internal control structure had been considered.
   d. unusual matters were resolved.

_____ 13. The permanent file of the auditors' working papers generally should include:
   a. time and expense reports.
   b. names and addresses of all audit staff personnel on the engagement.
   c. a copy of key customer confirmations.
   d. a copy of the corporate charter.

_____ 14. The third general auditing standard requires that due professional care be exercised in the performance of the audit and preparation of the report. The matter of due professional care deals with what is done. For example, due care in the matter of working papers requires that working paper:

    a. format be neat and orderly and include both a permanent file and a general file.
    b. content be sufficient to provide support for the auditors' report, including the auditors' representation as to compliance with auditing standards.
    c. ownership be determined by the legal statutes of the state where the auditors practice.
    d. preparation be the responsibility of assistant accountants whose work is reviewed by senior accountants, managers, and partners.

_____ 15. Which of the following is a primary function of audit working papers?

    a. Provide a source of information for internal auditors.
    b. Facilitate peer review.
    c. Aid seniors, managers, and partners in supervising and reviewing the work.
    d. Provide primary support for the financial statements.

_____ 16. Differences of opinion between members of the audit staff about auditing matters should:

    a. never be documented in the working papers because to do could lead to legal liability problems.
    b. be documented along with the manner in which they were resolved.
    c. be included in a note to the financial statements.
    d. be described in the auditors' report.

_____ 17. Tracing a sample of documents from the source documents to the ledgers is designed to test the financial statement assertion of:

    a. completeness.
    b. validity.
    c. existence.
    d. valuation.

EXERCISES

1. Match the following audit terms with their definitions.

_g___ 1. Inspection

a. Proving the accuracy of a client-performed activity.

_d___ 2. Physical Examination

b. Establishing the validity of a balance by direct communication with an outside party.

_b___ 3. Confirmation

c. Following a transaction from a source document to recorded entries.

_a___ 4. Reperformance

d. Observing assets that have physical existence.

_f___ 5. Reconciliation

e. Establishing the validity of a transaction by examining supporting documents.

_c___ 6. Tracing

f. Establishing the agreement between two sets of related accounting records.

_e___ 7. Vouching

g. Critical review of a document.

2   Analytical procedures must be used by auditors in planning audit engagements.

a.   Define analytical procedures.

b.   List the two major benefits derived from using analytical procedures in planning an engagement.

(1)

(2)

3.   The auditors have two types of working paper files, the current file (**CF**) and the permanent file (**PF**). Using the initials and the spaces provided, indicate which file each of the following documents would most likely be filed.

_P_   1.   A lease agreement.

_C_   2.   A confirmation of financial institution deposits.

_P_   3.   Articles of incorporation.

_P_   4.   An analysis of long-term debt.

_P_   5.   A pension agreement.

_C_   6.   An adjusted trial balance.

_C_   7.   Adjusting journal entries.

_C_   8.   An analysis of miscellaneous expenses.

_P_   9.   An analysis of owners' equity accounts.

_P_   10.   A chart of accounts.

CHAPTER 6

Planning the Audit; Linking Audit Procedures to Risk

Highlights of the Chapter

1.   The first standard of field work requires that the audit engagement be adequately planned. Adequate planning includes investigating the prospective client, obtaining an understanding of the client's business, and developing an overall strategy to organize, coordinate, and schedule the audit staff.

2.   In addition to determining that the CPA firm has the necessary skills to effectively audit a prospective client in accordance with GAAS, CPAs must consider other factors of **engagement risk** such as the possibility of litigation arising from investors who sustain a loss. For example, auditors consider the reputation of management, the company's financial strength and its credit rating in investigating and considering a prospective client.

3.   Successor auditors must attempt certain inquiries of the predecessor auditors before accepting a new engagement. These inquiries are designed to determine whether the successor auditors should accept the engagement, and include questions regarding disagreements with management, the integrity of management, and the predecessor auditors' understanding of the reason for the change in auditors.

4.   Another useful preliminary step for the auditors is to arrange a tour of the plant and offices of the prospective client. This tour provides the auditors with an understanding of the plant layout, manufacturing process, principal products, and physical safeguards. The auditors also meet key personnel and learn the location of various accounting records.

5.   For prospective clients that are SEC registrants—as well as for a number of other companies—the company's audit committee is responsible for appointment, compensation and oversight of the auditors. Audit committees usually consist of 3 to 5 directors that are not officers of the company.

6.   A conference with the audit committee and management prior to beginning the engagement is a useful step in avoiding misunderstandings between the client and the auditors, concerning the scope and purpose of the audit. The conference should include a discussion of such matters as the objective of the audit, the audit fee, the timing of the audit work, and the work which will be performed by the client's staff to reduce the time and cost of the audit.

7.   The preliminary arrangements reached with the client should be set forth in an engagement letter prepared by the auditors, making clear the nature of the engagement, any limitations on the scope of the audit, work to be performed by the client's staff, and the basis for computing the auditors' fee. The letter should also explain the auditors' responsibilities for detecting fraud.

8.   To understand a client and its environment, the auditors must have a thorough understanding of the client's industry, including economic conditions and financial trends, inherent risks, government regulations, barriers to entry, strength of competitors, and the bargaining power of suppliers and customers. The auditors' knowledge of the client's business should include an understanding of such factors as the client's organizational structure, accounting policies and procedures, capital structure, product lines, and methods of production and distribution. These factors will be considered in relation to the client's operating and financing strategies.

9.   After obtaining a knowledge of the client's business, the auditors should formulate an efficient and effective strategy for the audit engagement. In developing this strategy, the auditors make a preliminary estimate of the levels of risk and materiality for the engagement. Where the risk of the engagement is higher, the auditors must increase the intensity of their audit procedures.

10.   **Analytical procedures** involve evaluations of financial information by examination of relationships among financial and nonfinancial data. In planning the engagement, analytical procedures must be performed to provide the auditors with a better understanding of the financial characteristics of the client's business, and identify financial statement amounts that may contain material misstatement.

11.   Materiality for planning purposes is the auditors' preliminary estimate of the smallest amount of misstatement that would be material to any one of the client's financial statements. The auditors must plan the audit to achieve a low level of audit risk that a material misstatement in the financial statements will not go undetected. Various rules of thumb are used to develop estimates of materiality. The materiality estimate may then be allocated to specific accounts in a number of manners.

12.   To identify fraud risks the auditors perform the following procedures:

        a.   Hole a discussion among the audit team members about fraud risk.
        b.   Make inquires of audit committee, management, internal auditors, and other employees about knowledge or reports of fraud.
        c.   Perform planning analytical procedures to identify fraud risks.
        d.   Consider fraud risk factors and the conditions necessary for fraud: (1) incentive or pressure, (2) opportunity, and (3) attitude or ability to rationalize the act. Appendix 6B, which begins on page 215 of the textbook, provides examples of fraud risk factors.
        e.   Identify fraud risks by considering results of a. through d. above.
        f.   Responses to fraud risks—described in detail in following sections.
        g.   Evaluate the results of audit tests.

13.   An overall response to fraud risk may include modification of the audit by

        a.   Application of increased professional skepticism and the designing of procedures to obtain more reliable evidence.
        b.   Assigning of personnel with specialized skills and increased supervision of staff.
        c.   Further consideration of management's selection and application of accounting principles
        d.   Performing less predictable auditing procedures.

14.   Audit procedures may be altered in specific areas to provide more reliable evidence, to shift tests from the interim period to near year-end, and by increasing sample sizes for substantive procedures.

15.   On all audits CPA should consider the possibility of management override of controls by including procedures such as reviewing journal entries for propriety and accounting estimates for biases, and by evaluating the business rationale for significant unusual transactions.

16.   When fraud has been discovered or is suspected the auditors should communicate it to an appropriate level of management, at least one level above the level involved. If the fraud involves senior management (even immaterial) or material misstatement of the financial statements committed by others, it should be reported to the audit committee.

17.   The planning process is documented in the working papers by audit plans, audit programs, and time budgets. An **audit plan** provides an overview of the engagement, describing the characteristics of the client's business and industry, identifying special problems for the engagement, and outlining the overall audit strategy. An **audit program** is a detailed outline of all auditing procedures to be performed during the audit, which serves as a tool for scheduling and controlling the audit work. A **time budget** is a detailed schedule of the estimated amount of time to complete each major audit procedure or audit area. The budget is used to control the audit work and measure the efficiency of the audit staff.

18.   Audit procedures should be focused (linked) to the risks identified. In developing audit procedures directly related to the client's accounting records, the direction of audit testing is often of importance.
       a.   Tests for overstatements (existence)—ordinarily start from recorded entries and vouch to source documents.
       b.   Tests for understatements (completeness)—ordinarily start from source documents and trace to recorded entries.

19.   The audit program must be tailored to the individual circumstances of each audit engagement. Although a final audit program cannot be developed until the auditors have completed their consideration of internal control, a preliminary program is developed prior to beginning the audit. This tentative program is modified as the audit work is performed.

20.   An audit program is a working paper listing the specific auditing procedures to be performed during an audit. The first part of the audit program consists of the tests of controls, and is organized around the major transaction cycles in the client's internal control.

21.   The second part of the audit program is aimed at substantiating financial statement amounts, and it is usually organized around the balance sheet accounts. This balance sheet organization is efficient because the evidence available to substantiate balance sheet accounts is of higher quality than the evidence available to substantiate income statement accounts. By substantiating the changes in asset and liability accounts, the auditors indirectly verify revenues and expenses.

22.   The objectives that an audit program must accomplish follow directly from the assertions that are contained in the financial statements. Recall that the five assertions are: (1) Existence or occurrence, (2) completeness, (3) rights and obligations, (4) valuation or allocation, and (5) presentation and disclosure.

23.   Although the specific audit objectives and audit procedures are somewhat different for each balance sheet account, the general objectives for the major types of accounts (asset, liability, and owners' equity) are the same. The audit program for every asset account includes procedures to accomplish the following general objectives:

       a.   Establish the existence of the assets.
       b.   Establish the client's rights to the assets.
       c.   Establish the completeness of recorded assets.
       d.   Determine the proper valuation of the asset.
       e.   Establish the clerical accuracy of the records.
       f.   Determine proper financial statement presentation and disclosure of the assets.

24.   Although specific audit procedures vary form one audit to the next, the fundamental steps are:

      a.   Obtain an understanding of the client and its environment.
      b.   Identify and assess inherent risks of material misstatement, including risks of fraud.
      c.   Obtain an understanding of internal control sufficient to plan the audit.
      d.   Determine the planned assessed level of control risk and design additional tests of controls and planned substantive procedures.
      e.   Perform additional tests of controls.
      d.   Reassess control risk and modify planned substantive procedures.
      e.   Perform substantive procedures and complete the audit.
      f.   Form an opinion and issue the audit report.

25.   To facilitate an early release of the audit report, auditors normally perform certain audit work before the balance sheet date, during the interim period. Audit work that can always be performed during the interim period includes the consideration of internal control, issuance of the management letter, and tests of transactions that have occurred to the interim date.

26.   Substantive procedures of financial statement balances, such as inventories, can also be performed at an interim date, but this results in additional audit risk that must be controlled by the auditors. Significant misstatements could arise in these accounts during the remaining period from the dab that the test is performed to the balance sheet date. Thus, the auditors must be able to rely on internal control to prevent misstatements during the remaining period, or conduct additional substantive procedures of the activity affecting the account during the remaining period.

Test Yourself on Chapter 6

TRUE OR FALSE

For each of the following statements, circle the T or the F to indicate whether the statement is true or false.

T   F   1.   CPAs cannot ethically refuse to provide auditing services to any prospective client which the CPAs are competent to audit, if the prospective client is willing to pay the CPAs' standard audit fees.

T   F   2.   Successor auditors are required by professional standards to attempt certain inquiries of the predecessors before accepting a new audit client.

T   F   3.   Auditors are required to specifically assess the risk of material misstatement of the financial statements due to fraud on every audit.

T   F   4.   An engagement letter represents a written contract between the auditors and the client.

T.   F.   5.   A declining industry with increasing business failures is an industry condition that is indicative of increased risk of fraudulent financial reporting.

T   F   6.   Audit risk is the risk of issuing an inappropriate opinion because the auditors' procedures fail to detect a material misstatement in the financial statements.

T   F   7.   A written audit program is required on all audits.

T   F   8.   Since characteristics differ with every audit engagement, the auditors should tailor the audit program to the particular engagement.

T   F   9.   The more recommendations made in the management letter, the less effort the auditors must devote to substantive procedures.

T   F   10.   Auditors should never spend more time on an audit than is called for in a conscientiously developed time budget.

T   F   11.   Analytical procedures are optional procedures that may be useful to the auditors in planning the audit.

T   F   12.   Substantive procedures are generally completed before the auditors assess control risk.

T   F   13.   Tests of controls are designed to determine whether the client's controls are operating effectively.

T   F   14.   The audit program generally must be modified if the auditors revise their estimate of risk for the engagement.

T   F   15.   The substantive procedures portion of the audit program generally is organized around income statement accounts.

T   F   16.   A systems approach to an audit emphasizes tests of controls.

T   F   17.   An audit program should indicate which auditing procedures have been completed and which remain to be done.

T   F   18.   One basic reason that audit programs usually focus on balance sheet accounts is because users of financial statements are likely to rely more heavily upon the balance sheet than the other financial statements.

T   F   19.   An audit program includes procedures for verifying the client's cutoff of transactions to be included in the financial statements of the current period.

T   F   20.   Completeness of an asset account can best be established by vouching recorded entries in the asset account.

COMPLETION

Fill in the necessary words to complete the following statements.

1.   Auditors of SEC registrants are selected by the _____ _____ of the board of directors, that usually consists of from 3 to 5 directors that are not _____ or _____ of the client organization.

2.   The auditors must assess the risk of material misstatement of financial statements due to the two types of fraud, _____ _____ _____ and _____ _____ _____.

3.   Audit risk at the account balance level consists of three components: (1) _____ _____, (2)_____ _____, and (3) _____ _____.

4.   Audit planning is documented by: (1) the _____ _____, which provides an overview of the engagement; (2) the _____ _____, which is a listing of the audit procedures for the engagement; and (3) the _____ _____, which is a schedule of the estimated time for each major audit procedure or area.

5.   The two major types of audit procedures are (1) _____ _____ _____, which are tests of internal control; and (2) _____ _____, which are tests used to substantiate financial statement accounts and balances.

6.   Performing certain audit procedures at an _____ _____ rather than at the balance sheet date, results in additional _____ that must be controlled by the auditors.

7.   The authenticity and accuracy of an account receivable may be tested by _____ _____ with the debtor, or by _____ entries in the account to supporting documents.

8.   The _____ procedures portion of the audit program is normally organized around the balance

      sheet accounts because highly competent _____ is generally available for such accounts.

9.   Assertions are _____ of _____ that are set forth in the financial statements.

10.   The term _____ refers to the process of determining that transactions are reflected in the proper

      accounting period.

MULTIPLE CHOICE

Choose the best answer for each of the following questions and enter the identifying letter in the space provided.

_____   1.   Which of the following is the best example of a substantive procedure?

          a.   Examining a sample of cash disbursements to test whether expenses have been properly
                approved.
          b.   Confirming balances of accounts receivable.
          c.   Comparing signatures on checks to a list of authorized check signers.
          d.   Flowcharting a client's cash receipts system.

_____   2.   Which of the following topics is not normally included in an engagement letter?

          a.   The auditors' responsibilities with respect to the audit.
          b.   A request that the client sign a copy of the letter.
          c.   Client responsibilities regarding the audit.
          d.   A schedule of individual audit team member billing rates.

_____   3.   Which of the following statements is **not** correct regarding the auditor's determination of
                materiality?

          a.   It is the smallest amount of misstatement that would probably influence the judgment of a
                reasonable person relying upon the financial statements.
          b.   Auditing standards require auditors to consider materiality in planning the audit.
          c.   The planning level of materiality will normally be the larger of the amount considered for
                the balance sheet versus the income statement.
          d.   The appropriate financial statement base for computing materiality may vary based on the
                nature of the client's business.

_____   4.   A successor auditor **must** attempt communication with a predecessor auditor:

          a.   prior to accepting the engagement.
          b.   after the engagement has been accepted.
          c.   both prior to acceptance of the engagement and after the engagement has been accepted.
          d.   is not required to do so.

_____   5.   The systems (internal control) portion of an audit program is generally organized around the:

     a.   major transaction cycles.
     b.   substantive procedures.
     c.   analytical procedures.
     d.   inherent risk assessment.

_____   6.   The first standard of field work, which states that the work is to be adequately planned, and assistants, if any, are to be properly supervised, recognizes that:

     a.   early appointment of the auditors is advantageous to the auditors and the client.
     b.   acceptance of an audit engagement after the close of the client's fiscal year is generally not permissible.
     c.   acceptance of an audit engagement after the close of the client's fiscal year requires a disclaimer of opinion.
     d.   performance of substantial parts of the examination is necessary at interim dates.

_____   7.   Which of the following is an effective audit planning and control procedure that helps prevent misunderstandings and inefficient use of audit personnel?

     a.   Arrange to make copies, for inclusion in the working papers, of those client supporting documents examined by the auditors.
     b.   Arrange to provide the client with copies of the audit programs to be used during the audit.
     c.   Arrange a preliminary conference with the client to discuss audit objectives, fees, timing, and other information.
     d.   Arrange to have the auditors prepare and post any necessary adjusting or reclassification entries prior to final closing.

_____   8.   Which of the following is the most likely first step the auditors would perform at the beginning of an initial audit engagement?

     a.   Prepare a rough draft of the financial statements and of the auditors' report.
     b.   Consider internal control.
     c.   Tour the client's facilities and review the general records.
     d.   Consult with and review the work of the predecessor auditors prior to discussing the engagement with the client management.

_____   9.   Which of the following is a basic tool used by the auditors to control the audit work and review the progress of the audit?

     a.   Time and expense summary.
     b.   Engagement letter.
     c.   Progress flowchart.
     d.   Audit program.

_____   10.   Hawkins, CPA, requested permission to communicate with the predecessor auditors of a prospective client. The prospective client's refusal to permit this will bear directly on Hawkins' decision concerning the:

     a.   adequacy of the preplanned audit program.
     b.   ability to establish consistency in application of accounting principles between years.
     c.   apparent scope limitation.
     d.   integrity of management.

_____ 11. Which of the following risk factors indicates an increased risk of misappropriation of assets?

   a. High turnover of senior management.
   b. Strained relationships between management and auditors..
   c. Overly complex organizational structure..
   d. Lack of mandatory vacations for employees performing key functions.

_____ 12. Which of the following is most likely to be an overall response to fraud risks identified in an audit?

   a. Decrease the use of professional skepticism and increase the use of internally generated evidence.
   b. Use predictable, well established audit procedures.
   c. Consider further management's selection and application of significant accounting principles.
   d. Supervise members of the audit team less closely and rely more upon judgment.

_____ 13. Which of the following is most likely to be included in an auditor's inquiry of management while obtaining information to identify the risk of material misstatement due to fraud?

   a. Are financial reporting operations controlled by and limited to one location?
   b. Does it have knowledge of fraud or suspect fraud?
   c. Has the possibility of management override been assessed?
   d. Does the company have insurance against all forms of fraud?

_____ 14. Audit programs are modified to suit the circumstances of a particular engagement. A final audit program for an engagement generally should be developed:

   a. prior to beginning the actual audit work.
   b. after the auditors have completed their consideration of the existing internal control.
   c. after reviewing the client's accounting records and procedures.
   d. when the audit engagement letter is prepared.

_____ 15. An audit committee's responsibilities normally would not include:

   a. discussing the meaning and significance of audited financial statements.
   b. discussing problems and experience with independent auditors in completing the audit of annual financial statements.
   c. nominating the independent auditors.
   d. discussing all details of the audit programs of the independent auditors.

_____ 16. Tracing of a transaction from source documents to the accounting records is generally an audit procedure that is designed to establish:

   a. completeness.
   b. valuation.
   c. existence.
   d. presentation.

EXERCISES

1. Listed below are the management assertions that are contained in financial statements, and several financial statement misstatements. For each misstatement, indicate with the appropriate letter the assertion by management that is being violated.

    Assertion

    A   Existence and occurrence
    B   Completeness
    C   Rights and obligations
    D   Valuation or allocation
    E   Presentation and disclosure

    Misstatements

    _____   a.   The client failed to include in their financial statements inventory that was consigned to others.

    _____   b.   The client had a significant amount of damaged goods that were presented at cost.

    _____   c.   The client failed to describe in the financial statements significant debt restrictions.

    _____   d.   The client recorded receivables that were fictitious.

2. Listed below are audit objectives for the audit of assets, and audit procedures designed to achieve certain of those objectives. Match the procedure with the primary objective or objectives that it is intended to achieve.

    Audit Objectives

    A   Establish the existence of the assets
    B   Establish the rights to the assets
    C   Establish the completeness of recorded assets
    D   Determine the appropriate valuation of the assets
    E   Establish the clerical accuracy of the underlying records
    F   Determine the appropriate financial statement presentation

    Audit Procedures

    _____   a.   Confirm a sample of accounts receivable by direct communication with the customers.

    _____   b.   Observe the client's physical inventory.

    _____   c.   Obtain a lawyer's letter from the client's attorney.

    _____   d.   Vouch purchases of property, plant and equipment made during the year.

    _____   e.   Foot the subsidiary accounts receivable ledger.

CHAPTER 7

Internal Control

Highlights of the Chapter

1. A number of years ago the major accounting organizations commissioned a study to develop a comprehensive set of criteria for evaluating internal control. This set of criteria is referred to as *Internal Control--Integrated Framework*, and was developed by the committee of sponsoring organizations (COSO) of the Treadway Commission. The study defines internal control as:

   > A process effected by the entity's board of directors, management, and other personnel, designed to provide reasonable assurance regarding the achievement of objectives in the following categories:
   >
   > - Effectiveness and efficiency of operations.
   > - Reliability of financial reporting.
   > - Compliance with applicable laws and regulations.

2. Not all controls are relevant to an audit of financial statements. Generally, the controls relevant are those that pertain to the reliability of financial reporting.

3. The Foreign Corrupt Practices Act of 1977 prohibits the making of payments to foreign government officials to obtain business and requires all companies under SEC jurisdiction to maintain an adequate system of internal control.

4. A company's internal control may be divided into five components: (1) the control environment, (2) risk assessment, (3) the accounting information system, and (4) control activities, and (5) monitoring.

5. The **control environment** is the foundation for other components of internal control, and consists of the following factors:

   Integrity and ethical values--The behavioral and ethical standards established by management to discourage employees from engaging in improper acts. These values should be communicated through appropriate means, such as *codes of conduct.*

   Commitment to competence--Management's commitment to hiring employees with appropriate levels of education and experience, and providing them with adequate supervision and training.
   Board of directors or audit committee--An effective board of directors or audit committee is important to ensuring that management is acting in the best interest of the stockholders.

   Management philosophy and operating style--The reliability of financial statements is affected by the philosophy of management toward financial reporting, and management's attitudes toward taking business risks.

   Organizational structure--An entity's organizational structure refers to the division of authority, responsibilities, and duties among departments of the organization. The major principle that should be applied in designing a plan of organization is effective segregation of duties among functional departments.

Human resource policies and procedures--Management's policies and practices for hiring, training, evaluating, promoting, and compensating employees.

Assignment of authority and responsibility--Methods of communicating to personnel their level of authority and responsibilities, such as job descriptions.

6. An important step in achieving an effective control environment is separation of the accounting function from custody of the related assets. When the accounting and custodial departments are relatively independent, periodic comparisons of the accounting records to the existing assets serves to check the work of both departments.

7. When the principle of subdivision of duties is applied to a large company, separate and independent departments are necessary for such functions as purchasing, receiving, manufacturing, selling, accounting, and finance. Departments should be organized so that one department has an incentive to monitor the efficiency of another.

8. It is important for the accounting and finance departments to be adequately separated in a company. The finance department should have custody of the liquid assets and responsibility for financial operations of the company, while the accounting department is responsible for all accounting functions and the design and implementation of internal control.

9. The second component of internal control is **risk assessment,** which is management's process for identifying and responding to business risks faced by the organization.

10. An effective **accounting information system** (the third component of internal control) should include methods to achieve the following objectives: (1) identify and record all valid transactions, (2) describe on a timely basis the transactions in sufficient detail to permit proper classification in the financial statements, (3) measure the appropriate value of the transactions, (4) permit recording of transactions in the proper accounting period, and (5) present properly the transactions and related disclosures in the financial statements.

11. Management establishes other **control activities** to help ensure that management's directives are carried out. Major types of control activities that are relevant to the audit of financial statements include:

Performance reviews--Controls that evaluate the performance of departments or individuals by comparison of actual performance to standards, budgets or forecasts.

Information processing--Control activities designed to check the accuracy, completeness, and authorization of transactions. The two broad categories of information processing controls include *general control activities* and *application control activities.*

Physical controls--Controls that restrict access to assets and records to authorized personnel.

Segregation of duties--The assignment of responsibilities among personnel so that no one individual is in a position to perpetrate an error or irregularity and prevent the error or irregularity from being detected. Generally, the functions of authorizing transactions, recording transactions, and maintaining transactions (custody of assets) should be segregated. Also, to the extent possible, individuals executing the transactions should be segregated from these functions.

12.   The last component of internal control is **monitoring**, which involves assessing the quality of internal control over time. An important aspect of the monitoring component is the internal audit function.

13.   An important role of the internal auditors is to investigate and appraise internal control and the efficiency with which various units of a business carry out their functions.

14.   Internal auditors are not independent of the employer and, therefore, cannot attest to the fairness of the company's financial statements. In performing their evaluations, however, the internal auditors should be independent of the departments being investigated. If the internal auditors report directly to the audit committee of the board of directors or to a high-level executive, they may achieve a greater degree of independence than if they report to an official of lesser rank.

15.   In addition to evaluating controls, many internal auditing departments conduct operational audits. **Operational auditing** involves evaluation of the **efficiency** and **effectiveness** of an operating department within the business.

16.   Internal control has certain limitations. The extent of the controls is limited by cost considerations; to maintain internal control that would make errors and fraud "impossible" would cost more than the benefits it would provide. Also, controls may be rendered ineffective by collusion or may be overridden by management of the company.

17.   When auditing financial statements, auditors consider those controls that are designed to prevent or detect misstatements of the financial statements.

18.   The auditors consider internal control to: (1) **plan the audit** and (2) **assess control risk**.

19.   In every audit, the auditors must obtain a sufficient understanding of internal control to plan the audit. In planning the audit, the knowledge is used to: (a) identify types of potential misstatements, (b) consider factors that affect the risk of material misstatement, (c) design tests of controls, when applicable, and (d) design substantive procedures.

20.   The auditors must also assess control risk, using a process that may be summarized as: (a) determine the planned assessed level of control risk, (b) design and perform additional tests of controls, (c) reassess control risk and modify planned substantive procedures, and (d) document the assessed level of control risk.

21.   In every audit, the auditors must obtain an understanding of the five components of a client's internal control. In obtaining this understanding, the auditors will determine whether the controls have been **placed in operation.** This understanding enables the auditors to plan the engagement and provides them with a basis for their preliminary assessment of control risk.

22.   In obtaining an understanding of a client's accounting information system and the related control activities, auditors generally find it useful to subdivide the overall system into its major transaction cycles, such as the sales and collection cycle, the purchase or acquisition cycle, the production or conversion cycle, the payroll cycle, and the financing cycle.

23.   Three methods commonly used to record the auditors' understanding of the client's internal control are: questionnaires, written narratives, and flowcharts.

24.   **Internal control questionnaires** inquire into the existence of controls and provide a space for explanatory comments in the event a yes or no answer is insufficient. The advantages of questionnaires are that they are comprehensive, and "no" answers help the auditors to identify weaknesses in internal control.

25.   **Written narratives** usually follow the flow of each major transaction cycle, identifying the employees performing various tasks, documents prepared, records maintained, and the division of duties.

26.   A **systems flowchart** is a diagram symbolic representation of a system or a series of procedures with each procedure shown in sequence. The advantage of a flowchart over a questionnaire is that a flowchart provides a clearer, more specific, portrayal of the system.

27.   To clarify their understanding of a system, the auditors will normally trace (walk) one or more of each major type of transaction through the processing steps.

28.   After completing their working paper description of internal control, the auditors perform their preliminary assessment of control risk. At this point the auditors will decide whether additional tests of controls should be performed or whether it is more efficient to proceed directly to the design of substantive procedures.

29.   **Tests of controls** are performed by observation, inquiry, inspection, and reperformance. In some cases, the test will involve the use of audit sampling. In order to use sampling to test a procedure, performance of that procedure must leave some form of **evidence of performance**, such as a completed document or the signature of the person performing the procedure.

30.   After the auditors have completed their tests of controls, they reassess control risk and design other audit procedures. Based upon this assessment, the auditors generally find it necessary to modify the preliminary audit program. Substantive audit procedures are expanded in areas of weak internal control (high control risk) and limited in areas in which tests of controls reveal strong controls (low control risk).

31.   CPA firms have attempted to add more structure to these audit program decisions by developing decision aids. A decision aid is a check list or standard form that helps ensure that auditors consider all relevant information and/or appropriately combine that information in making a decision.

32.   In assessing the contribution of the internal audit function to internal control, the auditors obtain an understanding of the internal auditors' work and its relevance to the audit. If the independent auditors conclude that the internal auditors' work is relevant and it would be efficient to consider it, the independent auditors assess the **competence** and **objectivity** of the internal audit staff, and evaluate the **quality of their work**. In evaluating the objectivity of the internal auditors, the auditors consider the level in the organization to which the director of internal audit reports, consider the policies for assigning internal audit staff to activities, and compare the content of selected reports to related audit findings. Competence is evaluated by examining a sample of the work of auditors, and considering the educational level, professional experience, and professional certifications of the internal audit staff. They also investigate the internal auditors' policies, programs, procedures, working papers, and reports.

33.   SAS No. 60 (AU 325) requires the auditors to communicate significant deficiencies in the design or functioning of internal control **(reportable conditions)** to the audit committee of the board of directors. A reportable condition may be significant enough to be considered a material weakness. That is, a weakness that results in a higher than acceptable risk of material misstatement of financial statements.

34.   The Sarbanes-Oxley Act of 2002 requires auditors of public companies to report on the effectiveness of management's internal control over financial reporting. More guidance on this topic is included in Chapter 19.

Test Yourself on Chapter 7

TRUE OR FALSE

For each of the following statements, circle the T or the F to indicate whether the statement is true or false.

T F   1.   The basic purpose of internal control is to prevent fraud.

T F   2.   The five components of internal control are risk assessment, control activities, the accounting information and communication system, general controls, and the control environment.

T F   3.   In performing an audit, the auditors are concerned with those controls that prevent or detect financial statement misstatements.

T F   4.   The establishment of sales terms is an example of a control.

T F   5.   Establishing and maintaining internal control is a responsibility of the stockholders of the company.

T F   6.   The Foreign Corrupt Practices Act applies only to corporations that have foreign operations.

T F   7.   An employee has incompatible duties if the person is in a position to perpetrate and conceal errors or fraud in the normal course of performing his or her duties.

T F   8.   For well controlled operations, the same employee that maintains custody of assets should also keep the accounting records for the assets.

T F   9.   The accounting department should maintain custody of the company's marketable securities.

T F   10.   Internal auditors normally are responsible for reconciling the company's bank accounts to monitor the controls over cash.

T F   11.   Internal control is not generally effective at preventing all fraud by top management of the company.

T F   12.   The internal audit function is an important part of the monitoring component of internal control.

T F   13.   Auditors are required to test all strengths in an audit client's internal control.

T F   14.   The controls over a client's sales cycle are part of that client's control environment.

T F   15.   Internal control should provide management with reasonable assurance that they are achieving the objectives related to effectiveness and efficiency of operations, reliability of financial reporting, and compliance with laws and regulations.

T F   16.   An advantage of an internal control questionnaire is that weaknesses in internal control are highlighted by the questionnaire.

T F   17.   Flowcharts are generally a less flexible method of depicting a system of internal control than an internal control questionnaire.

T F   18.   To be effective, a walk-through test must involve tracing at least 60 transactions through each cycle.

T F   19.   A control activity that leaves evidence of compliance is usually tested by inquiry and observation.

T F   20.   Reportable conditions noted by the auditors must be communicated to management in writing.

COMPLETION

Fill in the necessary words to complete the following statements.

1.   The five components of a client's internal control include the _____ _____, _____ _____, the _____ _____ ____ _____ _____, _____ _____, and _____.

2.   The Foreign Corrupt Practices Act of 1977 prohibits _____ to foreign officials to obtain business and requires companies to maintain an effective system of _____ _____.

3.   No single employee in a company should have _____ _____, allowing the employee to both perpetrate and conceal errors or fraud in the normal course of performing his or her job.

4.   The two broad categories of information processing controls are _____ _____ and _____ _____.

5.   Controls that rely on segregation of duties may be circumvented by _____ among employees.

6.   A client's _____ _____ factors include such things as management philosophy and operating style, and organizational structure.

7.   A form of insurance in which an insurance company agrees to reimburse an employer for losses attributable to employee theft is referred to as _____ _____.

8.   A "no" answer in an _____ _____ _____ indicates a weakness in the client's internal control.

9.   Controls that leave evidence of performance may be tested by _____ whereas other controls must be tested by _____ and _____.

10. Auditors are required by professional standards to communicate reportable conditions to the client's _____ _____ of the _____ _____ _____.

MULTIPLE CHOICE

Choose the best answer for each of the following questions and enter the identifying letter in the space provided.

_d_ 1. Before assessing control risk at a level lower than the maximum, the auditor obtains reasonable assurance that controls are in use and operating effectively. This assurance is most likely obtained in part by:

a. preparing flowcharts.
b. performing substantive procedures.
c. analyzing tests of trends and ratios.
d. inspecting documents.

_b_ 2. Auditors must communicate internal control reportable conditions to:

a. management.
b. the audit committee.
c. the shareholders.
d. the SEC.

_d_ 3. A significant deficiency in the design or functioning of internal control that could adversely affect the organization's ability to record, process, summarize, and report financial data is referred to as a:

a. material weakness in internal control.
b. inherent limitation of internal control.
c. management override.
d. reportable condition.

_C_ 4. Which of the following is most likely to provide an auditor with the most assurance about the effectiveness of the operation of internal control?

a. Inquiry of client personnel.
b. Recomputation of account balance amounts.
c. Observation of client personnel applying the control.
d. Confirmation with outside parties.

_a_ 5. Monitoring is considered:

a. a component of internal control.
b. an element of the control environment.
c. the primary asset safeguarding technique.
d. a portion of the information and communication system.

_C_ 6. Which of the following is not a control environment factor?

a. Board of directors.
b. Human resource policies.
c. Communication system.
d. Commitment to competence.

_b_ 7.   Effective internal control requires organizational independence of departments. Organizational independence would be impaired in which of the following situations?

   a.   The internal auditors report to the audit committee of the board of directors.
   b.   The controller reports to the vice president of production.
   c.   The payroll accounting department reports to the chief accountant.
   d.   The cashier reports to the treasurer.

_b_ 8.   The purpose of tests of controls is to provide reasonable assurance that the:

   a.   accounting treatment of transactions and balances is valid and proper.
   b.   controls are operating effectively.
   c.   entity has complied with disclosure requirements of generally accepted accounting principles.
   d.   entity has complied with requirements of quality control.

_c_ 9.   Tests of controls are most likely in which of the following situations?

   a.   Evidence to support a reduction of the assessed level of control risk below the maximum is not available.
   b.   The cost of tests of controls is likely to exceed the savings brought about by a resulting decrease in the scope of substantive procedures.
   c.   The planned assessed level of control risk is low.
   d.   Few transactions have occurred, but for very material amounts.

_a_ 10.   An auditor's flowchart of a client's internal control is a diagrammatic representation which depicts the auditors':

   e.   understanding of the system.
   f.   program for tests of controls.
   g.   documentation of control risk.
   h.   understanding of the types of fraud which are probable, given the present system.

_c_ 11.   Which of the following is ordinarily considered a test of a control?

   a.   Send confirmation letters to financial institutions.
   b.   Count and list cash on hand.
   c.   Examine signatures on checks.
   d.   Obtain or prepare reconciliations of bank accounts as of the balance sheet date.

_d_ 12.   Taylor Sales Co. maintains a large full-time internal audit staff which reports directly to the chief accountant. Audit reports prepared by the internal auditors indicate that internal control is functioning as it should and that the accounting records are reliable. The independent auditor will probably:

   a.   eliminate tests of controls.
   b.   increase the depth of the consideration of administrative controls.
   c.   avoid duplicating the work performed by the internal audit staff.
   d.   make limited use of the work performed by the internal audit staff.

_____d_____ 13. Of the following statements about internal control, which one is not valid?

    a. No one person should be responsible for the custodial responsibility and the recording responsibility for an asset.
    b. Transactions must be properly authorized before such transactions are processed.
    c. Because of the cost benefit relationship, a client may apply controls on a test basis.
    d. Control activities reasonably insure that collusion among employees cannot occur.

_____d_____ 14. Which of the following statements regarding auditor documentation of the client's internal control is correct?

    a. Documentation must include flowcharts.
    b. Documentation must include procedural write-ups.
    c. No documentation is necessary although it is desirable.
    d. No one particular form of documentation is required, and the extent of documentation may vary.

EXERCISES

1.   List four control environment factors.

        a.

        b.

        c.

        d.

2.   Define each of the following terms.

        a.   Internal control questionnaire

        b.   Internal control flowchart

        c.   Walk-through of the system

        d.   Management letter

CHAPTER 8

Consideration of Internal Control in an Information Technology Environment

Highlights of the Chapter

1. Audit clients use information technology (IT) for most accounting functions. In a traditional IT environment a large mainframe computer may be used, with data sent by user departments to an information systems department. With the advent of microcomputers, data processing has become more decentralized in many companies, with users processing much of their own data.

2. Commercially available accounting software varies from applications costing less than $100 that are in essence electronic checkbooks to basic general ledger systems, to enterprise resource planning (ERP) systems costing into the tens, and even hundreds of millions of dollars

3. An IT-based system consists of a computer and peripheral equipment, known as hardware, and various programs and materials used to operate the system, termed software. A typical large business has client/server computer architecture in which a number of "client" microcomputers are connected to either the corporate mainframe system or to another "server" computer.

4. The major hardware component is the central processing unit (CPU), consisting of a control unit, an arithmetic unit, and a primary storage unit. Peripheral to the CPU are input devices such as card readers, optical scanners, electronic cash registers, and intelligent terminals. Auxiliary storage devices, such as magnetic tape drives and magnetic disk drives, augment the storage capacity of the CPU. Peripheral equipment is said to be either on-line or off-line depending on whether it is in direct communication with the CPU.

5. Software is of two types: system software and application software. **System software** consists of programs that control the hardware and provide other support to application programs. An important element of system software is the computer's **operating system**, which may be programmed to monitor computer activities or control access to other programs and stored data. Programs that are designed to perform a specific task, such as updating the accounts receivable files, are referred to as **application programs**.

6. IT-based systems have various characteristics that affect the nature of the appropriate controls. In **batch processing systems**, transactions are collected in groups (batches) and processed at periodic intervals. Control totals, hash totals, and item counts can be used to assure that the transactions are processed accurately.

7. In **on-line systems** users have direct (on-line) access to the data stored in the system. On-line systems may be divided into (1) online transaction processing (OLTP) and online analytical processing (OLAP) systems. In **on-line, real-time** systems transactions are processed immediately and all accounting records are updated instantaneously. To insure the accuracy of processing of these transactions, the operating system must verify user identification numbers and passwords, and apply various input validation checks to the data as it is entered.

8.   A **database storage** system avoids the data redundancy that is characteristic of traditional systems, as each element is stored only once in an integrated **database**. It is essential that the integrity of the **database** be assured by restricting access through a system of user identification numbers and passwords. Also, terminal activity should be logged to provide evidence that data has not been improperly altered.

9.   **Computer networks** link together computers both between companies and within a company. A **wide area network** covers a large geographical area, while a **local area network** covers a smaller area (e.g., computers within one building). **Distributed data processing** involves computers located throughout an organization that are linked to a main computer.

10.   In **end user computing** user groups are responsible for the development and execution of certain computer applications. End user computing generally involves user development of programs on microcomputers rather than development of programs by an information systems department.

11.   While many components of the **control environment** may be affected by IT-based processing, the organizational structure is often modified to include an information systems department, with the primary activities of application systems development, operations, and technical services. **Application systems development** may include the functions of systems analysis, application programming and **database** administration. **Operations** may include data entry, computer operations, a program and file library, and a data control group. Finally, **technical services** often consists of the functions of telecommunications and systems programming.

12.   Many cases of computer fraud have involved personnel with knowledge of programs and unsupervised access to the computer. At a minimum, the functions of programming the computer should be segregated from both operating the computer and entering data into the system. Also, computer operators should not have access to details regarding specific programs.

13.   The **accounting information system** in an IT-based environment may vary from systems in which microcomputers with off-the-shelf accounting software are used to large main-frame systems with software developed by the information systems department.

14.   **Information processing controls** in an IT-based system include general control activities, application control activities, and user control activities.

15.   **General control activities**, which affect all IT applications, include controls over (1) developing or customizing new programs and systems, (2) changing existing programs and systems, (3) access to programs and data, and (4) computer operations.

16.   When data are transmitted over telecommunications facilities, data transmission controls should be established to prevent unauthorized access or changes to information when it is being transmitted. These controls may include parity checks, data encryption, message acknowledgment techniques, and private lines.

17.   **Application control activities** relate to a specific application (e.g., payroll). Programmed control activities are written into the computer programs and help ensure the accuracy of computer input and processing. Examples include limit tests, validity tests, and self-checking numbers. Manual application control activities include manual follow-up activities, such as the analysis of exception reports.

18.   **User control activities** are performed by users of the computer output through either extensive review and testing of the output or though overall reasonableness checks.

19.   The control of microcomputers is difficult because the machines are located in user departments and operated by user personnel. Internal control over microcomputers is enhanced when operating procedures are documented and operators are well-trained. Back-up diskettes or tapes of files should be made frequently and stored away from the originals. To prevent unauthorized use of microcomputers, authorization codes should be required to gain access to programs and files, the machines should be equipped with locking operating switches, and critical software should be locked away overnight.

20.   Valid business reasons exist for inclusion of an adequate audit trail in all systems. However, in an IT-based system, the audit trail may only exist in machine readable form. For example, consider electronic commerce conducted over the Internet. Very limited printed output exists related to the transactions which are often stored on a long term basis on magnetic tape. The auditors should consider the form of the trail and the client's retention policy when designing the nature and timing of their audit tests.

21.   The use of computer processing by a client does not affect the audit requirement to obtain an understanding of internal control and to assess control risk. It is efficient for auditors to begin their consideration of internal control with a review of generally controls because satisfactory general control activities are necessary for the effectiveness of application control activities.

22.   Auditors may have to rely on IT specialists to describe the flow of transactions or assess control risk on complex engagements. Still, the auditor in charge of the engagement must have sufficient IT knowledge to review the specialist's work and evaluate its audit implications.

23.   The auditors must document their understanding of IT controls in the working papers. Controls typically are documented by flowcharts or specially designed computer control questionnaires.

24.   General control activities are generally tested by inquiry and observation. To test the effectiveness of program controls, auditors examine error reports and activity logs generated by the computer. A commonly used approach to assessing application control activities is to test the manual follow-up activities by inspecting the exception reports generated by the computer, and reviewing the way in which the exceptions are handled. The auditors might also use computer-assisted audit techniques (CAATS) to test the controls included in the software. Computer-assisted audit techniques include the use of test data, controlled programs, program analysis, tagging and tracing, and parallel simulation.

25.   The **test data** approach involves processing of test data that are erroneous and contain other exceptions to test the operation of programmed control activities.

26.   The **controlled program** technique involves testing program controls by processing real and/or test data with a copy of the client's application program controlled by the auditors.

27.   The **program analysis** technique involves the examination of computer generated flowcharts of the logic of a client's application program.

28.   **Tagging and tracing** involves the examination of computer generated details of the steps in processing transactions that were tagged when they were entered.

29.   The auditors may elect to write a program that processes data in a manner similar to the client's program. This technique, known as **parallel simulation** involves comparing the results of processing real and test data by the two programs to provide evidence that the client's program is operating properly.

30.   Generalized computer audit programs are simple programming languages that assist in the audit of clients' computer systems. The programs generally are used to assist in the performance of substantive procedures by performing such functions as reviewing computer files for completeness and valid conditions, performing mathematical computations on computer records, selecting audit samples, and comparing data from two or more sources.

31.   Computer service centers provide data processing services for clients that do not have their own computer facilities. The auditors of a client that uses a computer service center must consider the controls applied at the center if those controls are necessary to achieve the client's control objectives. This may require that the auditors visit the service center to obtain an understanding of the internal control for processing client transactions and, perhaps, to perform tests of controls.

32.   The service center may engage its own auditors (termed **service auditors**) to perform a study of their internal control over the processing of their customers' (users') transactions. This study may result in a report on the design of the system or a report on the design of the system and the results of certain tests of controls. The auditors of a particular user (termed **user auditors**) may use the report to complete their understanding of internal control. If the service auditors' report communicates the results of tests of controls at the center, the user auditors may elect to consider the center's controls without conducting their own tests.

Test Yourself on Chapter 8

TRUE OR FALSE

For each of the following statements, circle the T or the F to indicate whether the statement is true or false.

T F 1. Data stored by a device with direct access must be stored sequentially.

T F 2. Programs designed to perform specific data processing tasks are known as application software.

T F 3. Segregation of duties is not a feasible method to help establish control over computer systems.

T F 4. Application control activities include controls over making changes to programs and systems.

T F 5. The computer operator may also be the librarian without adversely affecting control over a computer system.

T F 6. A weakness in internal control would exist if the data control group also operated the computer.

T F 7. An echo check is an example of a control that is performed by a user.

T F 8. Back-up copies of files and records should be filed conveniently with the originals.

T F 9. A limit test is a program control that is used to test the reasonableness of a particular transaction.

T F 10. Internal file labels are printed labels that are placed on the inside of a tape container.

T F 11. Internal auditors are not necessary when the client has a data control group.

T F 12. Microcomputers are generally operated by user personnel.

T F 13. Distributed data processing systems have data communication capabilities.

T F 14. Elimination of data redundancy is a chief advantage of a database system.

T F 15. Advanced computer systems do not generally produce audit trails.

T F 16. The objective of the auditor's consideration of internal control is different for a client with a computer system.

T F 17. Using "test data" is primarily a substantive procedure approach.

T F 18. The program analysis technique involves examination of the details of the processing steps for tagged transactions.

T F 19. Generalized computer audit software is used for both substantive procedures and tests of controls.

T F 20. A service auditor's report on the design of the service center's controls does not provide a basis for the user auditors' reliance on the operating effectiveness of those controls.

COMPLETION

Fill in the necessary words to complete the following statements.

1. The two types of software used by a computer system are known as _____ software and _____ software.

2. Application control activities may be classified as either _____ or _____.

3. In well-staffed computer systems, a _____ should maintain custody of programs and files that may be checked out to the _____ _____ when processing is to be performed.

4. The only type of program documentation that should be provided to the computer operator is the _____ _____ that contains processing _____.

5. In the _____ _____ technique, known as _____ _____, a receiving device sends a message back to the sending device that verifies a transmission.

6. A _____ _____ is an _____ _____ check that involves the comparison of an account number against a master file of account numbers to test its authenticity.

7. Microcomputers generally use _____ _____ _____ for secondary storage on the computer.

8. When testing controls written into computer programs, auditors often use _____ _____ _____ techniques.

9. Many CPA firms use _____ _____ _____ that may be used to perform audit tests directly on their clients' computer records.

10. The auditors of a service center, known as _____ _____, may review the controls at the center and issue a report that may be relied upon by _____ _____.

MULTIPLE CHOICE

Choose the best answer for each of the following questions and enter the identifying letter in the space provided.

c 1. Which of the following is an example of a validity test?

a. The computer ensures that a numerical amount in a record does not exceed some predetermined amount.
b. As the computer corrects errors and data are successfully resubmitted to the system, the causes of the errors are printed out.
c. The computer flags any transmission for which the control field value did not match that of an existing file record.
d. After data for a transaction are entered, the computer sends certain data back to the terminal for comparison with data originally sent.

b 2. Clico uses an online sales order processing system to process its sales transactions. Clico's sales data are electronically sorted and subjected to edit checks. A direct output of the edit checks most likely would be a:

a. report of missing sales invoices.
b. file of all rejected sales transactions.
c. printout of all user code numbers and passwords.
d. list of all voided shipping documents.

a 3. Processing data through the use of simulated files provides an auditor with information about the operating effectiveness of controls. One of the techniques involved in this approach makes use of:

a. an integrated test facility.
b. controlled reprocessing.
c. input validation.
d. program code checking.

d 4. Which of the following is not a characteristic of a batch processed IT system?

a. The collection of like transactions which are sorted and processed sequentially against a master file.
b. Data input, followed by machine processing.
c. Production of numerous printouts.
d. Posting of a transaction, as it occurs, to several files, without intermediate printouts.

a 5. Which of the following is an example of application control activities in IT systems?

a. Programmed control activities.
b. Hardware controls.
c. Documentation procedures.
d. Controls over access to equipment and data files.

_c_

_____ 6.   Which of the following situations is compatible with good internal control in an information systems department?

   a.   Computer programmers have unsupervised access to computer terminals.
   b.   Computer operators have detailed knowledge of computer programs.
   c.   Computer librarians have physical control of program documentation.
   d.   Computer programmers have access to input data.

_a_

_____ 7.   What is the IT process called when data processing is performed concurrently with a particular activity and the results are available soon enough to influence the particular course of action being taken or the decision being made?

   a.   Real-time processing.
   b.   Batch processing.
   c.   Random access processing.
   d.   Integrated data processing.

_c_

_____ 8.   A customer inadvertently ordered part number 12368 rather than part number 12638. In processing this order, the error could be detected by the vendor with which of the following controls?

   a.   Batch totals.
   b.   Key verifying.
   c.   Self-checking digit.
   d.   Limit test.

_d_

_____ 9.   Data control group activities in an information systems department would appropriately include:

   a.   reviewing error listings and maintaining error logs and reports.
   b.   investigating deviations from standard procedures in data handling.
   c.   supervising distribution of output.
   d.   all of the above.

_c_

_____ 10. A computer master file that is the output of the most recent updating operation is referred to as the:

   a.   grandfather file.
   b.   father file.
   c.   son file.
   d.   scratch file.

_d_

_____ 11. When auditing an IT based system, the auditors may use the "integrated test facility" technique, sometimes referred to as the mini–company approach, as an audit tool. This technique:

   a.   is more applicable to independent audits than internal audits.
   b.   involves using test decks.
   c.   is the most commonly used audit tool for "auditing through the computer."
   d.   involves introducing simulated transactions into a system simultaneously with actual transactions.

_____ 12. Independent auditors obtain an understanding of a client's computer system and perform tests of controls. The latter phase might include which of the following?

    a. Examination of systems flowcharts to determine whether they reflect the current status of the system.
    b. Examination of the systems manuals to determine whether existing procedures are satisfactory.
    c. Examination of the machine room log book to determine whether control information is properly recorded.
    d. Examination of organization charts to determine whether electronic data processing department responsibilities are properly separated to afford effective control.

_____ 13. The auditors may decide not to perform tests of the controls within the computerized portion of the client's internal control. Which of the following would not be a valid reason for choosing to omit such tests?

    a. The controls appear adequate.
    b. The controls duplicate operative controls existing elsewhere in the system.
    c. There appear to be major weaknesses that would preclude reliance on the stated procedures.
    d. The time and dollar costs of testing exceed the time and dollar savings in substantive testing if the tests show the controls to operating effectively.

EXERCISES

1.   Match the following computer controls with the error or fraud that the control is designed to prevent

	Control		Error or Fraud
___	1. Item counts	a.	Processing a transaction that is unreasonable in amount.
___	2. Passwords	b.	An error when entering an account number.
___	3. Limit tests	c.	Loss of data as it is processed internally by the computer.
___	4. Self-checking numbers	d.	Interception of data when it is transmitted.
___	5. Internal file label	e.	Alteration of data by an unauthorized terminal user
___	6. Parity check	f.	Update of the wrong master file of accounts
___	7. Locking operating switch	g.	Loss of a transaction during processing of data
___	8. Private lines	h.	Unauthorized entry of data after business hours.

2.   Define the following computer-related terms.

a.   Hash total

b.   Validity test

c.   System software

d.   Echo check

e.   Microcomputers

CHAPTER 9

Audit Sampling

Highlights of the Chapter

1. Audit sampling is applying audit procedures to less than 100 percent of the items in a population under audit to form a conclusion about a characteristic of the population.

2. Sampling risk is the risk that the auditors will reach a different conclusion from the sample results than they would if they tested all the items in the population.

3. Nonsampling risk is the risk that the auditors will draw an erroneous conclusion for any reason not related to audit sampling. For example, the auditors may erroneously perform a test that does not meet the desired audit objective.

4. Sampling procedures may be applied on either a statistical or nonstatistical (judgmental) basis. In nonstatistical sampling, the determination of sample size and interpretation of sample results are left entirely to the auditors' professional judgment.

5. The use of **statistical sampling** allows the risk of material sampling error to be measured and controlled. Thus, statistical sampling may allow the auditors to design more efficient samples, to measure the sufficiency of the evidence obtained, and to evaluate the results. However, statistical sampling involves additional costs in applying the statistical sampling techniques.

6. Regardless of whether statistical or nonstatistical sampling is used, sample items should be selected in such a way that the sample can be expected to be representative of the population. Also, misstatements that are found in a sample should be used to estimate the total amount of misstatement in the population.

7. **Random selection** is a procedure for selecting a sample in such a manner that every item in the population has an equal chance of being included in the sample. Random selection can be used with statistical or nonstatistical sampling.

8. Techniques often used for selecting random samples include the use of random number tables and random number generators, and systematic selection. In using **systematic selection,** every nth item in the population (beginning from one or more random starting points) is included in the sample. An advantage of systematic selection is that it does not require the auditors to develop a correspondence between random numbers and items in the population.

9. Smaller sample sizes result from using stratified sampling. In using a **stratified sampling,** the population is divided into several more homogeneous subpopulations (called strata). Different selection methods may then be applied to each strata, and the sample results combined.

10. If the auditors sample without replacement, the population size has a small effect on the required sample size. As the population increases in size, the sample size necessary to represent the population will increase, but not proportionately to the increase in the population size.

11.   The population variability, as measured by the expected population occurrence (deviation) rate in attributes sampling and the standard deviation in variables sampling, has a large effect on the required sample size. The larger the variability, the greater the required sample size.

12.   The set of sampling procedures used to accomplish a specific audit objective is called a sampling plan. Two major types of statistical sampling plans that are used in auditing are variables sampling plans and attributes sampling plans. **Variables sampling plans** are widely used in substantive procedures because they provide auditors with an estimate of a numerical quantity, such as an account balance. **Attributes sampling plans**, on the other hand, are used in tests of controls where the auditors are interested in estimating the rate of deviation from a prescribed policy or procedure.

13.   The use of a statistical sampling technique does not eliminate the need for auditors to exercise professional judgment. Auditors must make several judgmental decisions before the mathematical relationships among sampling risk, allowance for sampling risk (precision), and sample size may be applied.

14.   Although the allowance for sampling risk and sampling risk are not independent of one another, auditors may view the **allowance for sampling risk** as the margin of error and **sampling risk** as establishing the risk of being wrong. For example, sampling risk of 10 percent means the auditors face a 10 percent chance that they will make a wrong conclusion from the sample.

15.   **Allowance for sampling risk** (precision) is the range from the sample results within which the true value of the population characteristic being measured is likely to lie. For example, if a sample result indicates an occurrence rate of deviations in the population of 2 percent, we have little assurance that the true deviation rate in the population is exactly 2 percent. However, we may set an interval around the sample results within which we expect the population deviation rate to be. An allowance for sampling risk of 1 percent would indicate that the true population deviation rate is expected to lie between 1 and 3 percent.

16.   In sampling to estimate an account balance, the allowance for sampling risk may be stated as a dollar value interval. In such cases, the auditors will determine the allowance in light of the amount of the tolerable misstatement in the account under audit (materiality).

17.   Sampling is used in tests of controls to estimate the frequency of deviations or exceptions from a prescribed internal control procedure, when performing the procedure leaves evidence of performance.

18.   Audit sampling tests of controls generally involves the following procedures:

     a.   Determine the objective of the test.
     b.   Define the attributes and deviation conditions.
     c.   Define the population to be sampled.
     d.   Specify the risk of assessing control risk too low and the tolerable deviation rate.
     e.   Estimate the expected population deviation rate.
     f.   Determine the sample size.
     g.   Select the sample.
     h.   Test the sample items.
     i.   Evaluate the sample results.
     j.   Document the sampling procedure.

19.   In performing tests of controls, the auditors are concerned with two aspects of sampling risk:

    a.   **The risk of assessing control risk too high**—the possibility that the sample results will cause the auditors to conclude that control risk is higher than it actually is.

    b.   **The risk of assessing control risk too low**—the possibility that the sample results will cause the auditors to conclude that control risk is lower than it actually is.

20.   The risk of assessing control risk too high relates to the **efficiency** of the audit, while the risk of assessing control risk too low relates to the **effectiveness** of the audit. The auditors should design tests of controls to allow for a low level risk of assessing control risk too low.

21.   Attributes sampling enables the auditors to estimate the occurrence rates of specified characteristics in a population. The technique is especially useful for evaluating the effectiveness of internal control procedures by estimating the deviation rates for significant internal control policies and procedures. In using attributes sampling, the auditors must specify the tolerable deviation rate and the desired risk of assessing control risk too low for the test, and they must estimate the expected population deviation rate. The **tolerable deviation rate** is determined based on the auditors' planned assessed level of control risk. The lower the planned assessed level of control risk, the lower the tolerable deviation rate. Since the test results is the only direct evidence that the auditors obtain regarding the effectiveness of an internal control procedure, the risk of assessing control risk too low is typically set at 5 or 10 percent.

22.   The **expected population deviation rate** is significant because it represents the rate of deviation that the auditors expect to observe in their sample. When the sample contains that rate (or less) the sample results support the auditor's planned assessment of control risk. The assessed level of control risk must be increased if the sample contains a deviation rate that is greater than the expected rate.

23.   In evaluating the sample results, the auditors must consider not only the percentage of deviations in the sample, but also the nature of those deviations. Exceptions that indicate fraud or intentional circumvention of internal control should be investigated thoroughly.

24.   Some auditors use a **sequential (stop or go) attributes sampling plan** to test an internal control procedure. Under a sequential sampling plan, the audit sample is taken in several stages. After each stage, the auditors decide whether to: (1) accept the planned assessed level of control risk, (2) increase the assessed level of control risk, or (3) examine additional sample items to get more information.

25.   The purpose of **discovery sampling** is to assure the auditors, with a predetermined level of confidence, of locating at least one example of an exception, providing the exception exists in the population with a specified occurrence rate. An important use of discovery sampling is to locate an example of a critical exception, such as fraud.

26.   Sampling plans that are used for substantive procedures are designed to estimate the dollar amount of misstatement in a particular balance. Statistical plans that typically are used for substantive procedures include **variables sampling plans** and **probability–proportional–to–size sampling**.

27.   Designing and implementing a mean–per–unit estimation plan involves the following procedures:

      a.   Define the objective of the test.
      b.   Define the population and sampling unit.
      c.   Choose an audit sampling technique.
      d.   Determine the sample size.
      e.   Select the sample.
      f.   Test the sample items.
      g.   Evaluate the sample results.
      h.   Document the sampling procedures.

28.   In determining the appropriate allowance for sampling risk (precision) for a substantive procedure, the auditors should consider the materiality of the tolerable misstatement in the account.

29.   In performing substantive procedures of account balances, auditors are faced with two types of sampling risk:

      a.   **The risk of incorrect rejection**—the possibility that the auditors may conclude, based on the sample results, that a balance contains material misstatement when, in fact, it does not.

      b.   **The risk of incorrect acceptance**—the possibility that the auditors may conclude that the balance is free from material misstatement when, in fact, material misstatement exists.

     If the auditors make the first type of error, and incorrectly reject an acceptable balance, their audit will lack **efficiency**. The risk of incorrect acceptance, on the other hand, relates to the **effectiveness** of the audit in detecting material misstatement.

30.   **Mean–per–unit estimation** is a variables sampling plan which enables auditors to estimate the average dollar value of items in a population with specified sampling risk and allowance for sampling risk by determining the average dollar value of the items in the sample. An estimate of the total dollar value of the population then may be obtained by multiplying the sample average by the number of items in the population.

31.   When the auditors' estimate of the population's standard deviation used to calculate the sample size turns out to be exactly the amount that is calculated for the audited values in the sample, the planned allowance for sampling risk may be used for evaluation purposes. The auditors calculate an acceptance interval by adding and subtracting the allowance for sampling risk to and from the estimated total audited value of the account (mean audited value x population size). If the book value is in this interval the auditors "accept" the population.

32.   When the auditors' estimate the population's standard deviation used to calculate the sample size differs from that found in the audited values of the sample, the auditors must modify their procedure. One method is to calculate an adjusted allowance for sampling risk that holds the planned risk of incorrect acceptance at the desired level.   This technique is described on pages 332-333.

33.   Two other variables sampling plans are **ratio estimation** and **difference estimation**. In ratio estimation, the auditors use a sample to estimate the ratio of the audited (correct) value of the population to its book value. In applying difference estimation, the auditors use a sample to estimate the average difference between the audited value and book value of the items in the population.

34.   The use of ratio or difference estimation techniques requires that (1) each population item has a book value, (2) an audited value may be ascertained for each sample item, and (3) differences between audited and book values be relatively frequent.

35.   Auditors may use a nonstatistical sampling approach for substantive procedures. They may use unassisted judgment for determining the sample size and for evaluating sample results, or they may use structured approaches that are based on statistical methods.

36.   In a structured nonstatistical sample, the ratio and difference methods are frequently used to evaluate the sample results.

Highlights of the Appendices

1.   In **probability-proportional-to-size (PPS) sampling**, the sampling unit is defined as $1, rather than an item with a variable dollar balance, such as an account balance. For example, a population of 10,000 accounts receivable with a total value of $2,500,000 is viewed as a population of 2,500,000 items (dollar) rather than a population of 10,000 items (accounts).

2.   PPS sampling automatically stratifies the population, and is especially efficient in populations with very few misstatements in the recorded amounts. Auditors frequently use systematic selection when using PPS sampling.

3.   The PPS sample is selected based on aggregating the dollars of the individual accounts as illustrated in Figure 9-17 (page 351). As such, all accounts with a book value as large or larger than the sampling interval are included in the sample. Accordingly, when evaluating sample results, no allowance for sampling risk is calculated for such items since they have not been sampled--all of them are included in the sample.

4.   The audit risk model originally presented in Chapter 5 is:

$$AR = IR \times CR \times DR$$

where: AR =   Audit Risk
         IR =   Inherent Risk
         CR =   Control Risk
         DR =   Detection Risk

Detection risk in the formula may be further divided into two components--the risk that analytical procedures and any other substantive procedures will fail to detect a material misstatement (AP) and the allowable risk of incorrect acceptance for the substantive procedure (TD). Substituting into the above formula one may derive:

$$AR = IR \times CR \times AP \times TD$$

Solving for TD, we derive:

$$TD = AR / (IR \times CR \times AP)$$

Thus, at least conceptually, it is possible to derive a formula for the appropriate risk of incorrect acceptance.

Test Yourself on Chapter 9

TRUE OR FALSE

For each of the following statements, circle the T or the F to indicate whether the statement is true or false.

T F 1. The allowance for sampling risk for a substantive procedure is determined based in part on the tolerable misstatement in the account.

T F 2. Nonstatistical sampling may be used for tests of controls but should never be used for substantive procedures.

T F 3. Statistical sampling techniques permit the auditors to eliminate sampling risk.

T F 4. Nonsampling risk may be reduced by increasing the size of the sample.

T F 5. A difference between nonstatistical and statistical sampling is reflected in the methods used to interpret sample results.

T F 6. Random sampling is another term for statistical sampling.

T F 7. Selecting every 50th invoice for inclusion in a sample is termed systematic sampling.

T F 8. Block samples are used extensively in auditing.

T F 9. The risk of assessing control risk too high relates to the effectiveness of the audit.

T F 10. Attributes sampling is often used in conjunction with tests of the client's internal control.

T F 11. In performing tests of controls, the auditors focus on the risk of assessing control risk too high rather than the risk of assessing control risk too low.

T F 12. In using a sequential sampling plan for tests of controls, the auditors are concerned with critical misstatements.

T F 13. Discovery sampling is best suited to discovering examples of commonplace errors, such as the wrong price entered on a sales invoice.

T F 14. To estimate the total audited dollar value of a population of 10,000 items, using the mean-per-unit estimation method, one would multiply the sample mean audited value times 10,000.

T F 15. Mean–per–unit estimation is often used in tests of controls, because an estimate of the misstatement is usually desired.

T F 16. If the variability of the population increases, as measured by the standard deviation, the required sample size increases.

T F 17. The risk of incorrect rejection relates to the efficiency of a substantive procedure, but not to the effectiveness of the test.

T F 18. Auditors may determine the risk of incorrect rejection, but they cannot determine the risk that their sample will cause them to accept a population which contains material misstatement.

T   F   19.   The tolerable misstatement is an estimate of the maximum monetary amount that may exist in an account and still not lead to a material misstatement in the financial statement.

T   F   20.   In attributes sampling, the risk of assessing control risk too high is often not controlled when using statistical sampling.

COMPLETION

Fill in the necessary words to complete the following statements.

1.   Inherent in the use of sampling is the risk of _____ _____ which is the possibility of selecting a sample that is not representative of the _____.

2   When the auditors estimate sampling risk using professional judgment rather than by using the laws of probability, they are said to be using _____ sampling.

3.   When using _____ _____ _____ an item from the population may be selected two or more times for inclusion in the sample.

4.   The term _____ refers to the process of dividing a population into relatively homogeneous subgroups called _____.

5.   In performing tests of controls, the auditors are primarily concerned with the critical aspect of sampling risk known as the _____ _____ _____ _____ _____ _____ _____.

6.   To use attributes sampling tables, the auditors must stipulate the desired _____ _____ _____ _____ _____ _____ _____, the expected deviation rate in the population, and the desired tolerable _____ _____.

7.   The _____ _____ _____ _____ is the range around the sample results, within which the true value of the population is likely to lie.

8.   If the variability of a population increases, as measured by the _____ _____, the required sample size for the population will _____.

9.   _____ _____ plans are typically used for tests of controls, whereas variables sampling plans are typically used for _____ _____.

10.   Detection risk may be separated into two risks, one relating to _____ procedures and the other is

the allowable risk of tests of _____.

MULTIPLE CHOICE

Choose the best answer for each of the following questions and enter the identifying letter in the space provided.

____ 1.   The estimated deviation rate obtained from attributes sampling is useful in satisfying the auditing standard which states:

a.   the work is to be adequately planned, and assistants, if any, are to be properly supervised.
b.   sufficient competent evidential matter is to be obtained through inspection, observation, inquiries, and confirmations to afford a reasonable basis for an opinion.
c.   the audit is to be performed by a person or persons having adequate technical training and proficiency as an auditor.
d.   a sufficient understanding of the internal control is to be obtained to plan the audit and determine the nature, timing, and extent of other audit tests.

____ 2.   For a large population of cash disbursement transactions, Smith, CPA, is testing internal control by using attributes sampling techniques. Anticipating an deviation rate of 3 percent, Smith found from a table that the required sample size is 400 with a desired tolerable deviation rate of 5 percent and risk of assessing control risk too low of 5 percent. If Smith anticipated an deviation rate of only 2 percent, the sample size would be closest to:

a.   200.
b.   400.
c.   533.
d.   800.

____ 3.   There are many kinds of statistical estimates that an auditor may find useful, but basically every accounting estimate is either of a quantity or of an occurrence rate. The statistical terms that roughly correspond to quantities and occurrence rate, respectively, are:

a.   attributes and variables.
b.   variables and attributes.
c.   constants and attributes.
d.   constants and variables.

____ 4.   How should an auditor determine the allowance for sampling risk required in establishing a statistical sampling plan for a substantive procedure?

a.   By the materiality of an allowable margin of misstatement the auditor is willing to accept.
b.   By the amount of reliance the auditor will place on the results of the sample.
c.   By reliance on a table of random numbers.
d.   By the amount of risk the auditor is willing to take that material misstatements will occur in the accounting process.

_b_ 5. The audit risk against which the auditors require reasonable protection is a combination of two separate risks. The first of these is that material misstatements will occur and the second is that:

    a. a company's internal control structure is not adequate to detect misstatements.
    b. those misstatements that occur will not be detected in the auditors' procedures.
    c. management may possess an attitude that lacks integrity.
    d. evidential matter is not competent enough for the auditors to form an opinion based on reasonable assurance.

_a_ 6. Which of the following best describes what the auditor means by the expected rate of deviation in an attributes sampling plan?

    a. The number of deviations that can reasonably be expected to be found in a population.
    b. The frequency with which a certain characteristic occurs within a population.
    c. The degree of confidence that the sample is representative of the population.
    d. The dollar range within which the true population total can be expected to fall.

_a_ 7. Auditors often utilize sampling methods when performing tests of controls. Which of the following sampling methods is most useful when testing controls?

    a. Attributes sampling.
    b. Variables sampling.
    c. Unrestricted random sampling with replacement.
    d. Stratified random sampling.

_a_ 8. Which of the following best describes the distinguishing feature of statistical sampling?

    a. It provides for mathematically measuring the degree of uncertainty that results from examining only a part of the data.
    b. It allows the auditor to have the same degree of confidence as with nonstatistical sampling, but with substantially less work.
    c. It allows the auditor to substitute sampling techniques for audit judgment.
    d. It provides for measuring the actual misstatements in financial statements in terms of reliability and precision.

_b_ 9. If certain forms are not consecutively numbered:

    a. selection of a random sample probably is not possible.
    b. systematic sampling may be appropriate.
    c. stratified sampling should be used.
    d. random number tables cannot be used.

_b_ 10. Jones, CPA, believes the industry–wide occurrence rate of client billing errors is 3 % and has established a tolerable deviation rate of 5 % . In the review of client invoices, Jones should use:

    a. discovery sampling.
    b. attributes sampling.
    c. stratified sampling.
    d. variables sampling.

_d___   11.   In attributes sampling, which one of the following must be known in order to appraise the results of the auditor's sample?

a.   Estimated dollar value of the population.
b.   Standard deviation of the values in the population.
c.   Actual occurrence rate of the attribute in the population.
d.   Sample size.

_c___   12.   Which of the following statistical selection techniques is least desirable for use by an auditor?

a.   Systematic selection.
b.   Stratified selection.
c.   Block selection.
d.   Sequential selection.

_a___   13.   Which of the following best illustrates the concept of sampling risk?

a.   A randomly chosen sample may not be representative of the population as a whole on the characteristic of interest.
b.   An auditor may select audit procedures that are not appropriate to achieve the specific objective.
c.   An auditor may fail to recognize misstatements in the documents examined for the chosen sample.
d.   The documents related to the chosen sample may not be available for inspection.

_b___   14.   Given random selection without replacement, the same sample size, and the same tolerable deviation rate for the testing of two unequal populations, the risk of assessing control risk too low for the smaller population is:

a.   higher than the risk of assessing control risk too low for the larger population.
b.   lower than the risk of assessing control risk too low for the larger population.
c.   the same as the risk of assessing control risk too low for the larger population.
d.   indeterminable relative to the risk of assessing control risk too low for the larger population.

_a___   15.   Holding all other factors constant, an increase in the planned allowance for sampling risk will occur if the:

a.   tolerable misstatement increases.
b.   incorrect acceptance coefficient increases.
c.   risk of incorrect acceptance decreases.
d.   population size increases.

Use the following information to answer questions 16 through 20.

Mean book value of items in sample:	$32
Mean audited value of items in sample:	$31
Mean book value of items in population:	$33
Number of items in population:	10,000

____ 16. The total book value of this population is:

    a. $310,000
    b. $320,000
    c. $330,000
    d. $347,222

____ 17. Using the mean-per-unit estimation, the estimated total audited value is:

    a. $310,000
    b. $320,000
    c. $330,000
    d. $347,222

____ 18. Using mean-per-unit estimation, the projected misstatement is:

    a. $10,000 overstatement
    b. $10,000 understatement
    c. $20,000 overstatement
    d. $20,000 understatement

____ 19. Using ratio estimation, the estimated total audited value is:

    a. $300,606
    b. $310,000
    c. $319,688
    d. $320,000

____ 20. Using difference estimation, the estimated total audited value is:

    a. $300,000
    b. $310,000
    c. $320,000
    d. $330,000

EXERCISES

1. Listed below are statistical sampling techniques and audit situations. Match each technique with the audit situation in which use of the technique would be most appropriate.

    Sampling Technique

    A   Difference estimation
    B   Discovery sampling
    C   Attributes sampling
    D   Probability-proportional-to-size sampling

    Situation

    _____   a.   The auditors wish to test the operating effectiveness of a control, and expect a 2 percent deviation rate in the population.

    _____   b.   The auditors wish to estimate the dollar value of 1,000 inventory items that have been priced by the client; the auditors expect a moderately high misstatement rate in the client's pricing of the items.

    _____   c.   The auditors wish to estimate the value of accounts receivable by confirmation; the auditors expect a very low deviation rate in recorded amounts.

    _____   d.   The auditors wish to test for the existence of a critical deviation in internal control.

2. Define each of the following terms.

    a.   Audit sampling:

    b.   Sampling risk:

    c.   Nonsampling risk:

    d.   Risk of assessing control risk to low:

CHAPTER 10

Cash and Financial Investments

Highlights of the Chapter

1. In the examination of cash, the auditors' principal objectives are to: (1) consider the **inherent risks** related to cash, including fraud risks, (2) consider **internal control** over cash transactions, (3) substantiate the **existence** of recorded cash, (4) establish the **completeness** of recorded cash, (5) determine that the client has **rights** to recorded cash, (6) establish the **clerically accuracy** of cash schedules, and (7) determine that the **presentation and disclosure** of cash is appropriate.

2. Since cash has a high degree of inherent risk, and most financial statement items "flow through" the cash account, more audit time is devoted to cash than would be indicated by the materiality of the cash balance.

3. Control over cash receipts should provide assurance that all cash which should have been received was in **fact** received and recorded promptly and accurately. Rules for achieving control over cash receipts include:

    a. separate cash handling from recordkeeping,
    b. centralize the receiving of cash as much as possible,
    c. record cash receipts immediately,
    d. encourage customers to obtain receipts and observe cash register totals, and
    e. deposit each day's cash receipts intact.

4. Depositing daily receipts intact contributes to internal control because less cash will be on hand to invite theft or "borrowing," and the bank's independent record of deposits should correspond to the client's records of daily cash receipts. Also, undeposited receipts represent idle cash, which is not a revenue producing asset.

5. Control over cash sales is strongest when two or more employees (usually a salesclerk and cashier) participate in each transaction. Restaurants and auto repair garages often use a centrally located cashier who receives cash from the customer along with a serially numbered sales ticket prepared by another employee.

6. Cash sales may also be controlled through the use of a cash register. The protective features of cash registers include (1) visual display of the amount of the sale in full view of the customer, (2) a printed receipt, and (3) accumulation of a lock-in total of the day's sales.

7. Electronic point-of-sale systems provide control over cash receipts that is similar to that provided by cash registers. In addition, electronic systems often are programmed to perform other functions, such as verification of the credit status of customers, and updating of accounts receivable and inventory records.

8. In many businesses cash receipts consist largely of checks received through the mail. The employee who opens the mail should prepare a control listing of the checks received, showing the customer's name and the amount received. A copy of this list should be reconciled with daily bank deposits, entries in the cash receipts journal, and credits to customers' accounts. The employee who prepares the control listing must not perform the reconciliation functions, issue credit memoranda, or have access to the accounting records.

9. The mail room employee is prevented from abstracting the cash receipts because they consist of checks made payable to the company. Also, statements are mailed to customers who will complain when they do not receive credit for a payment.

10. The cashier uses the checks and customers' remittance advices to deposit the day's receipts intact in the bank. Control is exercised over the cashier by periodic reconciliation of the mail room control listings with the cash receipts journal and the detail of daily bank deposits.

11. The cashier forwards the remittance advices to the employee responsible for the customers' accounts ledger, who posts credits to the customers' accounts.

12. Control over cash disbursements should provide assurance that disbursements are made only for authorized business purposes and are properly recorded. The basic rule for achieving control over disbursements is to make all payments by check or from an imprest petty cash fund. The advantages of making disbursements by check include (1) the centralization of authority to make cash disbursements, (2) a permanent record of all disbursements, and (3) a reduction in the amount of cash kept on hand.

13. To determine that all disbursements have been recorded, checks should be sequentially numbered and all checks in the series accounted for. Voided checks should be defaced and filed in the regular sequence of paid checks. It is important to distinguish between a voided check and a cancelled check. A voided check was not cleared ("cashed") by a financial institution—perhaps because the preparer realized that the payee's name was misspelled or that the check was written for the wrong amount. A cancelled check was cleared by a financial institution and bears markings so indicating. Since voided checks were never cleared, the client ordinarily maintains them; cancelled checks may, or may not, be returned by the financial institution to the client.

14. Checks should be prepared by one person and signed by another. By separating these functions, no one person is in a position to make fictitious disbursements. The official signing checks should review the documents supporting the payment, and cancel the documents at the time the check is signed to prevent them from being reused. After checks have been signed, they should be mailed without being returned to the employee' who prepared them for signature.

15. A **voucher system** is one method of achieving strong internal control over cash disbursements by providing assurance that all disbursements are properly authorized and reviewed before a check is issued.

16. Periodic reconciliation of bank statements provides assurance that the client's records of cash receipts and disbursements correspond to the bank's independent record of deposits received and checks paid.

17. Internal control over payments from an imprest petty cash fund is achieved at the time the fund is replenished. At that time, the supporting documentation for expenditures is reviewed and canceled.

18. An audit program illustrating the general pattern of work performed by the auditors in the verification of cash is described on page 367 and 369 of the textbook.

19. The audit procedures of tracing the detail of a cash receipts listing to the posting to individual customers' accounts may uncover a fraud known as **lapping**. Lapping refers to abstracting cash by delaying the recording of cash receipts. Lapping is most likely to occur when an employee receiving collections from customers has access to the accounts receivable records.

20. Reconciling the bank activity for one or more months with cash activity per books is known as a **proof of cash.** The working paper generated is a four column bank reconciliation which reconciles the cash receipts and disbursements for the period, and provides evidence as to the reliability of the client's cash records.

21. Confirmation of amounts on deposit with financial institutions is a common audit procedure. An important element of the standard confirmation is a confirmation of indebtedness of the client to the financial institution. If the auditors consider it necessary they may decide to send additional specially designed letters to confirm the details of the client's financial arrangements with the financial institution (e.g., the terms of a line of credit arrangement).

22. When cash on hand is counted, the auditor should insist that the custodian of the funds be present throughout the count. The custodian should sign the working paper, indicating that the fund was returned intact.

23. **A cutoff bank statement** is a statement covering a specified number of business days (usually seven to ten) following the end of the client's fiscal year. The auditors use the bank cutoff statement to verify the accuracy of the items appearing on the bank reconciliation (e.g., deposits in transit and outstanding checks).

24. Manipulations causing an amount of cash to be included simultaneously in the balance of two or more bank accounts is referred to as **kiting.** Auditors can detect kiting by preparing and verifying a schedule of bank transfers for a few days before and after the balance sheet date. This working paper lists all bank transfers and shows the dates that the receipt and disbursement of cash were recorded in the cash journals and on the bank statements.

25. Any restrictions on bank deposits, such as required compensating balances or restrictions against removing cash in foreign banks, should be disclosed in notes to the financial statements.

26. Financial investments consist principally of government bonds and notes and listed corporate securities which can readily converted into cash. Because most financial investments are readily negotiable, the need for their physical protection and for strong internal controls is almost as great as in the case of cash. The auditors must also be concerned with derivatives, which are financial instruments that derive their value from other financial instruments, underlying assets, or indices.

27. The audit of financial investments can be very complex requiring specialized skill or knowledge in performing such tasks as: (1) identifying controls at service organizations that provide financial services and are part of the client's information system, (2) obtaining an understanding of information systems for securities and derivatives that are highly dependent on computer technology, (3) applying complex accounting principles, (4) understanding the methods of determining fair values of financial investments, and (5) assessing inherent and control risk for assertions about derivatives used in hedging activities.

28. The auditors' objectives in the examination of financial investments are to: (1) consider **inherent risks,** including fraud risks, (2) consider **internal control** over financial investments, (3) determine the **existence** of financial investments and that the client has **rights** to the securities, (4) establish the **completeness** of recorded financial investments, (5) determine that the **valuation** of financial investments is appropriate, (6) establish the **clerical** accuracy of schedules of investments, and (7) determine that the **presentation and disclosure** of financial investments is adequate.

29.   The major elements of adequate internal control over financial investments include the following:

    a.   Formal investment policies that limit the nature of investments in securities and other financial instruments.

    b.   An investment committee of the board of directors that authorizes and reviews investment activities.

    c.   Separation of duties between the executive authorizing purchases and sales of securities and derivative instruments, the custodian of the securities, and the person maintaining the records of investments.

    d.   Complete detailed records of all securities and derivative instruments owned, and the related provisions and terms.

    e.   Registration of securities in the name of the company.

    f.   Periodic physical inspection of securities by an internal auditor or other independent official.

    g.   Determination of appropriate accounting for complex financial instruments by competent personnel.

30.   Purchases and sales of securities should be authorized in advance by a responsible official. Regular internal reports should be prepared for the investment committee of the board of directors showing securities owned, current transactions, investment revenue, and gains and losses. The custody of the securities should lie with an independent safekeeping agent, or the securities should be kept in a bank safe-deposit box under the **joint control** of two or more of the company's officials.

31.   A typical audit program for the examination of financial investments is illustrated on page 384-385 of the textbook.

32.   Inherent risk for financial instruments is often high due to their liquidity, and due to complex accounting requirements.   The use of derivatives almost always increase the risk of material misstatement.

33.   The count of securities on hand should be made concurrently with the verification of other liquid assets, such as cash.

34.   Comparison of the serial numbers on securities with those recorded in the prior year's audit working papers may bring to light any substitution or "borrowing" of securities.

35.   Securities held by brokers or by banks as collateral for loans should be confirmed by use of a request signed by the client but mailed by the auditors with the reply directed to the auditors' office.

36.   Dividend and interest revenue is usually verified by independent computations by the auditors, or by tests of reasonableness of the amount of revenue earned. Dividend record books published by investment advisory services show the amounts of dividends and dates of declaration, of record, and of payment. Bond interest can be recomputed from the interest rates and payment dates shown on the bonds.

37.   If the client has securities that are valued on the equity basis of accounting, the auditors should obtain recent audited financial statements of the investee to verify the client's share of net assets and income from the investment. If such financial statements are not available, the auditors may find it necessary to perform audit procedures to verify the unaudited financial statements of the investee.

38.   Since most financial investments are valued at current market values, the auditors must obtain current market quotations for financial investments owned by the client from sources such as the *Wall Street Journal* and various Internet sources.

Test Yourself on Chapter 10

TRUE OR FALSE

For each of the following statements, circle the T or the F to indicate whether the statement is true or false.

T   F   1.   In relation to its materiality, the audit of cash requires little audit time.

T   F   2.   Designating the cashier to be custodian of the petty cash fund is more acceptable from the standpoint of internal control than making the cashier responsible for maintenance of accounts receivable records.

T   F   3.   A salesperson who uses a cash register to record over-the-counter sales should, at the end of each work day, turn over to a supervisor the cash register tape and a corresponding amount of cash.

T   F   4.   An employee who prepares checks and submits them with supporting documents to the official authorized to sign checks should not be responsible for mailing the signed checks.

T   F   5.   Cash should be deposited weekly so it can be counted several times before being sent to the bank.

T   F   6.   The "lapping" of cash receipts is most likely to occur when one person has both responsibility for recordkeeping for cash receipts and custody of cash.

T   F   7.   An improper bank reconciliation designed to conceal a cash shortage is more likely to overstate than understate the amount of outstanding checks.

T   F   8.   Auditors should never count a cash fund with the custodian present because the custodian might be able to influence the count.

T   F   9.   The standard financial institution confirmation request used by the auditors is a means of obtaining documentary evidence about both assets and liabilities.

T   F   10.   Confirmation letters should be mailed by the auditors in envelopes bearing the auditors' return address.

T   F   11.   The audit working paper known as a "proof of cash" is a means of proving that checks paid by the bank during the test period were not in excess of authorized cash disbursements during that same test period.

T   F   12.   A cutoff bank statement provides assurance to the auditors that all checks outstanding at year-end were included in the list of outstanding checks in the year-end bank reconciliation.

T   F   13.   The practice of "kiting" as a means of overstating cash is possible only if the client maintains two or more bank accounts.

T   F   14.   A client has $100,000 on deposit at year-end and owes the bank $250,000 on a note payable. The borrowing agreement calls for the client to maintain a minimum (compensating) balance of $40,000 on deposit during the life of the bank loan. On the balance sheet, the asset cash should be stated at $60,000, the excess of the deposit over the compensating balance.

T   F   15.   Good internal control over financial investments requires that the treasurer obtain certificates for all securities and keep them in the company safe.

T   F   16.   The inspection of securities on hand should be coordinated with the verification of inventories because both involve counting and inspection and can conveniently be combined.

T   F   17.   A derivative is a financial instrument that derives its value from another financial instrument, an underlying asset, or indices.

T   F   18.   An official of the client company took securities from the safe deposit box and sold them to obtain cash to meet a personal financial crisis. Even with proper internal control, if the official purchased identical securities before the year-end and placed them in the safe deposit box, this improper "borrowing" would probably go undetected during the annual audit.

T   F   19.   Auditors normally verify the amount of dividends earned on the client's security investments by writing directly to the companies which paid the dividends.

T   F   20.   Marketable equity securities should be valued at cost.

COMPLETION

Fill in the necessary words to complete the following statements.

1.   Control over cash sales is increased if a centrally located _____ participates in each transaction.

2.   Collection of accounts receivable through the mail should be initially listed by personnel in the _____

 _____ .

3.   Checks in payment of a company's payables should be _____ by one person and

_____ by another.

4.   A standard form to _____ _____ _____ _____ _____ _____

 _____ _____ requests the financial institution to confirm the balance in the client's

deposit accounts as well as any _____ due to the bank.

5.   A _____ _____ _____ is a bank statement covering a few days after year-end which is used

by the auditors to verify the client's bank reconciliation.

6.   A _____ _____ is a required minimum account balance that may be required by a

bank when making a loan to a customer.

7.   If a client's financial investments are maintained in a _____ _____ _____, the box should be

      under the _____ control of two or more officials.

8.   Financial investments should be registered in the name of the _____.

9.   The count of securities on hand by the auditors should be made concurrently with the count of other

      _____ _____.

10.   Verification of dividend revenue can be achieved by independent computation using _____ _____

      published by investment advisory services.

MULTIPLE CHOICE

Choose the best answer for each of the following questions and enter the identifying letter in the space provided.

_____   1.   The least crucial element of internal control over cash is:

              a.   separation of cash record keeping from custody of cash.
              b.   preparation of the monthly bank reconciliation.
              c.   canceling the supporting documents for disbursements.
              d.   separation of cash receipts from preparing deposits.

_____   2.   Internal control over cash receipts is weakened when an employee who receives customer mail receipts also:

              a.   prepares initial cash receipts records.
              b.   records credits to individual accounts receivable.
              c.   prepares bank deposit slips for all mail receipts.
              d.   maintains a petty cash fund.

_____   3.   Contact with banks for the purpose of opening company bank accounts should normally be the responsibility of the corporate:

              a.   board of directors.
              b.   treasurer.
              c.   controller.
              d.   executive committee.

_____ 4. Which of the following is a frequent control over cash disbursements?

a. Checks should be signed by the controller and at least one other employee of the company.
b. Checks should be sequentially numbered and the numerical sequence should be accounted for by the person preparing bank reconciliations.
c. Checks and supporting documents should be marked "Paid" immediately after the check is returned with the bank statement.
d. Checks should be sent directly to the payee by the employee who prepares documents that authorize check preparation.

_____ 5. Operating control over the check signature plate normally should be the responsibility of the:

a. secretary.
b. chief accountant.
c. vice president of finance.
d. treasurer.

_____ 6. Under which of the following circumstances would an auditor be most likely to intensify an examination of a $500 imprest petty cash fund?

a. Reimbursement vouchers are not prenumbered.
b. Reimbursement occurs twice each week.
c. The custodian occasionally uses the cash fund to cash employee checks.
d. The custodian endorses reimbursement checks.

_____ 7. The auditors who are engaged to examine the financial statements of a business enterprise will request a cutoff bank statement primarily in order to:

a. verify the cash balance reported on the standard financial institution confirmation form.
b. verify reconciling items on the client's bank reconciliation.
c. detect lapping.
d. detect kiting.

_____ 8. Which of the following audit procedures is the most appropriate when internal control over cash is weak or when a client requests an investigation of cash transactions?

a. Proof of cash.
b. Bank reconciliation.
c. Cash confirmation.
d. Evaluation of ratio of cash to current liabilities.

_____ 9. In order to avoid the misappropriation of company-owned financial investments, which of the following is the best course of action that can be taken by the management of a company with a large portfolio of financial investments?

a. Require that one trustworthy and bonded employee be responsible for access to the safekeeping area where securities are kept.
b. Require that employees who enter and leave the safekeeping area sign and record in a log the exact reason for their access.
c. Require that employees involved in the safekeeping function maintain a subsidiary control ledger for securities on a current basis.
d. Require that the safekeeping function for securities be assigned to a securities broker that will act as a custodial agent.

_____   10.   The financial management of a company should take steps to see that company investment securities are protected. Which of the following is not a step that is designed to protect investment securities?

   a.   Custody of securities should be assigned to persons who have the accounting responsibility for securities.
   b.   Securities should be properly controlled physically in order to prevent unauthorized usage.
   c.   Access to securities should be vested in more than one person.
   d.   Securities should be registered in the name of the owner.

_____   11.   Which of the following is not one of the auditors' primary objectives in an examination of investments in securities?

   a.   To determine whether all securities are in proper, secure, files at year-end.
   b.   To determine whether securities are the property of the client.
   c.   To determine whether securities actually exist.
   d.   To determine whether securities are properly classified on the balance sheet.

_____   12.   A company holds bearer bonds as a short-term investment. Responsibility for custody of these bonds and submission of coupons for periodic interest collections probably should be delegated to the:

   a.   chief accountant.
   b.   internal auditors.
   c.   cashier.
   d.   treasurer.

EXERCISES

1.   Listed below are types of errors or fraud that might occur in financial statements and audit procedures. Match the audit procedure with the error or fraud that the procedure is likely to detect.

Error or Fraud

_____ 1. "Lapping" of accounts receivable

_____ 2. Using the company's securities during the year and replacing them.

_____ 3. "Kiting" of cash.

_____ 4. Understating the outstanding checks on the year-end bank reconciliation.

_____ 5. Recording fictitious cash sales.

Audit Procedure

a.   Preparing and verifying a schedule of bank transfers.

b.   Tracing remittance advices to postings in the accounts receivable records.

c.   Comparing the serial numbers of securities on hand to numbers recorded in the prior year's audit working papers.

d.   Review of the bank cutoff statement.

e.   Preparing a "proof of cash for the entire audit period.

2.   Explain the reason for each of the following controls:

a.   Canceling documents supporting cash disbursements--

b.   Preparing a mail room control listing of cash receipts--

c.   Separating the duties of cashier from the duties of posting accounts receivable records--

d.   Using a check protector--

CHAPTER 11

Accounts Receivable, Notes Receivable, and Revenue

Highlights of the Chapter

1.   The auditors' principal objectives in the examination of accounts receivable and revenue are to: (1) consider inherent risks, including fraud risks, (2) consider **internal control** over receivables and revenue transactions, (3) substantiate the **existence** of receivables and the occurrence of revenue transactions, (4) establish the **completeness** of receivables and revenue transactions, (5) determine that the client has **rights** to the recorded assets, (6) establish the **clerical accuracy** of records and supporting schedules of receivables and revenue, (7) determine that the **valuation** of receivables is at appropriate net realizable values, and (8) determine that the **presentation and disclosure** of receivables and revenue are appropriate.

2.   Revenue and receivables typically have a high degree of inherent risk. As discussed in Chapter 6, SAS No. 99 states that the auditors should generally conclude that there is a fraud risk with respect to revenue. Factors that may contribute to the inherent risk of revenue and receivables for a particular audit include (1) complex accounting methods, (2) estimates involved in determining revenue and the net realizable value of receivables, and (3) the possibility of management intentional misstatement of revenues.

3.   Strong internal control over sales transactions is best achieved by having separate departments (or individuals) responsible for preparing sales orders, approving credit, shipping merchandise, billing customers, maintaining the accounts receivable subsidiary ledger, approving of sales returns and allowances, and authorizing write-offs of uncollectible accounts. Also, the basic documentation of each transaction (shipping documents and sales invoices) should be controlled by serial numbers to assure that all transactions are accounted for.

4.   The sequence of procedures involved in a credit sales transaction may be referred to as the sales (revenue) cycle. The cycle begins with the preparation of a sales order which translates the terms of the customer's order into a specific instruction for the guidance of other divisions. Before the goods are shipped, the credit department must determine whether goods may be shipped to the customer on open account.

5.   Upon receipt of an approved sales order, the stores department issues the appropriate merchandise to the shipping department. When the merchandise is shipped, the shipping department prepares a serially numbered shipping document and obtains a **bill of lading** from the common carrier acknowledging receipt of the goods.

6.   The billing section accounts for the numerical sequence of shipping documents to assure that an invoice is prepared for all items shipped. An invoice is prepared using the sales order and price data from sales catalogs and price lists. After the sales invoice has been reviewed for accuracy of prices, discounts, credit terms, and other details, it is mailed to the customer.

7.   Daily totals of amounts invoiced should be transmitted to the general ledger section for entry to the accounts receivable control account. Copies of all sales invoices (or computer-readable details) are transmitted to the accounts receivable section for posting to the subsidiary ledger of accounts receivable.

8.   As receivables are collected, remittance advices are forwarded from the cashier to the accounts receivable section. The accounts receivable section reconciles the remittance advices with a cash receipt listing prepared by mail room personnel and will post the credits to customers' accounts. An aged trial balance of customers' accounts should be prepared periodically for use by the credit department in carrying out its collection efforts.

9.   The subsidiary ledger of accounts receivable should be balanced periodically with the controlling account by an employee from the operations control group.

10.   Receivables judged uncollectible should be written off and transferred to a separate ledger and control account. It is essential that written off accounts be properly controlled; otherwise, any subsequent collections may be abstracted by employees without the necessity of falsification of any records to conceal the theft.

11.   The basic element of internal control consists of the subdivision of duties. As applied to notes receivable, this principle requires that (1) the custodian of notes receivable not have access to cash or to the general accounting records, (2) the acceptance and renewal of notes be authorized in writing by a responsible official who does not have custody of the notes, and (3) the write-off of defaulted notes be approved in writing by responsible officials and effective procedures adopted for subsequent follow-up on such defaulted notes.

12.   A typical audit program for the audit of notes and accounts receivable appears on pages 412-413 of the textbook.

13.   To obtain assurance that **all shipments are billed**, and obtain evidence of the completeness of recorded sales and accounts receivable, it is necessary for the auditors to obtain a sample of shipping documents issued during the year and compare these to sales invoices.

14.   An **aged trial balance** of accounts receivable at the balance sheet date is normally prepared by the client, often in the form of a computer printout. This working paper is used by the auditors evaluating the adequacy of the client's allowance for uncollectible accounts. Examination of credit files for large accounts, review of subsequent collections, and analytical procedures are other techniques that are useful in evaluating the allowance for uncollectible accounts.

15.   Direct communication with debtors is generally regarded as the most important step in the verification of receivables. Acknowledgment of a debt by the debtor establishes the existence of the receivable and provides some assurance that no lapping or manipulation of receivables exists at the date of the confirmation.

16.   All confirmation requests are mailed in envelopes bearing the return address of the auditors. A stamped "business reply" envelope addressed to the office of the auditors is enclosed with the request. The requests should be mailed personally by the auditors. These procedures are designed to prevent the client's employees from having an opportunity to alter or intercept either a confirmation request or the customer's reply.

17.   Two forms of confirmation requests are widely used: (1) **positive confirmations**, which request the debtor to respond in every case, and (2) **negative confirmations**, which request the debtor to respond only if the balance shown is incorrect. Positive confirmations provide more competence evidence, because customers may not give the negative confirmations consideration. Negative confirmations should only be used when the account consists of a large number of small balances, the combination of inherent and control risk for accounts receivable is low, and the auditors have no reason to believe that the customer will not give the confirmation consideration.

18.   If responses are not received to positive confirmation requests, the auditors will follow up with a second request. When replies to follow-up requests are not received, the auditors should perform alternative auditing procedures for all significant nonrespondents. The best form of alternative verification is the examination of subsequent payments made to the account. The auditors may also examine documents substantiating the transactions making up the account balance, such as shipping documents and sales invoices.

19.   The size of the sample of accounts receivable confirmed varies with the materiality and risk of the account. The auditors should stratify the accounts receivable population and confirm a proportionately larger sample of the larger accounts.

20.   On a rare occasion it may be "impossible" to confirm accounts receivable. If the auditors are able to satisfy themselves by alternative procedures, there is no reason to refer to the omission of the procedure in the auditors' report. If the auditors are not able to satisfy themselves by alternative procedures, the omission of this procedure prevents the auditors from issuing an unqualified report.

21.   A common method of falsifying accounting records is to inflate the sales for the year by holding open the sales journal beyond the balance sheet date. The auditors' review of the cutoff of sales transactions consists primarily of reviewing the sales journal entries for several days before and after the **balance sheet date** and vouching these entries to the related shipping documents and bills of lading. In addition, the auditors should review all substantial sales returns subsequent to the balance sheet date.

22.   The most effective verification of the Interest Earned account consists of independent computation (or test of reasonableness) by the auditors of the interest earned during the year on notes receivable.

23.   Several ratios and trends can be computed (as analytical procedures) to indicate the overall reasonableness of the amounts shown for accounts receivable, sales, notes receivable, and interest revenue. Examples include: (1) the rate of gross profit, (2) accounts receivable turnover, (3) the ratio of the valuation allowance to the balance of accounts receivable, and (4) the ratio of interest revenue to the average balance of notes receivable.   As discussed in Chapter 6, SAS No. 99 requires the performance of analytical procedures on revenue.

24.   The auditors should include in their examination, procedures for the detection of related party receivables, and the determination of whether accounts or notes receivable are pledged or assigned as collateral securing loans.

25.   Appropriate balance sheet presentation requires that trade accounts receivable originating from sales be stated separately from other receivables, such as loans to related parties.

Test Yourself on Chapter 11

TRUE OR FALSE

For each of the following statements, circle the T or the F to indicate whether the statement is true or false.

T F 1. Credit approval should be obtained after the goods are shipped, but before the related sales invoice is prepared.

T F 2. When merchandise is shipped, the shipping department completes a document known as a sales order.

T F 3. The primary control that prevents the shipping department from making unauthorized shipments of merchandise is the use of serially numbered shipping documents.

T F 4. The use of serial numbers on shipping documents and sales invoices provides assurance that all goods shipped are billed to customers and recorded as sales.

T F 5. The accounts receivable section of the accounting department should open incoming mail and post collections to the customer's accounts.

T F 6. Sales can be recorded in the sales journal directly from serially numbered purchase orders, thus eliminating the need for sales invoices to be serially numbered.

T F 7. The person maintaining the accounts receivable subsidiary ledger should reconcile the subsidiary ledger to the accounts receivable controlling account at least once a month.

T F 8. Receivables judged to be uncollectible should be written off.

T F 9. Tracing a sample of shipping documents to recorded sales is designed to test the existence of recorded sales.

T F 10. The auditors should mail confirmation requests, and the enclosed envelope for the customer's reply should be addressed to the auditors' office.

T F 11. Since customers that cannot pay do not reply, mailing of confirmations is a test of collectibility of accounts receivable.

T F 12. The auditors should perform alternative auditing procedures on all negative confirmation requests that are not returned.

T F 13. The auditors will generally confirm a proportionately larger sample of accounts with large balances than accounts with small balances.

T F 14. Accounts with zero balances and accounts that have been written off as uncollectible are not confirmed by the auditors.

T F 15. When it is "impossible" to confirm accounts receivable, the auditors can never issue an unqualified opinion on the client's financial statements.

T F 16. Accounts receivable should be valued at their net realizable value.

T   F   17.   Inspection of notes receivable is adequate evidence of the existence of the notes.

T   F   18.   The best evidence of interest revenue on notes receivable is confirmation with the maker of the note.

T   F   19.   Accounts receivable that are pledged as collateral for loans should be reclassified as noncurrent assets.

T   F   20.   A note receivable from an officer is considered a related party receivable.

COMPLETION

Fill in the necessary words to complete the following statements.

1.   Before goods are shipped on open account, the sale should be approved by the _____ _____.

2.   A _____ ____ _____ is a shipping document that is prepared for goods shipped by a common carrier.

3.   Receivables written off are often turned over to a _____ _____.

4.   The _____ _____ should account for the serially numbered shipping documents to insure that an invoice is prepared for all shipments.

5.   An _____ _____ _____ of customers accounts receivable should be prepared at regular intervals for use by the credit department in carrying out its collection program.

6.   A test of the completeness of recorded sales involves tracing a sample of _____ _____ to recorded sales.

7.   A _____ confirmation requests the debtor to respond in all cases, while a _____ confirmation requests a response only when the debtor disagrees with the amount being confirmed.

8.   If a response to a _____ confirmation request is not received, the auditors should send a _____ _____.

9.   The best evidence of collectibility of accounts receivable is examination of subsequent _____ of the accounts.

10.   Loans by a company to its officers, directors, major stockholders, or affiliates require particular attention because these _____ _____ _____ are not the results of arm's length bargaining by independent parties.

MULTIPLE CHOICE

Choose the best answer for each of the following questions and enter the identifying letter in the space provided.

_b_   1.   Smith Manufacturing Company's accounts receivable clerk has a friend who is also Smith's customer. The accounts receivable clerk, on occasion, has issued fictitious credit memorandums to his friend for goods supposedly returned. The most effective procedure for preventing this activity is to:

       a.   prenumber and account for all credit memorandums.
       b.   require receiving reports to support all credit memorandums before they are approved.
       c.   have the sales department independent of the accounts-receivable department.
       d.   mail monthly statements.

_a_   2.   For effective internal control, the billing function should be performed by the:

       a.   accounting department.
       b.   sales department.
       c.   shipping department.
       d.   credit and collection department.

_d_   3.   Which of the following is an effective control over accounts receivable?

       a.   Only persons who handle cash receipts should be responsible for the preparation of documents that reduce accounts receivable balances.
       b.   Responsibility for approval of the write-off of uncollectible accounts receivable should be assigned to the cashier.
       c.   Balances in the subsidiary accounts receivable ledger should be reconciled to the general ledger control account once a year, preferably at year end.
       d.   The billing function should be assigned to persons other than those responsible for maintaining accounts receivable subsidiary records.

_b_   4.   The use of the positive (as opposed to the negative) form of receivables confirmation is indicated when:

       a.   control risk for accounts receivable is assessed as low.
       b.   there is reason to believe that a substantial number of accounts may be in dispute.
       c.   a large number of small balances are involved.
       d.   there is reason to believe a significant portion of the requests will be answered.

_e_ 5.   The auditor is examining copies of sales invoices only for the initials of the person responsible for checking the extensions. This is an example of a:

a.   test of controls.
b.   substantive procedure.
c.   dual purpose test.
d.   test of balances.

_c_ 6.   An auditor reconciles the total of the accounts receivable subsidiary ledger to the general ledger control account as of October 31, 200X. By this procedure, the auditor would be most likely to learn of which of the following?

a.   An October invoice was improperly computed.
b.   An October check from a customer was posted in error to the account of another customer with a similar name.
c.   An opening balance in a subsidiary ledger account was improperly carried forward from the previous accounting period.
d.   An account balance is past due and should be written off.

_c_ 7.   Which of the following audit procedures is most effective in testing credit sales for understatement?

a.   Age accounts receivable.
b.   Confirm accounts receivable.
c.   Trace sample of initial sales slips through summaries to recorded general ledger sales.
d.   Trace sample of recorded sales from ledger to initial sales slip.

_d_ 8.   The auditors have not been able to confirm a large account receivable, but they have satisfied themselves as to the proper amount of the receivable by means of alternative auditing procedures. The auditors' report on the financial statements should include:

a.   a description of the limitation on the scope of their examination and the alternative auditing procedures used, but an opinion qualification is not required.
b.   an opinion qualification, but reference to the use of alternative auditing procedures is not required.
c.   both a scope qualification and an opinion qualification.
d.   neither a comment on the use of alternative auditing procedures nor an opinion qualification.

_d_ 9.   To determine that sales transactions have been recorded in the proper accounting period, the auditors perform a cutoff review. Which of the following best describes the overall approach used when performing a cutoff review?

a.   Ascertain that management has included in the representation letter a statement that transactions have been accounted for in the proper accounting period.
b.   Confirm year-end transactions with regular customers.
c.   Examine cash receipts in the subsequent period.
d.   Analyze transactions occurring within a few days before and after year end.

_C_   10.   The confirmation of the client's trade accounts receivable is a means of obtaining evidential matter and is specifically considered to be a generally accepted auditing:

    a.   principle.
    b.   standard.
    c.   procedure.
    d.   practice.

_C_   11.   Which of the following would be the best protection for a company that wishes to prevent the "lapping" of trade accounts receivable?

    a.   Segregate duties so that the bookkeeper in charge of the general ledger has no access to incoming mail.
    b.   Segregate duties so that no employee has access to both checks from customers and currency from daily cash receipts.
    c.   Have customers send payments directly to the company's depository bank.
    d.   Request that customers' payment checks be made payable to the company and addressed to the treasurer.

_a_   12.   Which of the following statements regarding the examination of negotiable notes receivable is correct?

    a.   Confirmation from the customer of a note is not an acceptable alternative to inspection.
    b.   Notes receivable discounted without recourse are confirmed via the standard form for confirmation of deposits and loans at financial institutions used in the audit of cash.
    c.   Physical inspection of a note by the auditors provides conclusive evidence.
    d.   Notes receivable discounted with recourse need not be confirmed.

EXERCISES

1.   Listed below are types of errors and fraud that might occur in financial statements and audit procedures. Match the audit procedure with the error or fraud that the procedure is likely to detect.

Error or Fraud	**Audit Procedure**
____ 1. Recording of sales made in the subsequent period.	a. Confirming a sample of accounts receivable.
____ 2. Failing to record all sales transactions.	b. Reviewing standard confirmations from financial institutions.
____ 3. Recording fictitious accounts receivable.	c. Tracing a sample of shipping documents to recorded sales transactions.
____ 4. Failing to inform the auditors of pledged accounts receivable.	d. Comparing recorded sales several days before and after the balance sheet date with shipping documents.

2.   Explain the reason for each of the following internal control procedures.

   a.   Accounting for the numerical sequence of shipping documents--

   b.   Independence of the credit department from the sales department--

   c.   Maintaining a separate ledger account for accounts receivable that have been written off--

CHAPTER 12

Inventories and Cost of Goods Sold

Highlights of the Chapter

1. The principal objectives of the auditors in the examination of inventories and cost of goods sold are to: (1) consider **inherent risks**, including fraud risks, (2) consider **internal control** over inventories and cost of goods sold, (3) determine the **existence** of inventories and the occurrence of transactions affecting cost of goods sold, (4) establish the **completeness** of inventories, (5) establish that the client has **rights** to the recorded inventories (6) establish the **clerical accuracy** of records and supporting schedules for inventories and cost of goods sold, (7) determine that the **valuation** of inventories and cost of goods sold is appropriate, and (8) determine that the **presentation and disclosure** of inventories and cost of goods sold are adequate.

2. Inventories and cost of goods sold generally has a high degree of inherent risk because (1) inventories often constitute a large current asset of an enterprise and are very susceptible to major errors and fraud, (2) there are numerous alternative methods of valuation of inventories, (3) a misstatement of inventories and cost of goods sold directly affects net income, and (4) the determination of inventory quality, condition, and value is inherently complex and difficult.

3. Effective internal control over inventories is best achieved by having separate departments responsible for purchasing, receiving, custody of inventories, production, shipping, and maintaining the cost accounting records. When goods are transferred from one department to another, a receipt (or requisition) for the materials should be signed by both departments. Copies of these receipts serve as the basic documentation used by the accounting department in maintaining the perpetual inventory and cost of sales accounts.

4. Serially numbered purchase orders should be prepared by the purchasing department for all purchases and copies sent to the accounting and receiving departments. The copy that is sent to the receiving department should have the quantities blacked out to assure that the items are counted upon receipt.

5. All goods received by the company should be cleared through the receiving department where employees determine the quantity and condition of the merchandise and prepare a serially numbered receiving report.

6. The receiving department should transfer the goods to the stores department and obtain a receipt that is sent to the accounting department to be used to post the perpetual accounting records.

7. When the production department needs raw materials, a serially numbered **requisition** should be prepared to obtain them from the stores department. Responsibility for goods in production must be fixed, usually to factory supervisors or superintendents.

8. Shipments of goods should be made only after an authorized sales order has been received by the shipping department.

9. The key to a reliable cost accounting system is to insure that the basic documentation supporting costs incurred, interdepartmental transfers of goods, and sales transactions is reliable.

10.   **Perpetual inventory records** constitute a most important part of the system of internal control over inventories. Such records fix responsibility for inventories, and provide information essential to intelligent purchasing, sales and production planning policies.

11.   A typical audit program for the audit of inventories and cost of goods sold appears on page 477 of the textbook.

12.   Inherent risk and the risk of misstatement for inventories is relatively high due to factors such as its size, multiple acceptable valuation methods, and subjectivity of determination of inventory quality, condition and value.

13.   The auditors' tests of the cost accounting system are designed to determine that appropriate costs have been assigned to work-in-process, finished goods, and cost of goods sold.

14.   It is not the auditors' function to take inventory; the auditors observe the taking of the inventory to satisfy themselves as to management's representations about the existence and condition of the inventory.

15.   The auditors normally participate in the client's advance planning of the physical inventory and review the written instructions prepared by management for the employees who will make the counts.

16.   During the physical inventory, the auditors will note that all goods are being counted and that controls exist to prevent double counting of items. Also, the auditors will make test counts of numerous items and compare these counts with the quantities reported by the client's counting teams. They record the test counts and information regarding the sequence of tags used in their working papers for later comparison with the client's completed physical inventory listing.

17.   When a client maintains well-kept perpetual inventory records, the auditor's observation procedures may be performed during or after the year under audit. If the client uses statistical sampling techniques to estimate the total inventory, the auditors must satisfy themselves as to the **statistical validity** of the client's methods.

18.   If the auditors do not observe the taking of the inventory because it is impossible to do so, they may satisfy themselves as to the existence of the inventory by other audit procedures. For the auditors to be satisfied in such situations, the client generally must have effective internal control over inventories, and it is still necessary for the auditors to observe or make physical counts of the inventory.

19.   The auditors should be alert during their inventory observation for indications of goods that are damaged or otherwise unsaleable.

20.   Goods in the custody of public warehouses should be confirmed by direct communication with the custodian. When the amounts of inventory involved are significant, the auditors should consider performing supplementary procedures, including review of the client's procedures for investigating prospective warehouses and evaluating their performance, obtaining reports on internal control from the auditors of the warehouses, or observing the inventories at the warehouses.

21.   The auditors should verify the accuracy of the client's completed physical inventory listing by testing its clerical accuracy, tracing in the details of test counts made during the inventory observation, and comparing the inventory tag sequence to that noted during the observation.

22.   The auditors must determine that the methods of pricing inventory are in conformity with generally accepted accounting principles. The auditors also perform tests of prices applied to inventories to determine whether the inventory valuation method used by the client has been properly applied.

23.   If evidence exists that the utility of goods when sold will be less than cost, the prospective loss should be recognized in the current period. The lower-of-cost-or-market test is used by the auditors to determine whether there is a loss in value of the inventories.

24.   The cutoff of purchase transactions is verified by reviewing purchase invoices and receiving reports for several days before and after the balance sheet date, noting the date that title passed and the date the transaction was recorded in the accounting records.

25.   Material errors in counting, pricing, and calculating the physical inventory and indications of obsolete inventories may be disclosed by analytical procedures designed to establish the general reasonableness of the inventory figures. Typical analytical procedures include comparisons of inventories classified by major types to prior years' amounts, comparisons of gross profit percentages by product line to prior years' and industry statistics, and review of rates of inventory turnover.

26.   In the audit of a new client, the auditors must obtain evidence that the client's beginning inventories are fairly stated. This evidence may be obtained by review of the audit working papers of the predecessor CPA firm (if the client's financial statements were audited in the prior year), tests of the perpetual inventory records, tests of the documents used in the physical inventory, and tests of the overall reasonableness of the inventory figures. If the auditors cannot satisfy themselves as to the fairness of the beginning inventories, they will be unable to give an unqualified opinion on the income statement and the statement of cash flows, but they may issue an unqualified opinion on the ending balance sheet.

27.   One of the most important factors in proper presentation of inventories in the financial statements is disclosure of the inventory valuation methods in use. The financial statements should disclose inventories pledged for liabilities, and significant sales or purchase commitments.

Test Yourself on Chapter 12

TRUE OR FALSE

For each of the following statements, circle the T or the F to indicate whether the statement is true or false.

T   F   1.   The McKesson & Robbins case highlighted the need to directly verify the existence of a client's inventory.

T   F   2.   Since the employees in the purchasing department order inventory items, they should inspect and receive the items when the goods arrive.

T   F   3.   Serially numbered purchase orders should be issued for purchases of goods.

T   F   4.   The receiving department normally sends raw materials received to the production department and obtains a receipt from the supervisor.

T   F   5.   Factory overhead is normally assigned to work-in-process when overhead expenses are incurred.

T   F   6.   Perpetual inventory records not only help control theft of inventories, they also generally result in improved production planning.

T   F   7.   Testing the cost accounting system is a major step in determining the appropriate valuation of inventories in a manufacturing business.

T   F   8.   To assure that the physical inventory is taken properly, the auditors should prepare and take primary responsibility for the physical inventory instructions.

T   F   9.   Observation of inventory is a generally accepted auditing procedure.

T   F   10.   The auditors' observation of the taking of a client's physical inventory must be done on, or shortly after the balance sheet date.

T   F   11.   The extent of the auditors' test counts of inventory items should be based on the inherent risk of the client's inventory and the extent of the client's internal control.

T   F   12.   The auditors should record the details of their test counts in the audit working papers to be used to test the client's completed physical inventory listing.

T   F   13.   The auditors need never observe inventories stored in legitimate public warehouses.

T   F   14.   Management representations concerning inventories often include representations regarding purchase and sales commitments.

T   F   15.   If the auditors are unable to satisfy themselves regarding the fairness of the client's beginning inventories, they will be unable to give an unqualified opinion on any of the financial statements.

T   F   16.   Analytical procedures may reveal conditions indicating that the client has significant amounts of obsolete inventory.

T   F   17.   Goods in transit at the balance sheet date should never be included in the client's inventory.

T   F   18.   During the auditors' observation of the physical inventory, they often obtain information that may be used to test the cutoff of the client's purchase transactions.

T   F   19.   Auditors may use statistical sampling for their test counts, but the client should never use statistical sampling to estimate the quantities of goods on hand.

T   F   20.   Proper presentation of inventories includes disclosure of inventory that is pledged as collateral for loans.

COMPLETION

Fill in the necessary words to complete the following statements.

1.   To help insure that the physical inventory is taken accurately and completely, the auditors should participate in the _____ of the physical inventory, and review the written _____.

2.   The auditors observe the inventory taking primarily to obtain evidence of _____ and the client's _____ to the inventories.

3.   The details of the auditors _____ _____ made during the observation of the physical inventory should be recorded in their working papers to later check the accuracy of the final _____ _____.

4.   Inventories stored in public warehouses should be _____ with the custodians.

5.   The auditors' review of purchase invoices is generally performed in connection with tests of the _____ of the inventories.

6.   As a general rule, inventories should not be carried at an amount in excess of _____ _____ _____.

7.   Tracing _____ _____ for several days before and after year–end to recorded purchases is designed to test the proper _____ of purchase transactions.

8.   A decreasing rate of inventory turnover suggests the possibility of inventory _____.

9.   Even though the auditors are unable to obtain evidence regarding the fairness of beginning inventories, they may still issue an unqualified opinion on the client's _____ _____.

10.   Serially numbered _____ _____ should be prepared and sent to vendors when goods are ordered.

MULTIPLE CHOICE

Choose the best answer for each of the following questions and enter the identifying letter in the space provided.

_____ 1. On June 15, 200X, Ward, CPA, accepted an engagement to perform an audit of the Grant Co. for the year ended December 31,200X. Grant Co. has not previously been audited by a CPA and Ward has been unable to satisfy himself with respect to opening inventories. How should Ward report on his audit?

   a. He would have to disclaim an opinion or qualify his opinion on the December 31, 200X balance sheet, but could issue an unqualified opinion on the income statement and the statement of cash flows.
   b. He must disclaim an opinion on the financial statements taken as a whole.
   c. He could give an unqualified opinion on the financial statements taken as a whole so long as the change in the inventories from the beginning of the year to the end of the year was not material.
   d. He would have to disclaim an opinion or qualify his opinion on the income statement and the statement of cash flows, but could issue an unqualified opinion on the December 31, 200X balance sheet.

_____ 2. From which of the following evidence gathering audit procedures would an auditor obtain most assurance concerning the existence of inventories?

   a. Observation of physical inventory counts.
   b. Written inventory representations from management.
   c. Confirmation of inventories in a public warehouse.
   d. Auditor's recomputation of inventory extensions.

_____ 3. A client's physical count of inventories was lower than the inventory quantities shown in its perpetual records. This situation could be the result of the failure to record:

   a. sales.
   b. sales returns.
   c. purchases.
   d. purchase discounts.

_____ 4. An inventory turnover analysis is useful to the auditor because it may detect:

   a. inadequacies in inventory pricing.
   b. methods of avoiding cyclical holding costs.
   c. the optimum automatic reorder points.
   d. the existence of obsolete merchandise.

_d_   5.   When an auditor tests a client's cost accounting system, the auditors' tests are primarily designed to determine that:

    a.   quantities on hand have been computed based on acceptable cost accounting techniques that reasonably approximate actual quantities on hand.
    b.   physical inventories are in substantial agreement with book inventories.
    c.   the system is in accordance with generally accepted accounting principles and is functioning as planned.
    d.   costs have been properly assigned to finished goods, work–in–process, and cost of goods sold.

_c_   6.   An auditor would be least likely to learn of slow-moving inventory through:

    a.   inquiry of sales personnel.
    b.   inquiry of stores personnel.
    c.   vouching of year-end purchases.
    d.   review of perpetual inventory records.

_b_   7.   An auditor has accounted for a sequence of inventory tags and is now going to trace information on a representative number of tags to the physical inventory sheets. The purpose of this procedure is to obtain assurance that:

    a.   the final inventory is valued at cost.
    b.   all inventory represented by an inventory tag is listed on the inventory sheets.
    c.   all inventory represented by an inventory tag is bona fide.
    d.   inventory sheets do not include untagged inventory items.

_b_   8.   From the auditor's point of view, inventory counts are more acceptable prior to the year-end when:

    a.   internal control is weak.
    b.   accurate perpetual inventory records are maintained.
    c.   inventory is slow-moving.
    d.   significant amounts of inventory are held on a consignment basis.

_a_   9.   Purchase cutoff procedures should be designed to test whether or not all inventory:

    a.   owned by the company.
    b.   on the year-end balance sheet was carried at lower of cost or market.
    c.   on the year-end balance sheet was paid for by the company.
    d.   in the possession of the company.

_a_   10.   Which of the following is an effective control that encourages receiving department personnel to count and inspect all merchandise received?

    a.   Quantities ordered are excluded from the receiving department copy of the purchase order.
    b.   Vouchers are prepared by accounts payable department personnel only after they match item counts on the receiving report with the purchase order.
    c.   Receiving department personnel are expected to match and reconcile the receiving report with the purchase order.
    d.   Internal auditors periodically examine, on a surprise basis, the receiving department copies of receiving reports.

11. To strengthen the system of internal control over the purchase of merchandise, a company's receiving department should:

   a. accept merchandise only if a purchase order or approval granted by the purchasing department is on hand.
   b. accept and count all merchandise received from the usual company vendors.
   c. rely on shipping documents for the preparation of receiving reports.
   d. be responsible for the physical handling of merchandise but not the preparation of receiving reports.

12. A client's materials purchasing cycle begins with requisitions from user departments and ends with the receipt of materials and the recognition of a liability. An auditor's primary objective in reviewing this cycle is to:

   a. evaluate the reliability of information generated as a result of the purchasing process.
   b. investigate the physical handling and recording of unusual acquisitions of materials.
   c. consider the need to be on hand for the annual physical count if this system is not functioning properly.
   d. ascertain that materials said to be ordered, received, and paid for are on hand.

EXERCISES

1. Auditor's often provide the client with advice on planning the client's physical inventory. List four important considerations in planning an effective physical inventory.

   a.

   b.

   c.

   d.

2.   Listed below are errors and fraud that could affect the fairness of the client's financial statement balance for inventory. For each indicate a substantive procedure performed by the auditors to test for the occurrence of the error or fraud.

   a.   The client added items to the completed physical inventory that were not on hand at the time of the physical inventory. Procedure?

   b.   The client valued certain inventory items at their current replacement cost, rather than the item's historical cost. Procedure?

   c.   The client failed to include purchased goods in transit in their inventory. Procedure?

   d.   The client made significant errors in extending inventory quantities by their cost on the completed physical inventory listing. Procedure?

CHAPTER 13

Property, Plant, and Equipment; Depreciation and Depletion

Highlights of the Chapter

1. The title "Property, Plant, and Equipment" includes tangible assets with a useful life of more than one year which are used in the operation of the business. The major subgroups are land, buildings, machinery, equipment, land improvements, and natural resources.

2. The auditors' approach to examining property, plant, and equipment is to verify the changes (acquisitions and retirements) of the current period. The beginning balances of the accounts are determined by reference to the prior year's audit working papers.

3. In the examination of property, plant, and equipment, the auditors' objectives are to: (1) consider inherent risks, including fraud risks, (2) consider **internal control** over property, plant, and equipment, (3) determine the **existence** of recorded property, plant, and equipment, (4) establish the **completeness** of recorded property, plant, and equipment, (5) establish that the client has rights to the recorded property, plant, and equipment, (6) establish the **clerical accuracy** of schedules of property, plant, and equipment, (7) determine that the **valuation or allocation** of property, plant, and equipment is in accordance with GAAP, and (8) determine that the **presentation and disclosure** of property, plant, and equipment is appropriate.

4. One of the most important controls over plant and equipment is the plant and equipment budget. Use of a budget to forecast and control acquisitions and retirements of plant assets presupposes the maintenance of good detailed accounting records of plant and equipment. Other important controls include: (1) maintenance of a subsidiary ledger of property and equipment, (2) a system of authorizations or acquisitions of assets, (3) a reporting procedure assuring prompt disclosure and analysis of variations between authorized expenditures and actual costs, (4) a written statement of company policy distinguishing between capital and revenue expenditures (5) a policy requiring all purchases of plant and equipment to be made through normal purchasing procedures, (6) periodic physical inventories, and (7) a system of serially numbered retirement work orders.

5. The first audit of a client requires that the beginning balance of property plant, and equipment accounts be established by an historical analysis of the accounts. In subsequent examinations, the auditors can concentrate attention on additions and retirements during the year under audit.

6. A typical audit program for property, plant, and equipment is described on pages 513-514 of the textbook.

7. Although the dollar amounts are large, the audit work required to verify property, plant, and equipment accounts is usually a much smaller proportion of the total audit time spent on the engagement. This results from the relatively few transactions that typically affect the accounts during the year, and the **low inherent risk** that is typical of these assets.

8. To determine that the client owns assets, the auditors examine invoices, deeds, and title insurance policies. However, possession of a deed is not proof of present ownership of property; better evidence of continuing ownership is provided by examining current property tax bills, fire insurance policies, rent receipts from lessees, and mortgage payments for the year.

9.   A complete annual physical inventory of property, plant, and equipment is not usual practice. Instead, the auditors usually make a physical inspection of major units of plant and equipment acquired during the year under audit.

10.   The principal objective of analyses of repair and maintenance expense accounts is to determine whether the costs of assets acquired have been improperly treated as charges to expense.

11.   To locate unrecorded retirements of plant and equipment the auditors often perform the following procedures:

    a.   If major additions of plant and equipment have been made, ascertain whether old equipment was traded in or superseded by the new units.

    b.   Analyze the Miscellaneous Revenue account to locate cash proceeds from the sale of retired assets.

    c.   Investigate retirements related to any discontinued product lines or services.

    d.   Make inquiries of executives and supervisors regarding retired assets.

    e.   Examine retirement work orders prepared during the year.

    f.   Investigate any reduction of insurance coverage to determine whether this was caused by retired as sets.

12.   Analytical procedures may be used to judge the overall reasonableness of recorded amounts of plant and equipment.

13.   A plant asset must be written down to its fair market value when it is determined that the asset's value is impaired. Impairment of the asset is indicated if its future cash flows are not expected to be sufficient to recover the asset's cost.

13.   CPAs often encounter clients maintaining their records using federal income tax rules, such as accelerated cost recovery system (ACRS) or the modified accelerated cost recovery system (MACRS). Because the depreciable lives are often much shorter than the economic lives of many of the assets, these methods may for certain assets not be appropriate for financial purposes.

14.   Depreciation is an accounting estimate and auditors often use one or more of the basic approaches for auditing estimates: (1) Review and test management' process, (2) review subsequent events, (3) independently develop an estimate. The auditors' objectives in reviewing depreciation are to determine that: (1) the methods in use are appropriate, (2) the methods are being followed consistently, and (3) the computations have been accurately made.

15.   The auditors begin their audit of depreciation with a review of the depreciation policies set forth in company manuals or policy statements. A second step is to summarize the amounts of accumulated depreciation for the various groups of assets at the beginning of the year, the amounts provided for depreciation during the year, the amounts removed because of asset retirements, and the ending balances.

16.   Verification of the current year provision for depreciation may be carried out by comparing the rates used with those employed in prior years. Computations may then be reviewed for a representative number of units and traced to both the expense accounts and accumulated depreciation accounts.

17.   Audit programs for depreciation expense and accumulated depreciation emphasize the use of analytical procedures to test the overall reasonableness of the amounts.

18.   The pattern of audit work on properties subject to depletion (e.g., mines, oil and gas deposits, and timberlands) is similar to that described for properties subject to depreciation. The ownership and cost of natural resources can usually be verified by examination of deeds, leases, tax bills, contracts, and paid checks.

19.   The auditors should determine that the method of depletion is in conformity with generally accepted accounting principles and is being consistently applied. They may also make independent tests to establish the accuracy of the client's computations.

20.   The auditors often rely upon the opinions of such specialists as mining engineers and geologists to establish the reasonableness of the client's depletion rates.

21.   The balance sheet caption "Intangible Assets" includes a variety of assets, including goodwill, patents, franchises, and leaseholds. Because intangible assets lack physical substance, their existence cannot be established by physical examination. Their proper valuation lies in rules established by generally accepted accounting principles that are meant to reflect the values of the rights or economic advantages afforded by their ownership and yet to be objective.

22.   As part of an analysis of intangible asset accounts, the auditors should review the reasonableness of the client's amortization program.

23.   When property, plant and equipment or intangible assets have been impaired the auditors must evaluate the reasonableness of fair values of these assets. In some cases this may require the auditors to enlist the services of a specialist.

24.   Since the auditors' approach to the audit of plant and equipment is to audit the changes in the accounts, much of the work can be performed in advance of the balance sheet date.

Test Yourself on Chapter 13

TRUE OR FALSE

For each of the following statements, circle the T or the F to indicate whether the statement is true or false.

T   F   1.   The auditors' objectives in examining property, plant, and equipment ordinarily do not include a determination of net realizable value.

T   F   2.   Most companies that use a budget to forecast and control acquisitions and retirements of plant and equipment do not maintain detailed accounting records for plant and equipment.

T   F   3.   If property, plant, and equipment represent 40% of the total assets of a continuing audit client, the budget for property, plant and equipment will ordinarily less than 40% of the total audit effort devoted to assets.

T   F   4.   The department needing the assets should make plant and equipment purchases.

T   F   5.   An error in the year-end cutoff of plant and equipment transactions affects the company's income for the year in the same manner as an error in the year-end cutoff of sales or inventory transactions.

T   F   6.   Corporations should inventory their plant and equipment as least once a year.

T   F   7.   An important control for plant and equipment is the plant and equipment budget.

T   F   8.   The auditors should take exception to any accounting policy that involves the expensing of minor capital assets.

T   F   9.   In an initial audit engagement, the auditors must perform a historical analysis of the property accounts for one year prior to the year under audit.

T   F   10. Auditors typically observe the client's physical inventory of plant and equipment.

T   F   11. Physical inventories of plant and equipment assets almost never reveal missing assets.

T   F   12. The auditors typically vouch all additions to plant and equipment recorded during the period under audit and a sample of those recorded in prior years.

T   F   13. An essential step in the auditors' verification of the legal ownership of land and buildings listed on a client's balance sheet is examination of public records.

T   F   14. Evidence of continuing ownership of property is provided by examination of the deed.

T   F   15. Unrecorded retirements of plant and equipment are a more likely type of error than unrecorded acquisitions.

T   F   16. Loss payable endorsements on insurance policies may indicate the existence of liens on particular assets.

T   F   17. A typical audit procedure in examining plant and equipment is an analysis of the Miscellaneous Revenue account.

T   F   18.   The auditors' principal objective in analyzing depreciation expense is to discover items that should have been capitalized.

T   F   19.   The Accelerated Cost Recovery System cannot be used for financial statement purposes when the recovery periods differ significantly from the assets' useful lives.

T   F   20.   Goodwill should only be recorded if it was acquired as a part of a business combination.

COMPLETION

Fill in the necessary words to complete the following statements.

1.   A year–end _____ error in plant asset accounts usually does not result in a significant error in _____ _____.

2.   A company should maintain a _____ _____ for plant and equipment, consisting of a separate record for each unit of property.

3.   A dollar minimum ordinarily should be established to be used by accounting personnel for distinguishing between capital and _____ expenditures.

4.   To provide assurance that the accounting department is notified of property retirements, a system of serially numbered _____ _____ _____ should be used by the company.

5.   The auditors' principal objective in analyzing _____ _____ _____ expense accounts is to discover property items that should have been capitalized.

6.   In the auditors' first examination of a new client that has changed auditors, the beginning balances of property, plant, and equipment accounts may be substantiated by referring to the predecessor auditors' _____ _____.

7.   The plant and equipment budget is designed to control _____ and _____ of property items.

8.   Possession of a deed is not proof of present _____ of property. Better evidence is found by examining current _____ _____ bills.

9.   The intangible asset known as _____ arises in accounting for a business combination, and should be amortized over the years benefited, but not in excess of _____ years.

10.   A company may not actual own property recorded as an asset; instead the company may have rights to the asset under the terms of a _____ _____.

MULTIPLE CHOICE

Choose the best answer for each of the following questions and enter the identifying letter in the space provided.

___d___ 1.   An important consideration to the auditor in the audit of equipment is to determine:

      a.   that the equipment is properly maintained.
      b.   that theft of the equipment is impossible.
      c.   when the client should replace the equipment.
      d.   whether a recorded gain on trade of equipment is appropriate..

___b___ 2.   Tennessee Company violated company policy by erroneously capitalizing the cost of painting its warehouse. The auditors examining Tennessee's financial statements would most likely learn of this error by:

      a.   discussing Tennessee's capitalization policies with its controller.
      b.   reviewing the titles and descriptions for all construction work orders issued during the year.
      c.   observing, during the physical inventory observation that the warehouse has been painted.
      d.   examining in detail a sample of construction work orders.

___d___ 3.   To achieve effective internal control over fixed-asset additions, a company should establish procedures that require:

      a.   capitalization of the cost of fixed-asset additions in excess of a specific dollar amount.
      b.   performance of recurring fixed-asset maintenance work solely by maintenance department employees.
      c.   classification as investments of those fixed-asset additions that are not used in the business.
      d.   authorization and approval of major fixed-asset additions.

___a___ 4.   Which of the following policies is an internal control weakness related to the acquisition of factory equipment?

      a.   Acquisitions are to be made through and approved by the department in need of the equipment.
      b.   Advance executive approvals are required for equipment acquisitions.
      c.   Variances between authorized equipment expenditures and actual costs are to be immediately reported to management.
      d.   Depreciation policies are reviewed only once a year.

___d___ 5.   A normal audit procedure is to analyze the current year repairs and maintenance accounts to provide evidence in support of the audit proposition that:

      a.   expenditures for fixed assets have been recorded in the proper period.
      b.   capital expenditures have been properly authorized.
      c.   noncapitalizable expenditures have been properly expensed.
      d.   expenditures for fixed assets have been capitalized.

6. Which of the following is the best evidence of real estate ownership at the balance sheet date?

   a. Title insurance policy.
   b. Original deed held in the client's safe.
   c. Paid real estate tax bills.
   d. Closing statement.

7. Which of the following audit procedures would be least likely to lead the auditors to find unrecorded fixed asset disposals?

   a. Examination of insurance policies.
   b. Review of repairs and maintenance expense.
   c. Review of property tax files.
   d. Scanning of invoices for fixed-asset additions.

8. The auditors may conclude that depreciation charges are insufficient by noting:

   a. insured values greatly in excess of book values.
   b. large amounts of fully depreciated assets.
   c. continuous trade-ins of relatively new assets.
   d. excessive recurring losses on assets retired.

9. Patentex developed a new secret formula that is of great value because it resulted in a virtual monopoly. Patentex has capitalized all research and development costs associated with this formula. Greene, CPA, who is examining this account will probably:

   a. confer with management regarding transfer of the amount from the balance sheet to the income statement.
   b. confirm that the secret formula is registered and on file with the county clerk's office.
   c. confer with management regarding a change in the title of the account to "goodwill."
   d. confer with management regarding ownership of the secret formula.

10. In the examination of property, plant, and equipment, the auditors try to determine all of the following except the:

    a. adequacy of internal control.
    b. extent of property abandoned during the year.
    c. adequacy of replacement funds.
    d. reasonableness of the depreciation.

EXERCISES

1. Listed below are types of errors and fraud that might occur in financial statements and audit procedures. Match the audit procedure with the error or fraud that the procedure is likely to detect.

	Error or Fraud		**Audit Procedure**
____ 1.	Land was exchanged for a long–term note receivable, but the exchange was not recorded.	a.	Analyze the Miscellaneous Revenue account.
____ 2.	A machine was sold for cash, but the retirement was not recorded.	b.	Review expenditures charged to a repairs and maintenance account.
____ 3.	The cost of repairing a machine was improperly capitalized.	c.	Vouch additions to equipment accounts.
____ 4.	A lien exists on certain equipment.	d.	Review fire insurance policies.
____ 5.	An expenditure for equipment was improperly expensed.	e.	Review current property tax bills.

2. Explain the reason for each of the following internal control procedures.

    a. A system of retirement work orders

    b. Maintenance of a subsidiary ledger of plant and equipment

    c. Requiring all purchases of plant and equipment to be handled through normal purchasing procedures

CHAPTER 14

Accounts Payable and Other Liabilities

Highlights of the Chapter

1. In studying the audit of liabilities, it is important to remember that an understatement of liabilities will exaggerate the financial strength of a company just as effectively as an overstatement of assets. In addition, the **understatement** of liabilities often is accompanied by an understatement of expenses and an overstatement of net income.

2. The overstatement of assets usually requires an improper or fictitious entry, but the understatement of liabilities may be effected merely by failing to make an entry for a transaction creating a liability. The omission of an entry is less susceptible of detection than is a fictitious entry.

3. The term "accounts payable" is used to describe short-term obligations arising from the purchase of goods and services in the ordinary course of business.

4. The auditors' principal objectives in the examination of accounts payable are to: (1) consider **inherent risks**, including fraud risks, (2) consider **internal control** over accounts payable, (3) determine the **existence** of recorded accounts payable and that the client has **obligations** to pay them, (4) establish the **completeness** of accounts payable, (5) determine that the **valuation** of accounts payable is in accordance with GAAP, (6) establish the **clerical accuracy** of schedules of accounts payable, and (7) determine that the **presentation and disclosure** of payables is appropriate.

5. To achieve effective internal control over accounts payable, duties should be segregated so that a cash disbursement to a creditor will be made only after involving the purchasing, receiving, accounting, and finance departments. Separation of the functions of preparation of payments from that of cash disbursements tends to prevent errors and fraud. Also, monthly statements from vendors should be reconciled with the accounts payable ledger or list of open vouchers.

6. An audit program for accounts payable is presented on page 540 of the textbook.

7. Many of the inherent risks for accounts payable relate to business risks faced by management, such as the risk of paying unauthorized payables, and the failure to capture all accounts payable for financial reporting purposes.

8. The auditors should obtain a trial balance of accounts payable at the balance sheet date. To test the existence and accuracy of recorded accounts payable, the auditors may vouch a sample of the balances to supporting vouchers, invoices, purchase orders, and receiving reports.

9. The auditors may decide to reconcile vendors' statements to the client's trial balance of accounts payable. This procedure helps assure that an accurate year-end cutoff of accounts payable has been made. Cutoff of accounts payable can also be tested by tracing the details of the last receiving reports issued during the year (recorded during the year-end physical inventory) to recorded accounts payable.

10. Confirmation of accounts payable is **not** a generally accepted auditing procedure as is the confirmation of accounts receivable. One reason is that confirmation is generally a better test of existence than completeness of accounts. Also, valid evidence of the amounts of recorded accounts payable may be found in the client's possession in the form of vendors' invoices and statements.

11. If the auditors do elect to confirm accounts payable, they often mail confirmation requests to major vendors, even though the vendors' accounts show zero or small balances at year-end. Also, accounts payable confirmation requests ordinarily do not indicate a balance; they request the vendor to indicate the amount of the payable.

12. An important step in auditing accounts payables is the **search for unrecorded liabilities**--a comparison of cash payments made subsequent to the balance sheet date with items in the accounts payable trial balance. These payments may show that certain liabilities existed but were unrecorded at the balance sheet date.

13. Throughout the audit, the auditors should be alert for evidence of unrecorded liabilities, such as unmatched invoices and unbilled receiving reports in the accounting department, unpaid vouchers recorded subsequent to the balance sheet date, and invoices received by the client after the balance sheet date.

14. When unrecorded liabilities are discovered, the auditors must evaluate whether the omissions are sufficiently material to warrant proposing an adjusting entry. Some unrecorded liabilities affect only the balance sheet, while others affect both the balance sheet and the income statement.

15. To gain assurance as to the overall reasonableness of accounts payable, the auditors compute ratios such as accounts payable divided by purchases and accounts payable divided by total current liabilities. These ratios are compared with ratios for prior years to disclose variations that warrant investigation.

16. Proper presentation of accounts payable requires that material amounts of accounts with debit balances be reclassified as receivables. Material amounts of payables to related parties should be listed separately from accounts payable to trade creditors and the details of the related transactions should be disclosed in a note to the financial statements. Also, information about assets pledged as collateral for the payables should be disclosed in the balance sheet or a note thereto.

17. The auditors should obtain written representations from the client, stating that all known liabilities are reflected in the balance sheet. Although such representations do not reduce the auditors' responsibility, they remind executives that management is primarily responsible for the fairness of liabilities presented in the financial statements.

18. In addition to accounts payable, other items classified as current liabilities include (1) accounts withheld from employees' pay, (2) sales taxes payable, (3) unclaimed wages, (4) customers' deposits, and (5) accrued liabilities.

19. **Accrued liabilities** represent obligations payable sometime during the succeeding period for services received before the balance sheet date. Accrued liabilities are accounting estimates and auditors often use one or more of the basic approaches for auditing estimates: (1) Review and test management's process, (2) review subsequent events, (3) independently develop an estimate. The basic auditing steps for accrued liabilities are: (1) examine any contracts or other documents that provide the basis for the accrual, (2) appraise the accuracy of the detailed accounting records maintained for this category of liability, (3) identify and evaluate the reasonableness of the assumptions that underlie the computation of the liability, (4) test the computations made by the client in setting up the accrual, and (5) determine that accrued liabilities have been treated consistently at the beginning and end of the period, (6) consider the need for accrual of other liabilities not presently considered and (7) for significant estimates, comparing prior year estimated amounts with ultimate resolution of those estimates.

20.   Audit work on liabilities is primarily designed to detect understatements of the amounts at the balance sheet date. For that reason, most of the audit work on accounts payable must be performed after the balance sheet date.

Test Yourself on Chapter 14

TRUE OR FALSE

For each of the following statements, circle the T or the F to indicate whether the statement is true or false.

T   F   1.   In the audit of financial statements, the auditors are particularly on guard against the possible understatement of liabilities and the possible overstatement of revenues.

T   F   2.   To overstate net income requires the recording of an improper accounting entry.

T   F   3.   A company's receiving department should be independent of its purchasing department.

T   F   4.   Companies typically send statements to vendors detailing their accounts payable to the vendors.

T   F   5.   Vouching of selected accounts payable on the client's year-end trial balance is primarily a test of completeness of recorded accounts payable.

T   F   6.   Auditors may discover unrecorded liabilities by reconciling vendors' statements with the accounts payable trial balance.

T   F   7.   The audit procedure of confirmation by direct communication is just as important for accounts payable as it is for accounts receivable.

T   F   8.   Auditors often confirm vendors' accounts with zero balances at year-end.

T   F   9.   Accounts payable confirmations usually have the vendor indicate the amount of the payable from the client.

T   F   10.   Review of a client's cash payments subsequent to the balance sheet date is an important test of the completeness of recorded payables.

T   F   11.   All unrecorded liabilities have the same effect on the client's financial statements.

T   F   12.   Auditors are concerned with the discovery of receivables from related parties, but not with the discovery of payables from related parties.

T   F   13.   Accounts payable with debit balances should be reclassified as receivables.

T   F   14.   Since it is difficult to detect unrecorded liabilities, auditors rely primarily on the client's representations that no unrecorded liabilities exist.

T   F   15.   Accrued liabilities are substantiated by confirmation.

T   F   16.   Unless the auditors are engaged to prepare the client's tax return, there is no need for the auditors to review the return.

T   F   17.   The amount of accrued payroll is typically verified by confirmation with selected employees.

T   F   18.   When testing the amount of pension liability, the auditors typically rely on a specialist.

T   F   19.   Most of the audit work on liabilities is ordinarily performed during the interim period.

T   F   20.   Unclaimed payroll checks should be voided and the amount recorded in a special liability account.

COMPLETION

Fill in the necessary words to complete the following statements.

1   An _____ of liabilities or an _____ of assets will exaggerate the financial strength of a company.

2.   Auditors are primarily concerned with establishing the _____ of recorded accounts payable.

3.   Unlike in the case of accounts receivable, _____ of accounts payable is not a generally accepted auditing procedure.

4.   Accounts payable from important vendors should be confirmed, even though the accounts have _____ balances at year-end.

5.   When unrecorded liabilities are discovered by the auditors, they must evaluate whether the omission is sufficiently _____ to warrant proposing an _____ _____ _____.

6.   When observing the taking of a physical inventory at year-end, the auditors will record the serial number of the last _____ _____ issued to verify the accuracy of the cutoff of accounts payable.

7.   Proper balance sheet presentation of accounts payable requires that any material amounts payable to _____ _____, such as directors and officers, be disclosed separately from other accounts payable.

8.   Auditors often obtain written _____ from management regarding the existence of unrecorded payables.

9.   Most _____ _____ represent obligations payable sometime during the succeeding period for services of a continuing nature received before the balance sheet date.

10.   Because the auditors are primarily concerned with the _____ of recorded payables, most of the audit work on accounts payable is performed after the _____ _____ date.

MULTIPLE CHOICE

Choose the best answer for each of the following questions and enter the identifying letter in the space provided.

1. Bell's accounts-payable clerk has a brother who is one of Bell's vendors. The brother will often invoice Bell twice for the same delivery. The accounts-payable clerk removes the receiving report for the first invoice from the paid voucher file and uses it for support of payment for the duplicate invoice. The most effective procedure for preventing this activity is to:

   a. use prenumbered receiving reports.
   b. mail signed checks without allowing them to be returned to the accounts-payable clerk.
   c. cancel vouchers and supporting papers when payment is made.
   d. use dual signatures.

2. Auditor confirmation of accounts payable balances at the balance sheet date may be unnecessary because:

   a. this is a duplication of cutoff tests.
   b. accounts payable balances at the balance sheet date may not be paid before the audit is completed.
   c. correspondence with the audit client's attorney will reveal all legal action by vendors for nonpayment.
   d. there is likely to be other reliable external evidence available to support the balances.

3. The audit procedures used to verify accrued liabilities differ from those employed for the verification of accounts payable because:

   a. accrued liabilities usually pertain to services of a continuing nature while accounts payable are the result of completed transactions.
   b. accrued liability balances are less material than accounts payable balances.
   c. evidence supporting accrued liabilities is nonexistent while evidence supporting accounts payable is readily available.
   d. accrued liabilities at year–end will become accounts payable during the following year.

4. To avoid potential errors and fraud, a well-designed internal control in the accounts payable area should include a separation of which of the following functions?

   a. Cash disbursements and invoice verification.
   b. Invoice verification and merchandise ordering.
   c. Physical handling of merchandise received and preparation of receiving reports.
   d. Check signing and cancellation of payment documentation.

5. An examination of the balance in the accounts payable account is ordinarily not designed to:

   a. detect accounts payable which are substantially past due.
   b. verify that accounts payable were properly authorized.
   c. ascertain the reasonableness of recorded liabilities.
   d. determine that all existing liabilities at the balance sheet date have been recorded.

C   6.   Which of the following procedures relating to the examination of accounts payable could the auditors delegate entirely to the clients employees?

    a.   Test footings in the accounts payable ledger.
    b.   Reconcile unpaid invoices to vendors' statements.
    c.   Prepare a schedule of accounts payable.
    d.   Mail confirmations for selected account balances.

D   7.   Which of following audit procedures is least likely to detect an unrecorded liability?

    a.   Analysis and recomputation of interest expense.
    b.   Analysis and recomputation of depreciation expense.
    c.   Mailing of standard bank confirmation form.
    d.   Readings of the minutes of meetings of the board of directors.

C   8.   Which of the following procedures is least likely to be performed before the balance sheet date?

    a.   Observation of inventory.
    b.   Review of internal control over cash disbursements.
    c.   Search for unrecorded liabilities.
    d.   Confirmation of receivables.

C   9.   Under which of the following circumstances would it be advisable for the auditors to confirm accounts payable with creditors?

    a.   Internal control over accounts payable is adequate and there is sufficient evidence on hand to minimize the risk of a material misstatement.
    b.   Confirmation response is expected to be favorable and accounts payable balances are of immaterial amounts.
    c.   Creditor statements are not available and internal control over accounts payable is unsatisfactory.
    d.   The majority of accounts payable balances are with associated companies.

a   10.   Which of the following is the most efficient audit procedure for the detection of unrecorded liabilities?

    a.   Compare cash disbursements in the subsequent period with the accounts payable trial balance at year-end.
    b.   Confirm large accounts payable balances at the balance sheet date.
    c.   Examine purchase orders issued for several days prior to the close of the year.
    d.   Obtain a "liability certificate" from the client.

a   11.   In order to efficiently establish the accuracy of the accounts payable cutoff, the auditors will be most likely to:

    a.   coordinate cutoff tests with physical inventory observation.
    b.   compare cutoff reports with purchase orders.
    c.   compare vendors' invoices with vendors' statements.
    d.   coordinate mailing of confirmations with cutoff tests.

_____ 12. A client's procurement system ends with the assumption of a liability and the eventual payment of the liability. Which of the following best describes the auditors' primary concern with respect to liabilities resulting from the procurement system?

a. Accounts payable are not materially understated.
b. Authority to incur liabilities is restricted to one designated person.
c. Acquisition of materials is not made from one vendor or one group of vendors.
d. Commitments for all purchases are made only after established competitive bidding procedures are followed.

EXERCISES

1. Listed below are types of errors and fraud that might occur in financial statements and audit procedures. Match the audit procedure with the error or fraud that the procedure is likely to detect.

Error or Fraud		**Audit Procedure**	
_____ 1.	The existence of unrecorded accounts payable	a.	Reviewing unusual transactions during the year.
_____ 2.	The existence of an unrecorded accrued payable.	b.	Reviewing receiving reports issued near year–end.
_____ 3.	The existence of a fictitious account payable.	c.	Vouching selected accounts payable on the trial balance.
_____ 4.	An improper cutoff of accounts payable	d.	Comparing subsequent cash payments to the accounts payable trial balance.
_____ 5.	The existence of related party payables.	e.	Reviewing union contracts.

2.   For each of the following potential unrecorded liabilities, determine the effects of the omission on both the balance sheet and income statement of the client. Assume that the inventories recorded on the balance sheet reflect the results of a year-end (December 31) physical inventory.

   a.   An invoice for $3,000 worth of inventory items, dated January 1 and bearing terms of FOB destination, was not recorded. The goods were shipped December 27 and were received on December 30.

      (1)   Balance sheet effect:

      (2)   Income statement effect:

   b.   An invoice for $5,500 worth of inventory items, dated December 30 and bearing terms FOB destination, was not recorded. The goods were shipped December 28 and received January 2.

      (1)   Balance sheet effect:

      (2)   Income statement effect:

   c.   An invoice for $8,000 for a delivery truck, dated January 2 and bearing terms of FOB shipping point, was not recorded. The truck was shipped December 30 and received on January 3.

      (1)   Balance sheet effect:

      (2)   Income statement effect:

d.   An invoice for $1,000 for legal fees rendered in December was not recorded.

      (1)   Balance sheet effect:

      (2)   Income statement effect:

CHAPTER 15

Debt and Equity Capital

Highlights of the Chapter

1. Nearly all business enterprises issue notes payable for short-term bank loans as a means of financing inventories and other working capital requirements.

2. Long-term debt is usually substantial in amount and often extends for many years. The usual forms of long-term debt include debentures, secured bonds payable, and notes payable. Debentures are backed only by the general credit of the issuing corporation and not by liens on specific assets.

3. The formal document creating bonded indebtedness is called the indenture or trust indenture. These agreements usually place restrictions on the borrowing company. These restrictions often prohibit dividend payments unless working capital is maintained above a specified amount, and restrict managerial salaries and the acquisition of plant and equipment.

4. The auditors' principal objectives in the examination of interest-bearing debt are to: (1) consider inherent risks, including fraud risks (2) consider **internal control** over interest-bearing debt, (3) determine the **existence** of recorded interest-bearing debt, (4) establish the **completeness** of recorded interest-bearing debt, (5) determine that the client has **obligations** to pay the interest-bearing debt, (6) establish the **clerical accuracy** of the schedules of interest-bearing debt, (7) determine that the **valuation** of interest-bearing debt is in accordance with GAAP, and (8) determine that the **presentation and disclosure** of debt is appropriate.

5. Effective internal control over notes and bonds payable includes authorization by the board of directors for the issuance of these instruments. Also, it is desirable to appoint an **independent trustee** (usually a large bank) to handle the issuance of bonds and any subsequent redemptions or reacquisitions. The trustee assumes responsibility for protecting the creditors' interests and continually monitors the company's compliance with any restrictions in the debt agreement.

6. The most effective control over interest payments is created when the company assigns the task of making interest payments to the trustee. The company will then issue a single check to the trustee for the periodic interest payments, and the trustee makes payments to bondholders.

7. If a sinking fund is required by the debt contract, the fund should be maintained by the trustee. The records of interest-bearing debt maintained by the company should be regularly reconciled with the periodic reports from the trustee. In addition, the company should have a responsible official monitor compliance with the restrictions imposed by debt agreements.

8. Since transactions affecting interest-bearing debt are few in number but large in dollar amount, the auditors usually follow the approach of substantiating the individual transactions during the audit period. Audit procedures appropriate for the verification of interest bearing debt are listed on page 572 of the textbook.

9.   In the first audit of a client or upon the issuance of a new bond issue, the auditors will obtain a copy of the bond indenture for the permanent file and summarize the major provisions of the agreement. During each audit, the auditors will perform tests of compliance with these provisions. When the client is found to be in violation of a particular provision making the debt payable on demand, the client usually attempts to obtain a "waiver" of compliance with the provision. If a waiver is obtained for at least one year from the balance sheet date, the client can be allowed to continue to classify the debt as long-term liability.

10.   Although the auditors should be familiar with the Securities Act of 1933 and applicable state laws, they do not pass on the legality of a bond issue. When in doubt, they should consult the client's legal counsel.

11.   Notes payable to financial institutions are confirmed in connection with the confirmation of cash on deposit using the standard form to confirm account balance information with financial institutions. Bond transactions, including sinking fund transactions and year-end balances of bonds payable and sinking funds, are confirmed directly with the trustee. It is not customary to communicate with the individual bondholders.

12.   The auditors should be sure that interest payments correspond to the terms of recorded liabilities. Excessive interest payments may indicate the existence of unrecorded notes payable.

13.   Proper financial statement presentation requires that interest-bearing debt be fully described, including interest rates, maturity dates, a schedule of required future payments, assets pledged, and other major restrictions. Any debt maturing within the next year should be classified as a current liability if it is to be paid from current assets. Maturing long-term debt that is expected to be refinanced may continue to be classified as long term if management can demonstrate the **intent** and the **ability** to refinance the debt.

14.   The auditors' principal objectives in the examination of owners' equity are to: (1) consider **inherent risks**, including fraud risks. (2) consider **internal control** over owners' equity, (3) determine the **existence** of recorded owners' equity, (4) establish the **completeness** of owners' equity transactions, (5) determine that the **valuation** of owners' equity is in accordance with GAAP, (6) establish the **clerical accuracy** of schedules of owners' equity, and (7) determine that the **presentation and disclosure** of owners equity is appropriate.

15.   The three principal elements of strong internal control over capital stock and dividends are: (1) the proper authorization of transactions by the board of directors and corporate officers, (2) the segregation of duties in handling these transactions (especially the use of independent agents for stock registration and transfer and dividend payments), and (3) the maintenance of adequate records.

16.   The responsibility of the **stock registrar** is to avoid over-issuance of stock. The registrar verifies that stock certificates are issued in accordance with the articles of incorporation and formal authorizations by the board of directors.

17.   In addition to handling the stock transfers from one stockholder to another, the **stock transfer agent** maintains a record of the total shares outstanding and detailed records showing the holdings of individual stockholders.

18. In companies that do not use the services of an independent stock registrar and transfer agent, the board of directors usually delegates to the corporate secretary the responsibility for custody of stock certificates and recording stock transfers. Certificates should be issued in numerical sequence and signed and countersigned when issued. When outstanding shares are transferred from one stockholder to another, the old certificate should be canceled and attached to the corresponding stub in the stock certificate book. The corporation should also maintain a stockholders' ledger, containing a separate account for each stockholder.

19. Internal control over dividends is enhanced when an independent dividend-disbursing agent is used. The corporation provides the agent with a copy of the dividend declaration and a check for the total amount of the dividend. The agent issues checks to the individual stockholders and provides the corporation with a list of the payments made.

20. A typical audit program for the examination of owners' equity accounts is illustrated on page 581 of the textbook.

21. The auditors should verify the number of shares of stock outstanding by confirmation with the independent registrar and stock transfer agent. If the client corporation acts as its own transfer agent and registrar, the auditors should account for all stock certificates issued, and reconcile the stock certificate book and stockholders' ledger with the general ledger controlling account.

22. Audit work on retained earnings and dividends includes two major steps: (1) the analysis of retained earnings and any appropriations of retained earnings, and (2) the review of dividend procedures for both cash and stock dividends.

23. The balance sheet should contain a complete description of each issue of capital stock, including such data as title of the issue; par value; number of shares authorized, issued, and in the treasury; call provisions; conversion provisions; shares reserved for stock options; and cumulative preferred dividends in arrears.

24. Changes in retained earnings may be shown in a separate statement or combined with the income statement. If there have been numerous changes in owners' equity accounts, a statement of stockholders' equity may be used to present the changes.

Test Yourself on Chapter 15

TRUE OR FALSE

For each of the following statements, circle the T or the F to indicate whether the statement is true or false.

T F 1. Debentures are payables that are backed only by the general credit of the issuing company.

T F 2. The auditors should personally evaluate the legality of all new issues of debt by the client.

T F 3. The auditors have no responsibility to determine compliance with restrictions imposed by borrowing agreements since these restrictions do not affect accounting principles.

T F 4. The audit procedure of confirmation by direct communication with a creditor is more likely to be applied to a noteholder than to a bondholder.

T F 5. The authority to issue interest-bearing debt generally lies with the stockholders of the corporation.

T F 6. The audit of interest expense may reveal the existence of unrecorded debt.

T F 7. Since owner's equity accounts are typically large in amount, the audit time devoted to them is typically extensive in amount.

T F 8. The company stock registrar is responsible for transferring stock from one investor to another.

T F 9. In the audit of a corporation that does not utilize the services of an independent stock registrar and transfer agent, the auditors should always confirm all outstanding shares by direct communication with stockholders.

T F 10. When outstanding shares are transferred from one investor to another, the old certificate should be canceled and returned to the former investor for his or her records.

T F 11. The stock certificate book of a corporation provides a separate record of the total number of shares owned by each stockholder.

T F 12. In the verification of debit entries to retained earnings for small stock dividends, the auditors' only concern about dollar amounts is that the amount per share corresponds to the declaration by the board of directors.

T F 13. A complete set of financial statements includes both a statement of retained earnings and a statement of stockholders' equity.

T F 14. If the general partner of a partnership is unwilling to allow the auditors to examine the partnership contract, the auditors will not be able to issue an unqualified opinion on the partnership's financial statements.

T F 15. Treasury stock should be confirmed directly with shareholders.

T F 16. When a "sinking fund" exists the auditors should be able to identify cash or other assets set aside for the retirement of a debt.

T F   17. Notes payable to financial institutions are confirmed as a part of the confirmation of cash deposit balances.

T F   18. The discovery of related-party transactions is generally easier in the area of notes payable than in accounts payable.

T F   19. The use of a stockholders ledger eliminates the need for a stock certificate book.

T F   20. Multiplying the stock market price times the number of shares listed as outstanding by the registrar is a frequently used analytical procedure to test the completeness assertion for common stock.

COMPLETION

Fill in the necessary words to complete the following statements.

1. The formal document creating bonded indebtedness is called the _____ or the

    _____ _____.

2. If violation of a debt provision makes a debt payable on demand, the debt must be classified as a

    _____ _____ unless a _____ of compliance is obtained from the trustee or the

    financial institution.

3. To continue to classify a maturing debt as a long-term liability, the client must demonstrate both the

    _____ and the _____ to refinance the debt.

4. Unamortized _____ should be added to the face amount of the bonds or debentures in the

    liability section of the balance sheet, while unamortized _____ should be deducted from the face

    amount of the debt.

5. Internal control over the payment of dividends is enhanced when the company utilizes the services of

    an independent _____ _____ _____.

6. The primary responsibility of the independent stock _____ is to avoid any over–issuance of stock

    of the corporation.

7. The number of shares of stock _____ and _____ at the balance sheet date may be

    confirmed by direct communication with the independent stock _____ and _____

    _____.

8.   For a continuing audit client, the audit of retained earnings often consists of determining that the

_____ _____ was added to the beginning balance and that the _____ were

subtracted.

9.   In the audit of interest-bearing debt, the auditors' primary substantive procedures will include

_____ selected transactions occurring during the period to available support, examining

_____ _____, confirming balances and terms, and evaluating _____ with

restrictive covenants.

10.   The _____ of the corporation normally require that borrowing be approved by the _____

_____ _____.

MULTIPLE CHOICE

Choose the best answer for each of the following questions and enter the identifying letter in the space provided.

___C___ 1.   The auditors can best verify a client's bond sinking fund transactions and year-end balance by:

  a. recomputation of interest expense, interest payable, and amortization of bond discount or premium.
  b. confirmation with individual holders of retired bonds.
  c. confirmation with the bond trustee.
  d. examination and count of the bonds retired during the year.

___a___ 2.   Where no independent stock transfer agent is employed and the corporation issues its own stock and maintains stock records, canceled stock certificates should:

  a. be defaced to prevent reissuance, and attached to their corresponding stubs.
  b. not be defaced, but segregated from other stock certificates and retained in a canceled certificates file.
  c. be destroyed to prevent fraudulent reissuance.
  d. be defaced and sent to the secretary of state.

___a___ 3.   In the audit of a medium sized manufacturing concern, which one of the following areas would be expected to require the least amount of audit time?

  a. Owners' equity.
  b. Revenue.
  c. Assets.
  d. Liabilities.

_____ c   4.   If a company employs a capital stock registrar and/or transfer agent, the registrar or agent, or both, should be requested to confirm directly to the auditors the number of shares of each class of stock:

   a.   surrendered and canceled during the year.
   b.   authorized at the balance sheet date.
   c.   issued and outstanding at the balance sheet date.
   d.   authorized, issued, and outstanding during the year.

_____ a   5.   Florida Corporation declared a 100% stock dividend during 200X. In connection with the examination of Florida's financial statements, Florida's auditors should determine that:

   a.   the additional shares issued do not exceed the number of authorized but previously unissued shares.
   b.   stockholders received their additional shares by confirming year-end holdings with them.
   c.   the stock dividend was properly recorded at fair market value.
   d.   Florida's stockholders have authorized the issuance of 100% stock dividends.

_____ a   6.   In connection with the examination of bonds payable, the auditors would expect to find in a trust indenture:

   a.   the issue date and maturity date of the bond.
   b.   the names of the original subscribers to the bond issue.
   c.   the yield to maturity of the bonds issued.
   d.   the company's debt to equity ratio at the time of issuance.

_____ c   7.   An audit program for the examination of the retained earnings account should include a step that requires verification of the:

   a.   gain or loss resulting from disposition of treasury shares.
   b.   market value used to charge retained earnings to account for a two-for-one split.
   c.   authorization for both cash and stock dividends.
   d.   approval of the adjustment to the beginning balance as a result of a write-down of an account receivable.

_____ a   8.   A company guarantees the debt of an affiliate. Which of the following best describes the audit procedure that would make the auditor aware of the guarantee?

   a.   Review minutes and resolutions of the board of directors.
   b.   Review prior year's working papers with respect to such guarantees.
   c.   Review the possibility of such guarantees with the chief accountant.
   d.   Review the legal letter returned by the company's outside legal counsel.

_____ a   9.   During the course of an audit, a CPA observes that the recorded interest expense seems to be excessive in relation to the balance in the long-term debt account. This observation could lead the auditors to suspect that:

   a.   long-term debt is understated.
   b.   discount on bonds payable is overstated.
   c.   long-term debt is overstated.
   d.   premium on bonds payable is understated.

_____ 10. When auditing stockholders' equity accounts, the auditors determine whether there are restrictions on retained earnings resulting from loans or other causes. The primary audit objective of this procedure is normally to verify management's assertion of:

    a.   existence or occurrence.
    b.   completeness
    c.   valuation or allocation
    d.   presentation and disclosure.

EXERCISES

1.   Explain the functions of each of the following:

    a.   Indenture

    b.   Bond trustee

    c.   Stock registrar

    d.   Stock transfer agent

2.   List three procedures that auditors will usually perform in the verification of cash dividends.

    a.

    b.

    c.

CHAPTER 16

Auditing Operations and Completing the Audit

Highlights of the Chapter

1. Many revenue and expense accounts are conveniently substantiated in conjunction with the audit of various asset and liability accounts. However, auditors also perform audit procedures designed specifically to establish the fairness of certain revenues and expenses. These procedures include performing analytical procedures and analyzing specific accounts.

2. Analytical procedures involve evaluating financial information by examining relationships between financial and nonfinancial data. For example, the cost of goods sold expressed as a percentage of sales might be compared on a monthly basis. For any months in which this cost ratio appears unusually high or low, the auditors will perform additional procedures to determine that transactions during those months are not misstated.

3. Analytical procedures applied to income statement accounts often involve comparisons of revenue and expenses with budgeted amounts, comparable amounts from prior years, nonfinancial data, and industry averages. Whenever unusual variations in relationships are observed, the auditors investigate the accounts involved to determine that the variations are not caused by material misstatement.

4. The audit objectives for substantive procedures of revenues and expenses are to: (1) consider **inherent risks** of revenue and expenses, including fraud risks, (2) Consider **internal control** over revenue and expenses (3) determine the **occurrence** of recorded revenue and expense transactions, (4) establish the **completeness** of recorded revenues and expenses, (5) establish the **clerical accuracy** of supporting schedules, (6) determine that the **valuation** is in accordance with GAAP, and (7) determine that **presentation and disclosure** are appropriate.

5. Analyzing an account means verifying the individual debit and credit entries in that account. Auditors usually analyze accounts, such as miscellaneous revenue, in which accounting personnel might have recorded transactions that they did not thoroughly understand.

6. In the audit of payroll, selling expense, and general and administrative expense, the auditors consider the controls, and perform procedures to determine whether expenses are properly stated.

7. A significant control over revenue and expenses is a good system of budgeting that includes explanations of significant variances from budgeted amounts.

8. Auditors routinely analyze certain expense accounts, including the miscellaneous expense, travel and entertainment, and contributions accounts. Auditors analyze the professional fees expense account to determine that they have obtained a lawyer's letter from all attorneys that are handling litigation for the client.

9. For strong internal control over payroll transactions, the following functions should be segregated: (1) employment, (2) timekeeping, (3) payroll preparation and recordkeeping, and (4) distribution of pay to employees.

10. The function of timekeeping (performed by supervisory personnel) consists of determining the number of hours or days for which an employee is to be paid.

11.   The payroll department has the responsibility for computing the amounts to be paid to employees and preparing the payroll records and unsigned payroll checks.

12.   The company's paymaster should sign the checks and distribute them to the employees. Payroll checks should be drawn on an imprest payroll bank account, or the amounts should be directly deposited in the employees' accounts. If employees are paid by cash, they should be required to sign a receipt for their pay.

13.   A typical audit program for the audit of payroll appears on page 606 of the textbook.

14.   If control over payroll is weak, the auditors may decide to observe the distribution of paychecks on a surprise basis, as a test for payroll payments to fictitious employees.

15.   The Financial Accounting Standards Board requires public companies to include certain business segment information in their annual financial statements. The related auditing standards require the auditors to audit the information by performing the following procedures: (1) evaluate the reasonableness of management's methods of compiling the information, (2) consider whether the information is presented in sufficient detail and apply analytical procedures to test its reasonableness, and (3) evaluate the reasonableness of methods used in allocating operating expenses among segments.

16.   The amounts included in the statement of cash flows are audited in conjunction with the audit of balance sheet and income statement accounts. Additional procedures to examine the statement consist of review procedures to evaluate the presentation and clerical accuracy of the statement.

17.   In **completing the audit**, certain audit procedures and judgments must be performed at or near the end of field work. These audit procedures include: (1) search for unrecorded liabilities, (2) review the minutes of meetings, (3) perform final analytical procedures, (4) perform procedures to identify loss contingencies, (5) perform the review for subsequent events, and (6) obtain the representation letter.

18.   A **loss contingency** is a possible loss, stemming from past events, which will be resolved as to existence and amount by some future event. Such losses should be reflected in the financial statements if: (1) information available prior to the issuance of the financial statements indicates that it is **probable** that a loss had been sustained before the balance sheet date, and (2) the amount of the loss may be **reasonably estimated**. Loss contingencies that do not meet both of the above criteria should be disclosed when there is at least a reasonable possibility that a loss has been incurred.

19.   To assess the financial statement effects of pending litigation, the auditors rely primarily upon a representation from the client's legal counsel called a **lawyer's letter**. A lawyer's letter includes a description (or an evaluation of management's description) of all pending and threatened litigation of which the attorney has knowledge.

20.   Auditors must also inquire of management into the possibility of unasserted claims. An unasserted claim is a potential litigation situation in which no potential claimant has yet demonstrated the intent to initiate legal action.

21.   Other audit procedures for identifying and evaluating loss contingencies are presented on pages 611-612 of the textbook.

22.   Transactions or events occurring subsequent to the balance sheet date, but prior to issuance of the financial statements, may have a material effect on the financial statements and the auditors' report. These subsequent events may be described as follows:

    a.   **Type 1 subsequent events**—provide additional evidence regarding conditions existing at the balance sheet date and affect the estimates inherent in the financial statements. Management should adjust the financial statements to reflect this type of subsequent event.

    b.   **Type 2 subsequent events**—provide evidence about conditions that did not exist at the balance sheet date but arose subsequent to that date. The financial statements should not be adjusted to reflect these events, but disclosure of them in the notes of the financial statements may be necessary.

23.   The auditors have a responsibility to perform a review for material events occurring during the subsequent period (from the balance sheet date to the last day of field work). This review should include at least the following procedures:

    a.   Read the latest interim financial statements and minutes from meetings of stockholders, directors, and appropriate committees.

    b.   Make general inquiries of appropriate client officers and other personnel.

    c.   Obtain letters of representations from appropriate client officers and the client's legal counsel.

24.   The auditors' responsibility for performing procedures to discover subsequent events extends only to the date of the audit report (last day of field work). However, the auditors still have a responsibility to evaluate subsequent events that come to their attention after the date of the audit report.

25.   When a subsequent event that should be disclosed in the financial statements occurs after the last day of field work, but prior to the issuance of the report, the auditors may date their report in one of two ways. They may extend their subsequent events procedures to the date of the subsequent event and date their report as of that date, or they may **dual–date** the report, as for example, "February 11, 200X, except for Note 7 as to which the date is February 20, 200X."

26.   To issue an unqualified opinion, the auditors must conclude that there is a low level of risk of material misstatement in the financial statements. By accumulating (1) known misstatements that have not been corrected, (2) projected misstatements and (3) other estimated misstatements, the auditors obtain an estimate of the total likely misstatement that exists in the financial statements. Based on this estimate, the auditors conclude whether there is a sufficiently low level of risk on material misstatement in the financial statements to justify the issuance of an unqualified opinion.

27.   Audited financial statements are often included in three types of reports: (1) annual reports to shareholders, (2) reports to the SEC, and (3) auditor-submitted financial reports. Included in these reports is other information in addition to the audited financial statements. The auditors' responsibilities for this other information depends on the type of report and the nature of the information, as summarized below:

a.   **Required supplementary information.** The auditors are required to perform review procedures on the information. If the information is omitted or not appropriately presented, or the auditors are not able to complete the procedures, these facts should be set forth in an additional (not qualifying) paragraph of the audit report.

b.   **Other information in client-prepared documents**. The auditors must read this information for consistency with information known to the auditors, or other material misstatements. If the client refuses to revise misstated information, the auditors should consider revising the audit report to describe the inconsistency, withholding their opinion, or withdrawing from the engagement.

c.   **Information accompanying financial statements in auditor-submitted documents.** The auditors must report on all information included in auditor-submitted documents. If the auditors have audited the information, they express an opinion on the information. Otherwise, they provide a disclaimer of opinion on the information.

28.   If, after issuing their report, the auditors become aware of circumstances that cause them to question the appropriateness of their audit opinion, they should immediately perform an investigation. If the auditors find that circumstances that would have affected their report existed at the date of the report, the auditors should advise the client to make appropriate disclosure to persons relying on the financial statements or undertake to issue revised financial statements. If the client refuses to take such steps, the auditors should notify the board of directors that they no longer want their name to be associated with the financial statements and they intend to take steps to prevent further reliance on their report, such as notification of the SEC.

29.   Subsequent review of an audit engagement may reveal that certain essential procedures were omitted. In such cases, the auditors should attempt to perform the omitted procedures if they feel that their report is still being relied upon. The auditors should also consult their attorney as to the appropriate action to be taken.

Test Yourself on Chapter 16

TRUE OR FALSE

For each of the following statements, circle the T or the F to indicate whether the statement is true or false.

T   F   1.   Tests of revenue and expenses often involve analytical procedures.

T   F   2.   The auditors generally perform an analysis of the miscellaneous revenue account to determine the nature of the items recorded to the account.

T   F   3.   Budgets are an important internal control over revenue and expenses.

T   F   4.   Payroll frauds are easier to conceal today than they were in the past.

T   F   5.   For effective internal control over payroll, the personnel department should prepare the payroll records and checks.

T   F   6.   Maintaining records of attendance of employees for payroll should be performed by the employees' supervisors.

T   F   7.   The payroll department of a company should sign and distribute company paychecks.

T   F   8.   Payroll expenditures should be made from an imprest payroll bank account.

T   F   9.   Unclaimed payroll checks should be returned to the payroll department for safekeeping.

T   F   10.   A surprise observation of the distribution of paychecks is designed to detect employees that are paid for more hours than they worked.

T   F   11.   The auditors perform an analysis of professional fees in part to determine that they have obtained a lawyer's letter from all attorneys that are handling litigation for the client.

T   F   12.   Business segment information required by the FASB is supplementary and need not be audited to provide a basis for an opinion on the client's financial statements.

T   F   13.   Amounts included in the statement of cash flows are audited in conjunction with the audit of balance sheet and income statement accounts.

T   F   14.   The representations letter from management should be dated and signed on the balance sheet date.

T   F   15.   Second partner reviews of audit engagements should be performed prior to issuance of the audit report.

T   F   16.   Disclosure checklists are used to test the completeness of audit working papers.

T   F   17.   The auditors should accumulate known, projected, and other estimated misstatements in the financial statements to determine whether an unqualified opinion should be issued on the financial statements.

T   F   18.   The auditors generally perform review procedures on FASB-required supplementary information.

T   F   19.   All information included in a financial report prepared and submitted by the auditors must be audited.

T   F   20.   The loss of an account receivable because of a major customer declaring bankruptcy subsequent to the balance sheet date might or might not require adjustment of the financial statements, depending upon the cause of the customer's bankruptcy.

T   F   21.   Subsequent events, which provide additional evidence regarding conditions existing at the balance sheet date, may result in adjustment of the financial statements.

T   F   22.   The financial statements should not be adjusted for subsequent events that provide important evidence about conditions that did not exist at the balance sheet date but arose subsequent to that date.

T   F   23.   CPAs have no responsibility to perform audit procedures after the date of their report but must still investigate events that are brought to their attention and might have affected their report.

T   F   24.   Dual–dating of an audit report occurs when the auditors are not able to complete an audit engagement as of a particular date and must return to complete the audit work on a later date.

COMPLETION

Fill in the necessary words to complete the following statements.

1.   Revenue and expense accounts are audited in conjunction with related _____ and _____

       accounts.

2.   Material fluctuations revealed by analytical procedures should be investigated to determine whether

       they are indicative of material _____ in the financial statements.

3.   The _____ department of the company should authorize changes in employee pay rates.

4.   The company's _____ should distribute paychecks to the employees of the company.

5.   A _____ _____ is a list of all specific disclosures required by financial accounting

       standards.

6.   The primary purpose of the _____ _____ is to have the client's principal officers

       acknowledge that they are primarily responsible for the fairness of the financial statements.

7.   The auditors' opinion on the client's financial statement is based on all evidence gathered by the

       auditors up to the _____ _____ _____ _____ _____.

8.   In estimating the total likely misstatement in the financial statements, the auditors should combine

_____ misstatements, _____ misstatements, and _____ _____

misstatements.

9.   If the auditors conclude that their estimate of the total likely misstatement in the financial statements is

too high, they should request management to _____ the financial statements or issue a

_____ or an _____ opinion.

10.   Other information in client prepared reports should be _____ by the auditors for _____

and other misstatements.

11.   An event occurring after the date of the balance sheet, but prior to completion of the audit, is called a

_____ _____ .

12.   Financial statements that give effect to a subsequent event as though the event had occurred at the

balance sheet date are known as _____ financial statements.

MULTIPLE CHOICE

Choose the best answer for each of the following questions and enter the identifying letter in the space provided.

_____   1.   When examining a client's statement of cash flows, for audit evidence, an auditor will rely
                 primarily upon:

                 a.   determination of the amount of working capital at year-end.
                 b.   analysis of significant ratios of prior years as compared to the current year.
                 c.   cross referencing to balances and transactions audited in connection with the examination of
                      the other financial statements.
                 d.   the guidance provided by the FASB Statement on the statement of cash flows.

_____   2.   Which of the following situations has the best chance of being detected when a CPA compares
                 200X revenues and expenses with the prior year and investigates all changes exceeding a fixed
                 percentage?

                 a.   An increase in property tax rates has not been recognized in the company's 200X accrual.
                 b.   The cashier began lapping accounts receivable in 200X.
                 c.   Because of worsening economic conditions, the 200X provision for uncollectible accounts
                      was inadequate.
                 d.   The company changed its capitalization policy for small tools in 200X.

_____ 3. Overall analysis of income statement accounts may bring to light errors, omissions, and inconsistencies not disclosed in the overall analysis of balance sheet accounts. The income statement analysis can best be accomplished by comparing monthly:

a. income statement ratios to balance sheet ratios.
b. revenue and expense account balances to the monthly reported net income.
c. income statement ratios to published industry averages.
d. revenue and expense account totals to the corresponding figures of the preceding years.

_____ 4. The primary difference between an audit of the balance sheet and an audit of the income statement lies in the fact that the audit of the income statement deals almost completely with the verification of:

a. transactions.
b. authorizations.
c. costs.
d. cutoffs.

_____ 5. For which of the following ledger accounts would the auditor be most likely to analyze the details?

a. Service Revenue.
b. Sales.
c. Miscellaneous expense.
d. Sales salaries expense.

_____ 6. An example of an internal control weakness is to assign to a supervisor the responsibility for:

a. reviewing and approving time reports for subordinate employees.
b. initiating requests for salary adjustments for subordinate employees.
c. authorizing payroll checks for terminated employees.
d. distributing payroll checks to subordinate employees.

_____ 7. Which of the following best describes proper internal control over payroll?

a. The preparation of the payroll must be under the control of the personnel department.
b. The confidentiality of employee payroll data should be carefully protected to prevent fraud.
c. The duties of hiring, payroll computation, and payment to employees should be segregated.
d. The payment of cash to employees should be replaced with payment by checks.

_____ 8. A surprise observation by an auditor of a client's regular distribution of paychecks is primarily designed to satisfy the auditor that:

a. all unclaimed payroll checks are properly returned to the cashier.
b. the paymaster is not involved in the distribution of payroll checks.
c. all employees have in their possession proper employee identification.
d. names on the company payroll are those of bona fide employees presently on the job.

_____ 9. The date of the management representation letter should coincide with the:

a. date of the auditor's report.
b. balance sheet date.
c. date of the latest subsequent event referred to in the notes to the financial statements.
d. date of the engagement agreement.

_____ 10. Auditors perform interim work at various times throughout the year. The auditors' subsequent events work should be extended to the date of:

a. a postdated footnote.
b. the next scheduled interim visit.
c. the final billing for audit services rendered.
d. the auditors' report.

_____ 11. A client has a calendar year–end. Listed below are four events that occurred after December 31. Which one of these subsequent events might result in adjustment of the December 31 financial statements?

a. The client decided to change depreciation methods in the coming year.
b. A substantial portion of the company's inventory was written off as obsolete on January 31.
c. The factory building was damaged by a fire on January 19.
d. A major subsidiary was sold on February 7.

_____ 12. In connection with the annual audit, which of the following is not a "subsequent events" procedure?

a. Review available interim financial statements.
b. Read available minutes of meetings of stockholders, directors, and committees. With regard to meetings for which minutes are not available, inquire about matters dealt with at such meetings.
c. Make inquiries with respect to the financial statements covered by the auditors' previously issued report if new information has become available during the current examination that might affect that report.
d. Discuss with officers the current status of items in the financial statements that were accounted for on the basis of tentative, preliminary, or inconclusive data.

_____ 13. When obtaining evidence regarding litigation against a client, the CPA would be least interested in determining:

a. an estimate of when the matter will be resolved.
b. the period in which the underlying cause of the litigation occurred.
c. the probability of an unfavorable outcome.
d. an estimate of the potential loss.

EXERCISES

1. For each of the following balance sheet accounts listed below, list a related income statement account.

a.   Property, plant, and equipment

b.   Long–term debt

    c.   Inventories

    d.   Accounts receivable

2.   List three audit procedures that cannot be performed until the end of audit field work.

    a.

    b.

    c.

3.   For each of the following subsequent events, indicate whether the financial statements should be:

          (A)   adjusted;

          (D)   the event should be disclosed in the financial statements; or

          (ND)   the event need not be disclosed.

Subsequent Event

_____   1.   An employee strike is called

_____   2.   A lawsuit that was begun a year ago is settled.

_____   3.   A new subsidiary is purchased.

_____   4.   A major customer of the company is lost.

_____   5.   A significant decline in the value of inventories occurs.

_____   6.   A plant of the company is destroyed by fire.

CHAPTER 17

Auditors' Reports

Highlights of Chapter

1.   It is essential that all reports by auditors make clear the scope of the work performed and the extent of the responsibility assumed by the auditors.

2.   The auditors' report customarily expresses an opinion on the balance sheet, the income statement, the statement of retained earnings, and the statement of cash flows. The report also applies to the notes to the financial statements; adequate disclosure in the notes to the financial statements is necessary for the auditors to issue an unqualified opinion on the financial statements.

3.   The auditors' report is ordinarily addressed to the board of directors, the shareholders, the audit committee, and the company itself, signed in the CPA firm's name, and dated as of the last day of audit field work.

4.   The auditors' standard unqualified report consists of three paragraphs: (1) the **introductory paragraph** that clarifies the responsibilities of management and the auditors, (2) the **scope paragraph** that states that the audit was performed in conformity with auditing standards generally accepted in the United States of America and explains the nature of an audit, and (3) the **opinion paragraph** that expresses an opinion that the client's financial statements are presented fairly, in all material respects, in conformity with accounting principles generally accepted in the United States of America.

5.   The unqualified auditors' report may be issued only when the following conditions are met:

   a.   The financial statements are presented in conformity with generally accepted accounting principles, including adequate disclosure.
   b.   The audit was performed in accordance with generally accepted auditing standards, with no significant scope limitations preventing the auditors from gathering the evidence necessary to support their opinion.

6.   In addition to a standard, unqualified audit report, there are four other reporting options:

   a.   **An unqualified opinion—with explanatory language.** In certain circumstances explanatory language is added to the auditors' report with no effect on the opinion (e.g., when a client changes accounting principles).

   b.   **A qualified opinion.** Auditors issue this type of report when there is a limitation on the scope of the audit or the financial statements depart from generally accepted accounting principles. The limitation or exception is material, but not so material to necessitate the expression of an adverse opinion or a disclaimer of opinion.

   c.   **An adverse opinion.** Auditors issue this type of report when they believe that the financial statements do not present fairly the financial position, results of operations, or cash flows in conformity with generally accepted accounting principles.

      d.   **A disclaimer of opinion.** Auditors issue this type of report when they are unable to express an opinion on the financial statements taken as a whole. A disclaimer results from a very significant scope restriction. Also, the auditors are not precluded from issuing a disclaimer for the existence of a major uncertainty, including a going-concern uncertainty.

7.   Auditors must qualify their report whenever there are material deficiencies in the client's financial statements. The determination of whether an item is material to the client's financial statements is a matter of professional judgment that requires consideration of the dollar amount and the nature of the item. If a very material deficiency exists making the financial statements misleading, the auditors must issue an adverse opinion.

8.   Under certain circumstances explanatory language is added to what remains a report with an unqualified opinion. Auditors add additional explanatory language to their report to indicate a division of responsibility with another CPA firm, to refer to an uncertainty that could have a material impact on the financial statements, to indicate an inconsistency in the application of accounting principles, to emphasize a matter, and to justify a departure from an officially recognized accounting principle. These unqualified reports may be described as follows:

      a.   **Reliance on other auditors.** In some situations it may be necessary for the CPA firm principally responsible for an audit to rely on the audit work performed by another CPA firm. The principal auditors might make reference in the introductory, scope, and opinion paragraphs of their report to the reliance on the work of other auditors. Making reference to the other auditors divides the responsibility for the engagement among the participating CPA firms. If the principal auditors do not make reference to the other auditors, they assume responsibility for the adequacy of all work performed.

      b.   **Going Concern Question.** If the auditors become aware of conditions that indicate possible substantial doubt about going concern status (e.g., recurring losses), they should consider whether the conditions are mitigated by other factors (e.g., management plans). If, after considering such information, the auditors conclude that substantial doubt remains about the client's ability to continue as a going concern, they add an explanatory paragraph to their report.

      c.   **Changes in accounting principles.** When the client changes from one generally accepted accounting principle to another generally accepted accounting principle, the auditors add an additional paragraph to their report to highlight the lack of consistency in the application of acceptable accounting principles.

      d.   **Emphasis of a matter.** Auditors may also issue an unqualified opinion that includes an additional paragraph that emphasizes some element in the client's financial statements, such as related party transactions.

      e.   **Departure from an officially recognized accounting principle.** On rare occasions auditors may consider it appropriate to depart from an officially recognized principle (i.e., FASB and GASB statements and interpretations). The auditors may still issue an unqualified opinion, but they must disclose the departure in an explanatory paragraph of their report, the effects, and why application of the principle would result in materially misstated financial statements.

9.   Opinions are qualified "except for" the effects of a scope limitation or a departure from generally accepted accounting principles. The auditors' qualified report should include an additional paragraph explaining the reason for the qualification and its effects on the financial statements, if they can be determined. If the qualification results from a lack of disclosure in the financial statements, the auditors should disclose the matter in their report if it is practical and reasonable to do so.

10.   If the auditors find a departure from generally accepted accounting principles which is so material that a qualified report is not justified, they should issue an adverse opinion. The departure from generally accepted accounting principles and its effects (if determinable) should be set forth in a separate paragraph between the scope and opinion paragraphs.

11.   If a scope restriction is so severe that a qualified opinion is not appropriate, the auditors should issue a disclaimer of opinion. It is always advisable for the auditors to disclaim an opinion on the financial statements when a significant scope restriction is imposed by the client.

12.   The auditors should never issue a standard disclaimer of opinion when they believe that the financial statements are misstated. Even when the auditors issue a disclaimer of opinion, they should express in their report any reservations they have concerning the financial statements.

13.   In their annual reports, most companies issue the current year's financial statements with comparative financial statements for one or more prior periods. If the current auditors have audited all years' statements, they should report on all the financial statements. In doing so, the auditors may express differing opinions on the financial statements of different years, as well as differing opinions on the individual statements within a single year. Also, new information should be used to update the auditors' opinion on the prior years' financial statements.

14.   In some cases, the financial statements of the preceding year will have been examined by other auditors. In such situations, the auditors' report on the current year's financial statements typically contains explanatory language in the introductory paragraph referring to the audit report of the other auditors, and describing any qualification contained in that report. Alternatively, the predecessor auditors may be engaged to reissue their report on the prior year's financial statements (bearing its original date). Before reissuing their report, the predecessor auditors should read all financial statements and make inquiries of the current auditors to determine that nothing has occurred requiring revision of their original report.

15.   Most publicly owned corporations are subject to the financial reporting requirements of the federal securities laws, administered by the Securities and Exchange Commission (SEC). Many of the reports that must be filed under the federal securities laws require the inclusion of audited financial statements. The federal securities laws contain complex reporting requirements, and provide both civil and criminal penalties for any person, including auditors, who allow misrepresentations of the fact in financial statements filed with the SEC.

Test Yourself on Chapter 17

TRUE OR FALSE

For each of the following statements, circle the T or the F to indicate whether the statement is true or false.

T   F   1.   When the auditors' name is associated with financial statements, the audit report should contain a clear-cut indication of the degree of responsibility they are assuming.

T   F   2.   Supplementary information required by the FASB and the SEC must be presented in audited supplementary schedules accompanying the financial statements.

T   F   3.   When a client omits notes to audited financial statements, the auditor should add an explanatory paragraph to the report indicating such omission and issue an unqualified report.

T   F   4.   An auditor's report is in essence a guarantee by the auditors that the financial statements are correct.

T   F   5.   The phrase "generally accepted auditing standards" appears in the scope paragraph of the auditors' standard report.

T   F   6.   Qualifying language is ordinarily added to the introductory paragraph of an auditor's unqualified report.

T   F   7.   An adverse opinion is an opinion that the financial statements are not presented fairly in accordance with generally accepted accounting principles.

T   F   8.   The term material may be defined as "sufficiently important to influence decisions made by reasonable users of financial statements."

T   F   9.   Audit reports for shared responsibility engagements are considered to be qualified reports.

T   F   10.   An unqualified report should never contain an additional paragraph, because it would confuse the users of the report.

T   F   11.   Auditors may never issue an unqualified opinion when the financial statements materially depart from a *Statement of Financial Accounting Standards*.

T   F   12.   The introductory paragraph of the auditors' report clarifies management's responsibility for the financial statements.

T   F   13.   A qualified opinion that is issued because of a departure from generally accepted accounting principles should contain a separate paragraph explaining the departure and its effects.

T   F   14.   A qualified opinion is appropriate when a departure from generally accepted accounting principles is material enough to deserve mention in the auditors' report, but not material enough to call for expression of a disclaimer of opinion.

T   F   15.   A change in accounting principle from one generally accepted accounting principle to another normally would not prevent the issuance of an unqualified audit opinion, provided the effects of the change are set forth in a note to the financial statements and the change is justified.

T   F   16.   The auditors should generally issue a qualified opinion if the client is unwilling to permit the auditors to observe the physical inventory or to confirm accounts receivable.

T   F   17.   If a company is faced with any uncertainty such as the prospect of a strike or the possible imposition of wage and price controls, the auditors should issue a qualified opinion.

T   F   18.   The auditors may issue different opinions on financial statements for different years, or on different financial statements for the same year.

T   F   19.   The auditors are not allowed to change their opinion on financial statements that were reported on in prior years.

T   F   20.   A Form S-1 must be filed with the SEC if a company is planning to issue securities to the public.

COMPLETION

Fill in the necessary words to complete the following statements.

1.   The auditors' report is signed with the name of the _____ not the name of the individual _____ signing the report.

2.   The _____ paragraph of an auditors' report communicates the degree of responsibility that the auditors are taking for the fairness of the financial statements.

3.   An _____ opinion is an opinion that the financial statements fairly present financial position, results of operations, and cash flows, in conformity with generally accepted accounting principles.

4.   When the client elects to change accounting principles from one acceptable principle to another acceptable principle, the auditors should issue an _____ opinion with an _____ _____ that highlights the accounting change.

5.   When financial statements contain a material departure from generally accepted accounting principles, the auditors qualify their opinion _____ _____ the effects of the matter, or they issue a (an) _____ opinion depending on the materiality of the departure.

6.   Materiality depends upon both the _____ and the _____ of the item.

7.   The auditors issue a _____ opinion or an _____ opinion, if they consider the disclosure in the client's financial statements to be inadequate.

8.   If a scope restriction is so severe that a qualified opinion is inappropriate, the auditors should issue a

       _____ ____ _____ .

9.   All audit reports that are qualified should contain an _____ _____ explaining the

details of the qualification.

10.   If the auditors have examined the prior year's financial statements presented for comparative purposes,

they should _____ their opinion for any new information.

MULTIPLE CHOICE

Choose the best answer for each of the following questions and enter the identifying letter in the space provided.

_____   1.   The primary responsibility for the adequacy of disclosure in the financial statements of a publicly-held company rests with the:

      a.   partner assigned to the audit engagement.
      b.   management of the company.
      c.   auditor in charge of the field work.
      d.   Securities and Exchange Commission.

_____   2.   If the auditors indicate in the report that the opinion is based, in part, on the report of other auditors who were responsible for the examination of part of the total financial statement data, the auditors are:

      a.   in effect qualifying the opinion.
      b.   properly indicating a division of responsibility, and the report should further indicate in an appropriate quantitative form the proportionate responsibility being assumed by each set of auditors.
      c.   still held responsible for the work of the other auditors.
      d.   abrogating responsibility to those users who rely on the CPA firm's reputation as a basis for relying on the reported financial statements.

_____   3.   Which of the following is an authoritative body pronouncement source of generally accepted accounting principles when considering Rule 203 of the AICPA Code of Professional Conduct?

      a.   SEC Accounting Series Releases.
      b.   AICPA Industry Audit Guides.
      c.   Statements of the FASB.
      d.   AICPA Research Studies.

_____ 4.   Upon the advice of its auditors, Smith Company changed the method of computing depreciation from the straight-line method to an accelerated method with a material effect upon the financial statements. The auditors' report:

   a.   must be qualified for the accounting change.
   b.   should include an additional explanatory paragraph highlighting the accounting change.
   c.   should contain modifications in both the scope and opinion paragraph.
   d.   should be a standard unqualified report.

_____ 5.   If the auditors believe that related party transactions are not adequately described in the notes to the financial statements, they should:

   a.   disclaim an opinion.
   b.   qualify their opinion or issue an adverse opinion.
   c.   add an emphasizing paragraph to their unqualified opinion.
   d.   add an explanatory paragraph to their unqualified opinion.

_____ 6.   What is the objective of the reporting standard relating to consistency?

   a.   To give assurance that adequate disclosure will be made so that there will be comparability of financial statements between companies in the same industry.
   b.   To give assurance that users will be informed of the lack of comparability of financial statements between periods due to changes in accounting principles.
   c.   To give assurance that the comparability of financial statements between periods has not been materially affected by any type of change.
   d.   To give assurance only that the same accounting principles have been applied to all similar transactions within each period presented.

_____ 7.   Jones, CPA, accepts a new client late in Year 5 and therefore had no opportunity to observe the physical inventory taken at December 31, Year 4. Jones found it impossible to obtain evidence by other auditing procedures as to the beginning inventories for Year 5. Jones observed the physical inventory at December 31, Year 5 and completed the audit satisfactorily. The report to be issued should:

   a.   be unqualified.
   b.   be unqualified as to the balance sheet and with a disclaimer of opinion as to the income statement and the statement of cash flows.
   c.   be qualified as to all of the statements.
   d.   be a disclaimer of opinion.

_____ 8.   An auditors' opinion exception arising from a limitation on the scope of the audit should be explained in:

   a.   a note to the financial statements.
   b.   the auditors' report.
   c.   both a note to the financial statements and the auditors' report.
   d.   both the financial statements (immediately after the caption of the item or items which could not be verified) and the auditors' report.

_____ 9.   A note to the financial statements of the First Security Bank indicates that all of the records relating to the bank's business operations are stored on magnetic disks, and that there are no emergency back-up systems or duplicate disks stored since the First Security Bank considers the occurrence of a catastrophe to be remote. Based upon this, one would expect the auditors' report to express:

   a.   an adverse opinion.
   b.   an unqualified opinion with explanatory language.
   c.   a standard unqualified opinion.
   d.   a qualified opinion.

_____ 10.   Your independent examination of the Abbox Co. reveals that the firm's poor financial condition creates substantial doubt about its ability to continue as a going concern. Assuming that the financial statements have otherwise been prepared in accordance with generally accepted accounting principles, what disclosure should you make of the company's precarious financial position?

   a.   You should issue an unqualified opinion, but use an explanatory paragraph to direct the reader's attention to the poor financial condition of the company as described in the financial statements and the notes.
   b.   You should issue an adverse opinion on the financial statements.
   c.   You need not insist on any particular disclosure, since the company's poor financial condition is clearly indicated by the financial statements themselves.
   d.   You should provide adequate disclosure and appropriately qualify your opinion because of the uncertainty.

_____ 11.   A client company has changed its accounting practices during the year, materially affecting its financial statements so as to make them seriously misleading and not in conformity with generally accepted accounting principles. The CPAs examining these financial statements should:

   a.   render an adverse opinion and give reasons therefor.
   b.   modify the opinion with respect to the consistency standard and, in an explanatory paragraph of the report, explain the changes and their effects on the net income of the period.
   c.   disclaim an opinion and give reasons therefor.
   d.   modify the opinion with respect to the consistency standard, referring to explanatory notes of the financial statements to fulfill disclosure requirements.

_____ 12.   When an adverse opinion is expressed, the opinion paragraph should include a direct reference to:

   a.   a note to the financial statements which discusses the basis for the opinion.
   b.   the scope paragraph that discusses the basis for the opinion rendered.
   c.   the consistency or lack of consistency in the application of generally accepted accounting principles.
   d.   a separate paragraph that discusses the basis for the opinion expressed.

EXERCISES

1.   The five types of reports that may be issued by auditors include:

   (A)   An unqualified opinion
   (B)   An "except for" qualified opinion
   (C)   An unqualified opinion with explanatory language
   (D)   An adverse opinion
   (E)   A disclaimer opinion

   For each of the following situations indicate the letter(s) that corresponds to the appropriate type of auditors' report, both when the situation is "material" and when it is "very material."

Situation	Material	Very Material
a. The financial statements contain a departure from generally accepted accounting principles.	_____	_____
b. The financial statements reflect a change from one generally accounting principles to another generally accepted accounting principle.	_____	_____
c. The auditors wish to indicate in the report the reliance on the work of other auditors.	_____	_____
d. The scope of the auditors' examination is restricted.	_____	_____

2.   For each of the following types of audit reports, indicate whether the report is "unqualified" and whether the report typically contains additional explanatory language.

Situation	Qualified?		Additional Explanatory Language?	
a. A change in accounting principle	Yes	No	Yes	No
b. A scope limitation	Yes	No	Yes	No
c. The emphasis of a matter	Yes	No	Yes	No
d. A departure from a FASB Statement, because application of the principle would result in materially misleading financial statements.	Yes	No	Yes	No
e. Reliance upon other auditors	Yes	No	Yes	No

CHAPTER 18

Special Reports and Accounting and Review Services

Highlights of the Chapter

1. In performing accounting services, no explicit assurance is provided as the role is one of assisting the client, and not one of providing assurance to third parties about the information. The term auditor is most frequently used when discussing a CPA's role in providing an opinion on the fairness of historical financial statements. The term accountant refers to CPAs when they are performing other attestation services and accounting services

2. Auditors use the term special reports to describe auditors' reports on:

    a. Financial statements prepared on a comprehensive basis of accounting other than GAAP (for example, cash basis statements).
    b. Specified elements, accounts, or items within financial statements.
    c. Compliance with contractual agreements or regulatory requirements.
    d. Special-purpose financial presentations to comply with contractual or regulatory provisions.
    e. Audited financial information presented in prescribed forms or schedules.

3. When auditors issue a special report on financial statements presented on a comprehensive basis of accounting other than GAAP, their report must describe the basis of accounting being used and state that the statements are not presented in conformity with GAAP. In addition, the financial statements should be given appropriate names to reflect the basis of accounting being used.

4. An auditors' report on **cash–basis financial statements** is illustrated on page 671 of the textbook.

5. A report on specified elements of financial statements should indicate the item being reported upon, the basis of accounting used, and whether the item is fairly presented. The level of materiality for such engagements generally is less than would be used in a complete financial statement audit. If the CPAs' engagement is limited to performing procedures that have been agreed upon, the engagement is not sufficient to enable the CPAs to express an opinion. The report issued should indicate the procedures performed and the findings.

6. Regulatory requirements or debt agreements may require a company to provide a compliance report prepared by independent auditors. Auditors may issue such a special compliance report only if they have first audited the company's financial statements for the period.

7. When CPAs audit special–purpose financial presentations (based on contracts or regulatory agency requirements) they must restrict their report to use by the contracting parties or the regulatory agency. Since the financial statements are not in accordance with GAAP or some other comprehensive basis of accounting, they would not be appropriate for general use.

8. When auditing financial statements prepared for use in other countries, the nature of the auditors' report depends upon whether the report is for use primarily outside the United States or within the United States. If it is for primary use outside the United States, the auditors may issue either a U.S. report with appropriate modifications for the foreign accounting principles, or the report form of the other country. If the report is primarily for use in the United States, the auditor should issue the U.S. audit report with appropriate modifications.

9   Auditors sometimes issue auditors' reports on the personal financial statements of an individual or of a married couple. Generally accepted accounting principles require that assets in personal financial statements be valued at estimated current values, rather than at historical cost. In personal financial statements, the "balance sheet" is called a statement of financial condition and the "income statement" is called a statement of changes in net worth. A particular difficulty in the audit of personal financial statements is determination of the completeness of recorded assets and liabilities.

10.   The SEC requires certain public companies to have their auditors perform review procedures on their interim (quarterly) financial information before it is issued. A review is substantially less in scope than an audit; it consists of inquiries of management concerning operation of the accounting system and changes in internal control, analytical procedures, reading minutes of meetings, and obtaining letters of representation from management.

11.   The purpose of a **review** is to provide users of the statements with limited assurance that the statements are in conformity with generally accepted accounting principles. An example of a review report on interim statements is on page 677 of the textbook.

12.   CPAs also perform reviews of financial statements of nonpublic companies. A review for a nonpublic client is similar to the review of interim financial statements for a publicly owned client. However, a review of interim information for a public client includes a higher degree of understanding of internal control.

13.   The accountants' report on a **review** of the financial statements of a nonpublic client is illustrated on page 681 of the textbook. Since a review provides statement users with limited assurance as to the reliability of the statements, the CPAs must be independent to perform this service.

14.   Review reports must be modified to describe departures from generally accepted accounting principles, but not for changes in accounting principles, substantial doubt about going concern status, or uncertainties. A significant scope limitation results in auditor resignation; no report is issued because the review is considered incomplete.

15.   CPAs often issue letters for underwriters ("comfort letters") to help underwriters fulfill their obligation to perform a reasonable investigation of securities being purchased.

16.   Companies who have had their financial statements audited by a CPA may summarize the information and present it in *condensed financial statements*. CPAs may report on whether those condensed financials statements is fairly stated in all material respects in relation to the basic financial statements.

17.   The Auditing Standards Board issues professional standards for engagements involving the unaudited financial statements of public companies. Standards for compilations and reviews of the statements of *nonpublic companies* are issued by the Accounting and Review Services Committee.

18.   A compilation involves the preparation of financial statements for a nonpublic client directly from the client's accounting records and other representations of management. A compilation is not intended to provide any assurance that the financial statements constitute a fair presentation.

19   To perform a compilation, the accountants must first have knowledge of the accounting principles used in the client's industry and a general understanding of the client's business. The accountants must evaluate the client's representations in light of this knowledge and must also read the compiled statements for format and obvious material misstatement. Beyond these basic measures, however, the accountants have no responsibilities to perform any investigative procedures.

20.   Proper CPA reporting on compiled statements depends on whether the financial statements are expected to be used ay a party other than management. If not, the CPA may either (1) issue a compilation report or (2) not issue a report, but only document the understanding with the client through use of an engagement letter. When a compilation report is issued, it should be labeled as an accountants' report, not as an auditors' report. An example of the report is found on page 685 of the textbook. An additional paragraph may be added to the report (as a final paragraph) in the event that the client requests that the CPAs omit from the compiled statements the many disclosures required by generally accepted accounting principles. This special paragraph is illustrated on page 685 of the textbook.

21.   Since a compilation is not intended to provide any assurance to third parties as to the reliability of the financial statements, a CPA need not be independent of the client in order to perform a compilation. However, they must add a paragraph to the report indicating that "We are not independent with respect to [Company Name]."

22.   Accountants may also compile financial statements on prescribed forms and modify their compilation report to indicate that the information is compiled in accordance with the requirements of the body designing or adopting the form.

23.   When CPAs are associated with the financial statements of a *public company* that they have neither audited or reviewed, they should issue a disclaimer of opinion and mark each page of the statements as "unaudited." (recall that the compilation form of association exists for nonpublic companies).

Test Yourself on Chapter 18

TRUE OR FALSE

For each of the following statements, circle the T or the F to indicate whether the statement is true or false.

T   F   1.   If auditors are engaged to audit financial statements prepared on the cash basis of accounting, they must issue either a qualified report or an adverse report.

T   F   2.   Auditors may issue a special report indicating that they are not aware of violations of the terms of a loan agreement only if they have first audited the client's financial statements.

T   F   3.   When issuing a special report on cash-basis financial statements, the auditors' report must state that the financial statements are prepared on a basis of accounting other than generally accepted accounting principles.

T   F   4.   Auditors may not issue a report which covers only specified items or elements in the financial statements, such as net sales or working capital.

T   F   5.   When CPAs perform an audit they are acting as auditors, but when performing a compilation they are acting as accountants.

T   F   6.   When acting as accountants rather than as auditors, CPAs cannot be held liable to third parties for misstatements or omissions in the client's financial statements.

T   F   7.   Professional standards for compilations and reviews of the financial statements of nonpublic companies are issued by the Accounting and Review Services Committee, not by the Auditing Standards Board.

T   F   8.   Reviews of the interim financial statements of a public company are similar in scope to an audit, except that the CPAs are not required to observe the taking of physical inventory.

T   F   9.   The purpose of a review is to provide users of the financial statements with limited assurance that the statements are prepared in conformity with generally accepted accounting principles (or some other comprehensive basis of accounting).

T   F   10.   A compilation refers to the preparation of financial statements for a nonpublic client without performing investigative procedures to determine the reliability of the information.

T   F   11.   CPAs may perform a compilation even if they are not independent of the client.

T   F   12.   CPAs may perform a review even if they are not independent of the client.

T   F   13.   Engagement letters are required for review engagements and compilations.

T   F   14.   The accountants' report on either a review or a compilation engagement should disclaim an opinion on the financial statements.

T   F   15.   In compiled financial statements, management may omit substantially all of the disclosures required by generally accepted accounting principles if this omission is clearly indicated in the accountants' report.

T   F   16.   A review of the financial statements of a nonpublic client does not include a consideration of the client's internal control.

T   F   17.   The primary difficulty in the audit of personal financial statements is determining whether the individual involved has rights to the recorded assets.

T   F   18.   The requirements for performing a quarterly review of a public company are the same as those of a review of a nonpublic company.

T   F   19.   Letters for underwriters are commonly called comfort letters.

T   F   20.   Audits of condensed financial statements are often replacing audits of the basic (complete) financial statements..

COMPLETION

Fill in the necessary words to complete the following statements.

1.   An auditor's report on financial statements prepared on a comprehensive basis of accounting other than

GAAP is termed a _____ _____.

2.   Standards for a CPA's association with the unaudited financial statements of public companies are

issued by the _____ _____ _____, whereas standards for the _____ or review

of the financial statements of nonpublic companies are issued by the _____ _____

_____ _____ _____.

3.   The procedures applied by the CPAs in a review of financial statements consist primarily of

_____ of management and of applying _____ procedures.

4.   An engagement designed to provide users of financial statements with limited assurance that those

statements are presented in conformity with GAAP is termed a _____, whereas the preparation of

financial statements from the accounting records and other representations of management is termed a

_____.

5.   When performing an audit, CPAs properly may refer to themselves as auditors; when performing

compilation or review services, they should refer to themselves as _____.

6.   CPAs may not issue a special report regarding the client's _____ with the terms of a contract

unless the CPAs have first performed an _____ of the client's financial statements.

7.   Comfort letters help _____ in fulfilling their obligation to perform a _____ _____

      of the securities registration statement.

8.   At a minimum, the accountant must _____ the compiled financial statements for appropriate

      format and obvious material _____.

9.   The balance sheet of an individual is referred to as the statement of _____ _____. Of

      particular concern in the audit of such statements is the assertion of _____.

10.   Reviewed financial statements are modified for departures from _____ _____ _____

      _____, but not for changes in _____ _____.

MULTIPLE CHOICE

Choose the best answer for each of the following questions and enter the identifying letter in the space provided.

_____ 1.   Which of the following would not be considered a special report?

             a.   An audit of a company's cash basis financial statements.
             b.   An audit of the financial statements of an individual in which assets are valued at estimated
                  current values.
             c.   A report on specified elements of financial statements.
             d.   A report on the client's compliance with the terms of a bond indenture contract.

_____ 2.   An auditors' report on cash-basis financial statements should include a statement that:

             a.   the financial statements are not prepared in conformity with GAAP.
             b.   the auditors are disclaiming an opinion.
             c.   disclosure is inadequate.
             d.   the financial statements are misleading.

_____ 3.   Which of the following would not be included in a CPA's review report on the financial
             statements of a nonpublic company?

             a.   A statement that the review was performed in accordance with generally accepted auditing
                  standards.
             b.   A statement that all information is based upon representations of management.
             c.   A statement that a review is less in scope than an audit.
             d.   A statement describing the principal procedures performed during a review.

_____ 4.   Which of the following procedures is not included in a review of the financial statements of a nonpublic company?

a.   Inquiries of management.
b.   Obtaining a general understanding of the client's industry and business operations.
c.   Analytical procedures.
d.   A consideration of internal control.

_____ 5.   When CPAs are associated with the financial statements of a public company, but they have not performed an audit or a review, their report should include:

a.   negative assurance.
b.   limited assurance.
c.   a disclaimer of opinion.
d.   a list of the investigative procedures performed.

_____ 6.   CPAs who are not independent of the client may issue a:

a.   compilation report.
b.   review report.
c.   special report.
d.   report on internal control.

_____ 7.   Comfort letters help underwriters in fulfilling their obligation to perform a reasonable investigation of a(n):

a.   annual report filed with the Securities and Exchange Commission.
b.   annual report sent to shareholders.
c.   condensed financial statements.
d.   registration statement for the sale of securities.

_____ 8.   An engagement in which specified users agree with the CPAs on the procedures to be performed is:

a.   a form of special audit engagement.
b.   considered unethical under the professional standards.
c.   only allowable under engagements related to not-for-profit organizations.
d.   referred to as an agreed-upon procedures engagement.

_____ 9.   Which of the following is most likely to result in modification of a compilation report?

a.   A departure from generally accepted accounting principles.
b.   A lack of consistency in application of generally accepted accounting principles.
c.   A question concerning an entity's ability to continue as a going concern.
d.   A major uncertainty facing the financial statements.

_____ 10. In performing a compilation of the financial statements of a nonpublic company, the CPA concludes that modification of the accountants' report is not adequate to indicate the deficiencies in the statements. If the client is not willing to correct these deficiencies, the CPAs should:

     a. insist upon performing a review of the statements.
     b. express an adverse auditors' opinion.
     c. issue a special report with a negative assurance clause.
     d. withdraw from the engagement.

_____ 11. If information is for management's use only, which of the following forms of CPA association with financial information is most likely to result in no report being issued?

     a. An agreed-upon procedures engagement.
     b. An audit.
     c. A compilation.
     d. A review.

_____ 12. A CPA performing a compilation has discovered that the client refuses to present notes to the financial statements. The appropriate report is:

     a. adverse.
     b. qualified.
     c. a compilation report with an indication that all required disclosures under generally accepted accounting principle may not be presented with the statements.
     d. no report, auditor resignation is ordinarily required.

EXERCISES

1. Listed below are four types of reports issued by CPAs:

     1   Unqualified auditors' report
     2   Special report on cash-basis statements
     3   Review report
     4   Compilation report

Indicate the type of report (or reports) in which the following phrases appear by placing the identifying numbers in the spaces provided. A phrase may appropriately appear in more than one type of report. If the phrase should not appear in any of the five reports, place an "X" in the space provided.

_____ a. "in accordance with generally accepted auditing standards."

_____ b. A disclaimer of opinion phrase.

_____ c. "presenting in the form of financial statements, information that is the representation of management."

_____ d. "is in compliance with the requirements of the Foreign Corrupt Practices Act."

_____ e.   "Management has elected to omit substantially all of the disclosures required by generally accepted accounting principles."

_____ f.   "in accordance with standards established by the American Institute of Certified Public Accountants."

_____ g.   "is substantially less in scope than an audit in accordance with generally accepted auditing standards....."

_____ h.   "met those criteria."

_____ i.   "we are not aware of any material modifications that should be made"

_____ j.   "designed to obtain reasonable assurance."

_____ k.   "adequate informative disclosure....."

_____ l.   "which is a comprehensive basis of accounting other than generally accepted accounting principles."

2.   In the spaces provided, insert the words or phrases necessary to complete the following accountants' report on a review of the financial statements of a nonpublic company.

We have (a) _____ the accompanying balance sheet of X Company as of December 31, 20XX, and the related statements of income, retained earnings, and cash flows for the year then ended, in accordance with (b) _____ _____. All information included in these financial statements is the (c) _____ of X Company.

A review consists principally of (d) _____ of company personnel and (e) _____ applied to financial data. It is substantially (f) _____ than an audit in accordance with generally accepted auditing standards, the objective of which is the expression of an (g) _____ regarding the financial statements taken as a whole. Accordingly we (h) _____.

Based on our review, we are (i) _____ modifications that should be made to the accompanying financial statements in order for them to be in conformity with generally accepted accounting principles.

CHAPTER 19

Other Assurance Services

Highlights of the Chapter

1.   The Special Committee on Assurance Services defined assurance services as independent professional services that "improve the quality of information, or its context, for decision makers." Assurance services include, but go beyond attestation services in that they may involve analyzing data or putting it in a form to facilitate decision making.

2.   Attestation services are restricted to those services that involve issuing an examination, review, or agreed-upon procedures report on subject matter **or** an assertion about the subject matter that is the responsibility of another party.

   a.   The **subject matter** of an attest engagement may take many forms, including (1) historical prospective performance or condition information, (2) physical characteristics, (3) historical events, (4) analyses, (5) systems processes, or (6) behavior.

   b.   To perform an attestation engagement the practitioner generally must obtain an appropriate **assertion**—a declaration about whether the subject matter is presented in accordance with certain criteria.

   c.   The subject matter of an engagement is measured against **suitable criteria** that are objective and permit reasonably consistent measurements. Criteria are ordinarily suitable if they are developed by regulatory agencies or other bodes of experts that use due process. Criteria developed by management or industry groups without due process may or may not be suitable; the practitioner must make a determination of suitability. Some criteria are suitable in evaluating subject matter only for those who developed them (e.g., the terms of a contract between two parties).

   d.   Criteria must also be available and understandable to users. When criteria are only available to certain users, the practitioner's report should be restricted to those **specified parties.**

   e.   The eleven attestation standards provide a general framework for all attestation engagements.

3.   Like audit risk, **attestation risk** is the risk that the practitioners will unknowingly fail to appropriately modify their report on subject matter that is materially misstated. It also consists of the three components of inherent risk, control risk and detection risk.

4.   An attestation report should clearly describe the nature of the assurance being provided as an **examination**, a **review**, or **agreed-upon procedures** engagement.

   a.   An **examination** is designed to provide the highest level of assurance that CPAs provide—the same level provided by an audit of financial statements. Sufficient evidence is obtained to reduce attestation risk to an appropriately low level. Figure 19-4 on page 705 of the text provides an illustration of a standard unqualified examination report on subject matter.

   b.   A **review** involves performing limited procedures, such as inquiries and analytical procedures to gather sufficient evidence to reduce attestation risk to a moderate level and provide a report with limited assurance (also referred to as negative assurance). The report includes a statements such as "We are not aware of any material modifications that should be made in order for the information to be in conformity with the criteria." Figure 19-5 on page 705 of the text provides a standard unmodified review report on subject matter.

c.   An **agreed-upon procedures** engagement includes procedures agreed-upon by the specified users of the report and results in a report that includes a summary of the practitioners' findings. Reports on agreed-upon procedures are referred to as restricted use reports as contrasted to general use reports, such as those on examinations and reviews.

5.   CPAs may provide assurance on a client's internal control over financial reporting. This service has gained increased importance with the passage of the Sarbanes-Oxley Act of 2002, which requires that such an engagement be performed for SEC registrants as a part of the financial statement audit. In accordance with the attestation standards, CPA may examine (referred to as an audit when performed under the Sarbanes-Oxley Act's requirements) or perform agreed-upon procedures on these reports by management on internal control.

6.   When examining management's assertion about the effectiveness of an entity's internal control, the CPA (1) plan the engagement, (2) obtain an understanding of internal control, (3) evaluate the design and operating effectiveness of internal control, and (4) form an opinion on the fairness of management's assertion.

7.   A qualified report on internal control is issue when a **material weaknesses** in internal control exists, and that weakness is acknowledged in management's report. A disclaimer of opinion is issued if the scope of the accountants' procedures have been materially restricted, and an adverse opinion is issued if a material weakness of which the CPA is aware is not acknowledged in management's report.

8.   CPAs may be engaged to examine prospective financial statements (financial forecasts or projections) to provide third parties with assurance that the statements are presented in accordance with AICPA guidelines and that the underlying assumptions provide a reasonable basis for the statements. Prospective financial statements also may be compiled, or the accountants may be engaged to perform agreed-upon procedures on the them; a review service may not be performed on prospective financial statements. An example of a report on the **examination of a financial forecast** is presented on pages 707-708 of the textbook.

9.   Practitioners are permitted to perform an examination or agreed-upon procedures engagement on an entity's compliance with specified requirements of laws, regulations, rules, contracts or grants and may attest to the effectiveness of an entity's internal control over compliance with such specified requirements.

10.   **Management's discussion and analysis** (MD&A) of a public company is a required narrative explanation of financial results as reported in the financial statements filed with the SEC. When practitioners have audited the most recent financial statement period to which the MD&A relates, they may examine the company's MD&A. the objective of such an engagement is to provide assurance on whether (1) the presentation includes, in all material respects, the required elements of the rules and regulations adopted by the SEC, (2) the historical financial amounts included in the presentation have been accurately derived, in all material respects, from the entity's financial statements, and (3) the underlying information, determinations, estimates and assumptions of the entity provide a reasonable basis for the disclosures contained in the presentation.

11.   The public accounting profession is developing a set of **Trust Services** that are intended to address user and preparer needs regarding issues of security, availability, processing integrity, online privacy, and confidentiality within e-commerce and other systems.

12.   Trust Services address one or more of the following principles over a particular reporting period: (1) Security; (2) Availability; (3) Processing Integrity; (4) Online Privacy; and (5) Confidentiality. Each of the four principles have four criteria associated with them: (1) Policies; (2) Communication; (3) procedures; and (4) monitoring.

13.   At present two types of trust services have been developed. **WebTrust** provides assurance on electronic commerce systems. **SysTrust** provides assurance on any system.

14.   **ElderCare** services involve CPAs providing assurance to individuals that their elderly family members' needs are being met.

15.   Future assurance services are being developed in areas including risk assessment, business performance measurement, health care performance measurement and continuous auditing.

Test Yourself on Chapter 19

TRUE OR FALSE

For each of the following statements, circle the T or the F to indicate whether the statement is true or false.

T   F   1.   All attestation services are also assurance services.

T   F   2.   In an assurance engagement, a report may be oral, symbolic or in any other appropriate form.

T   F   3.   Attestation services are restricted to examinations, reviews, and agreed-upon procedures engagements.

T   F   4.   To perform an attestation engagement, the practitioners generally must obtain a low level of attestation risk.

T   F   5.   In an attestation engagement the practitioner's conclusion may be on the subject matter, the assertion, or on the suitability of criteria.

T   F   6   When an examination reveals material departures from suitable criteria, the practitioner should report directly upon the subject matter.

T   F   7   The AICPA attestation standards include standards of field work on planning, evidence and internal control.

T   F   8   Criteria developed by regulatory agencies that use due process are ordinarily suitable.

T   F   9   In addition to being suitable, criteria being followed must also be available to users in order for a practitioner to issue an examination report.

T   F   10   Attestation risk is composed of inherent risk, business risk, and detection risk.

T.   F   11   A limitation on the scope of an examination engagement will necessarily result in practitioner resignation.

T   F.   12   Reviews result in limited assurance, also referred to as positive assurance.

T   F.   13.   The purpose of a review is to provide users of the financial statements with reasonable assurance that the statements are prepared in conformity with generally accepted accounting principles (or some other comprehensive basis of accounting).

T   F   14.   A CPA's report on management's report on internal control must be modified for all reportable conditions that have been identified.

T   F   15.   The consideration of internal control performed as part of an audit generally is not sufficient to enable the CPAs to issue an opinion on management's report on internal control.

T   F   16.   CPAs may not examine financial forecasts prepared by a client.

T   F   17.   A financial projection represents expected future financial results for one or more future periods.

T   F   18.   A practitioner may be engaged to examine or review management's discussion and analysis.

T   F   19   WebTrust and SysTrust are both considered Trust Services.

T   F   20.   A Trust Services engagement may provide assurance on a system's security, availability, processing integrity, online privacy and confidentiality.

COMPLETION

Fill in the necessary words to complete the following statements.

1.   In an attestation engagement, the practitioner must evaluate the _____ _____ or an _____ about _____ _____ _____ that is the responsibility of another party.

2.   To perform an attestation engagement, the practitioner generally must obtain an appropriate _____ from the party responsible for the _____ _____.

3.   Suitable criteria are those that are _____ and permit reasonably _____ _____.

4.   Materiality for an attestation engagement may be considered in the context of _____ or _____ factors.

5.   When a practitioner is performing an examination, departure of subject matter from the criteria will generally result in a _____ or _____ opinion, depending on the _____ of the departure.

6.   The three forms of attestation engagements are _____, _____, and _____ _____.

7.   To present a report that includes an assertion about internal control, _____ should evaluate the company's internal control using some _____ _____.

8.   Estimates of the expected financial position, results of operations, and cash flows for a future period is termed a _____ _____.

9.   The practitioners' objective in an examination of management's discussion and analysis is to provide assurance on whether (1) the presentation includes, in all material respects, the required _____ of the _____ and regulations adopted by the SEC, (2) the historical _____ _____ included in the presentation have been accurately derived in all material respect from the financial

statements, and (3) the underlying information, determinations, estimates and assumptions of the entity

provide a _____ _____ for the _____ contained in the presentation.

10.   _____ _____ are intended to address user and preparer needs regarding issues of security,

availability, processing integrity, online privacy, and confidentiality within e-commerce and other

systems. At present the two types of services developed are _____ and _____.

MULTIPLE CHOICE

Choose the best answer for each of the following questions and enter the identifying letter in the space provided.

_____ 1.   Which of the following is not considered an attestation service?

   a. Agreed-upon procedures
   b. Compilation.
   d. Examinations.
   d. Review.

_____ 2.   Providing assurance using a series of reports provided simultaneously or shortly after the related information is released is referred to as:

   a. continuous auditing.
   b. reliability reporting.
   c. systems auditing.
   d. time intensive auditing.

_____ 3.   In which of the following circumstances is it **least** likely that an attest report will be restricted to specified parties?

   a. When reporting on subject matter and a written assertion has not been provided by the responsible party.
   b. When performing an examination and reporting directly upon the subject matter.
   c. When the criteria used to evaluate the subject matter are available only to specified parties.
   d. When the report is on an attest engagement to apply agreed-upon procedures to the subject matter.

_____ 4.   The practitioner may perform an attest engagement only if he or she has reason to believe that the

   a. subject matter is capable of evaluation against an assertion available to users.
   b. independence standards have been maintained by all practitioners within the client's controllership function.
   c. report to be issued is to be made publicly available,
   d. engagement is to be performed by a practitioner having adequate knowledge in the subject matter.

_____ 5.   Which of the following statements best describes a CPA's engagement to report on an entity's internal control over financial reporting?

a.   An attestation engagement to examine and report on management's written assertion about the effectiveness of its internal control.
b.   An audit engagement to render an opinion on the entity's internal control.
c.   A prospective engagement to project, for a period of time not to exceed one year, and report on the expected benefits of the entity's internal control.
d.   A consulting engagement to provide constructive advice to the entity on its internal control.

_____ 6.   The CPAs' examination report on a financial forecast should include all of the following except:

a.   a statement that the report will not be updated for future events.
b.   an indication that the CPAs' examination was in accordance with standards developed by the AICPA.
c.   the estimated probability of achieving the forecast results.
d.   whether the assumptions provide a reasonable basis for the forecast.

_____ 7.   The consideration of internal control made during an audit is generally:

a.   identical to that made in connection with an engagement designed to report on management's report on internal control.
b.   limited to controls rather than the accounting system.
c.   more limited than that made in connection with an engagement to report on management's report on internal control.
d.   less limited than that made in connection with an engagement designed to report on management's report on internal control.

_____ 8.   An examination of management's discussion and analysis (MD&A) is **least** likely to provide assurance on whether the

a.   presentation includes, in all material respects, the required elements of the rules and regulations adopted by the SEC.
b.   disclosures required by SEC requirements are properly presented.
c.   historical financial amounts included in the presentation have been accurately derived from the financial statements.
d.   the underlying information of the entity provides a reasonable basis for the discourses contained in the MD&A.

_____ 9.   Which of the following examinations is most likely to result in a CPA issuing a "restricted use" report?

a.   Financial projection.
b.   Internal control over financial reporting.
c.   Management's discussion and analysis.
d.   Trust Services.

_____ 10.   Which of the following is most likely to result in a CPA issuing a report that includes a seal or logo?

a.   Financial projection.
b.   Internal control over financial reporting.
c.   Management's discussion and analysis.
d.   Trust Services.

EXERCISES

1.   In the following figure, fill in the cells with "yes" if the statement is correct, and "no" if it is not correct.

	Assurance Services that are Attestation Services	Other Assurance Services
Are forms of engagements limited to examinations and reviews ?		
Must report form be written?		
Is independence required?		
Is conclusion only on reliability of information?		

2.   In the spaces provided, insert the words or phrases necessary to complete the following practitioners' examination report.

INDEPENDENT ACCOUNTANTS' REPORT

We have examined the accompanying schedule of investment performance statistics of Terrill Investment Fund for the year ended December 31, 20X2. This schedule is the responsibility of Terrill Investment Fund's management. Our responsibility is to (a)_____ on this schedule based on our examination.

Our examination was conducted in accordance with (b)_____established by the American Institute of Certified Public Accountants and, accordingly, included examining, on a test basis, evidence supporting the schedule and performing such other procedures as we considered necessary in the circumstances. We believe that our (c)_____ provides a (d)_____.

(e)_____, the schedule of investment performance statistics referred to above presents, (f)_____, the performance of Terrill Investment Fund for the Year ended December 31, 20X2, in conformity with the measurement and disclosure criteria set forth by the Association of Investment Management Research, Inc., as described in Note 1.

CHAPTER 20

Internal, Operational and Compliance Auditing

Highlights of the Chapter

1.   Internal auditing is an independent objective assurance and consulting activity designed to add value and improve an organization's operations.   It helps an organization accomplish its objectives by bringing a systematic, disciplined approach to evaluate and improve the effectiveness of risk management, control, and the governance processes.

2.   Originally, internal auditors work focused on financial controls. Gradually, their role expanded to encompass responsibilities for evaluating additional types of control, including both financial and operational controls.

3.   The expansion of internal auditing into operational activities required internal auditors with specialized knowledge in other disciplines, such as law, statistics, IT, engineering, and taxation.

4.   Several recent events have increased the demand for internal auditing, including

   a.   Foreign Corrupt Practices Act (1977)—requires public companies to establish and maintain effective internal accounting control.

   b.   *Report of the National Commission on Fraudulent Financial Reporting* (1987)—recommended that public companies establish an internal auditing function staffed with appropriately qualified personnel and fully supported by top management.

   c.   Blue Ribbon Committee Report on Audit Committee Effectiveness (1998)—concluded that oversight of financial integrity and accountability of public companies should be viewed as a three legged stool consisting of (1) management and internal audit, (2) the board of directors and its audit committee, and (3) the external auditors.

   d.   Sarbanes-Oxley Act (2002)—prohibited the same CPA firm from providing both internal and external auditing services for SEC reporting clients.

5.   The IIA's *Standards for the Professional Practice of Internal Auditing* sets forth the criteria by which the operations of an internal auditing department should be evaluated. These standards are presented in Figure 20-1 of the textbook.

6.   To achieve independence with respect to the activities audited:

   a.   the chief audit executive should report to a level within the organization that allows the internal audit activity to fulfill its responsibilities.

   b.   Internal auditors should have an impartial, unbiased attitude and avoid conflicts of interest.

   c.   If independence or objectivity is impaired, details should be disclosed to appropriate parties.

7.   To become a Certified Internal Auditor (CIA) an individual must: (1) successfully complete a two-day examination, (2) complete two years of work experience in internal auditing or its equivalent, and (3) have a baccalaureate degree from an accredited college.

8.   Operational audits focus on the **effectiveness**, **efficiency**, and **economy** of an organization or an operating unit.

9.   Operational audits are performed by internal auditors for top management and by government auditors for use by Congress and various regulatory agencies. CPAs also perform operational audits through their management advisory services departments.

10.   The steps in an operational audit include:

   a.   **Definition of purpose**—identification of the scope of the audit including the particular aspects of the organization, function, or group of activities to be audited.

   b.   **Familiarization**—obtaining a comprehensive knowledge of the objectives, organization structure, and operating characteristics of the unit being audited.

   c.   **Preliminary survey**—development of the auditors' preliminary conclusions about the critical aspects of the operations and potential problem areas.

   d.   **Program development**—development of a tailor-made program for the audit.

   e.   **Field work**—executing the operational audit program.

   f.   **Reporting the findings**—development of a report that includes suggested improvements in the operational policies and procedures of the unit and instances of noncompliance with existing policies and procedures. An example report appears on page 731.

   g.   **Follow–up**—determining whether the auditors' recommendations have been effectively implemented.

11.   Compliance auditing is designed to determine whether the organization is in compliance with particular laws and regulations.

12.   *Statement of Standards for Attestation Engagements 10* (SSAE 10) provides CPAs with guidance when they are engaged to attest to a organization's compliance with laws and regulations, or attest to a organization's internal control over compliance with laws and regulations. CPAs may be engaged either to apply agreed-upon procedures or perform an examination of an organization's compliance with specified requirements of laws or regulations, but they may not be engaged to perform a review of compliance.

13.   In a compliance engagement a CPA provides assurance on either management's assertion on compliance or directly on compliance.

14.   A major objective of compliance auditing is determining whether funds provided by the federal government (**federal financial assistance**) to state and local governments and certain nonprofit and business organizations are being spent in accordance with the requirements of the federal programs.

15.   A CPA's examination report on compliance is modified due to (1) material noncompliance with specified requirements, (2) scope restriction, and (3) involvement of another CPA firm in the examination.

16.   An organization receiving federal financial assistance may be required to obtain one of three types of audits: (1) an audit of its financial statements in accordance with generally accepted auditing standards, (2) an audit in accordance with *Government Auditing Standards*, or (3) an audit in accordance with the federal Single Audit Act of 1984.

17   In an audit in accordance with generally accepted auditing standards, the auditors have a responsibility to test for material misstatements resulting from violations of laws and regulations that have a **direct** and **material** effect on line-item financial statement amounts.

18.   State and local governments are subject to a variety of laws and regulations that have a direct effect on their financial statements--more than other types of organizations.

19.   Auditors identify the laws and regulations that affect the financial statements by (1) discussing laws and regulations with management, program and grant administrators, and government auditors, (2) reviewing grant or loan agreements, and (3) reviewing minutes of the legislative body of the governmental organization.

20.   The federal General Accounting Office (GAO) develops *Government Auditing Standards*, and an audit under these standards is often referred to as an audit in accordance with generally accepted governmental auditing standards (GAGAS), or the *Yellow Book*.

21.   In performing an audit in accordance with *Government Auditing Standards*, the auditors perform an audit of the financial statements in accordance with generally accepted auditing standards with a few additional requirements primarily related to communication, and report on two additional matters--on compliance with laws and regulations, and on the organization's internal control. This reports can be combined in various manners.

22.   Violations of a law or regulation that the auditors estimate to result in a material misstatement of the financial statements of the organization are referred to as **material instances of noncompliance**. Even if management corrects the financial statements for the effects of the violations, the auditors must still report the matter in their report on compliance with laws and regulations.

23.   An audit in accordance with the Single Audit Act of 1984 includes all of the requirements of an audit in accordance with *Government Auditing Standards* plus:

    a.   A supplementary schedule of federal financial assistance.

    b.   Compliance with requirements that may have a material effect on each major federal financial assistance program.

    c.   The controls relevant to federal financial assistance programs.

24.   State or local governments or not-for-profit organizations receiving $300,000 or more in federal financial assistance within a fiscal year must be audited in accordance with the Single Audit Act.

25.   Federal programs are classified as major based on a risk-based approach considering both the amount of the program's expenditures and their risk of material noncompliance. However, major programs, as determined by the auditors, must constitute at least 50 percent of the total federal expenditures of the organization.

26.   In a single audit the auditors must test compliance with the specific requirements of federal programs (activities allowed or unallowed, allowable costs, cash management, etc.)

27.   A summary of compliance auditing and reporting requirements is presented in Figure 20-6.

Test Yourself on Chapter 20

TRUE OR FALSE

For each of the following statements, circle the T or the F to indicate whether the statement is true or false.

T   F   1.   Internal auditors are considered to be an external control over top management.

T   F   2.   The primary users of internal auditors' reports are the independent auditors.

T   F   3.   Internal auditors first were used to help ensure the accuracy and timeliness of financial reports and prevent fraud.

T   F   4.   Ideally, the director of internal auditing should report directly to the audit committee of the board of directors.

T   F   5.   Independence and objectivity is one of the sections of the IIA's *Standards for the Professional Practice of Internal Auditing*.

T   F   6.   The American Institute of Certified Public Accountants issues the CIA designation.

T   F   7.   Most operational auditing is performed by CPAs.

T   F   8.   The operational auditors' understanding of the organization is documented with questionnaires, flowcharts, or written narratives.

T   F   9.   In performing an operational audit, the auditors typically use a standard audit program.

T   F   10.   Compliance auditing is designed to evaluate compliance with internal control.

T   F   11.   An example of a subrecipient is an individual who receives federal assistance from a legal aid society.

T   F   12.   Auditors perform compliance auditing procedures in audits in accordance with *Government Auditing Standards* but not in audits of financial statements under generally accepted auditing standards.

T   F   13.   State and local governments generally are subject to more laws and regulations that have a direct effect on their financial statements than business organizations.

T   F   14.   In an audit in accordance with *Government Auditing Standards*, the auditors must test compliance with all laws and regulations that affect major federal financial assistance programs.

T   F   15.   The specific requirements of federal programs are those that have a direct effect on the expenditures from the programs.

T   F   16.   Only state and local governments are required to have audits in accordance with *Government Auditing Standards*.

T   F   17.   In an audit in accordance with *Government Auditing Standards*, the auditors must perform more tests of compliance than in an audit in accordance with generally accepted auditing standards.

T   F   18.   Internal auditors may perform operational audits and financial audits for the same operating unit.

T   F   19.   Independence is required for performing compliance auditing.

T   F   20.   Audits in accordance with the Single Audit Act of 1984 focus on appropriate expenditures of funds among the various states.

COMPLETION

1.   Internal auditing is an _____, objective assurance and consulting activity designed to add value and improve an organization's _____.

2.   In 1977, passage of the _____ _____ _____ _____ increased the demand for internal auditing.

3.   The international organization of internal auditors is called the _____ _____ _____

      _____.

4.   An operational audit focuses on the _____, _____, and _____ of operations.

5.   The operational auditors' _____ _____ summarizes the auditors' preliminary conclusions about the critical aspects of the audit.

6.   An _____ _____ involves a meeting of the operational auditors and the persons directly concerned with the operations audited to discuss the audit findings.

7.   When auditing financial statements in accordance with generally accepted auditing standards, the auditors must test compliance with all laws and regulations that have a _____ and _____ effect on line–item amounts in the financial statements.

8.   In an audit in accordance with *Government Auditing Standards*, the auditors report on _____

      _____ _____ _____ _____, and on the organization's _____

      _____.

9.   Audits in accordance with the _____ _____ _____ are specifically designed to help ensure that the billions of dollars in federal financial assistance are appropriately spent.

10.   In an audit in accordance with the Single Audit Act, violations of laws and regulations that are

estimated to have a material effect on an organization's financial statements are referred to as

_____ _____ _____ _____ .

MULTIPLE CHOICE

Choose the best answer for each of the following questions and enter the identifying letter in the space provided.

_____   1.   When performing a financial type of audit for a governmental entity auditors generally do **not** report on:

a.   whether generally accepted accounting principles have been followed.
b.   economy and efficiency.
c.   compliance with laws and regulations.
d.   internal control.

_____   2.   The *Single Audit Act of 1984* applies to:

a.   only those state and local governments receiving specified levels of federal financial assistance.
b.   all state and local governments.
c.   all organizations required to have an audit in accordance with *Government Auditing Standards.*
d.   all organizations required to have an audit in accordance with *Government Auditing Standards* and other organizations that transact business with the federal government.

_____   3.   When performing financial statement audits the auditors perform tests of compliance with laws and regulations to determine that:

a.   civil statutes have not been violated.
b.   civil or criminal statutes have not been violated.
c.   any violations do not have a direct and material effect on line-item financial statement amounts.
d.   subrecipients of funds have appropriately spent funds prior to remitting them to recipients.

_____   4.   An internal auditor's independence is most likely to be assured if she reports to the:

a.   audit committee of the board of directors.
b.   controller.
c.   president.
d.   treasurer

_____   5.   Which of the following best describes the internal auditing function?

a.   A fraud prevention function.
b.   An integral part of the accounting system of an organization.
c.   A part of the organization's monitoring controls.
d.   A function that adds credibility to the financial information provided to third parties.

_____ 6. Which of the following is not one of the Attribute Standards of the IIA's *Standards for the Professional Practice of Internal Auditing?*

     a. Independence and objectivity.
     b. Proficiency and due professional care.
     c. Disclosure of noncompliance.
     d. Working papers.

_____ 7. Operational auditing focuses on all of the following, except:

     a. fairness.
     b. economy.
     c. efficiency.
     d. effectiveness.

_____ 8. During the field work stage of the operational audit, the auditors:

     a. develop the preliminary survey.
     b. perform various analyses.
     c. develop the audit program.
     d. familiarize themselves with the organization.

_____ 9. A typical objective of an operational audit is for the auditors to:

     a. determine that the financial statements fairly present the entity's operating results.
     b. evaluate the feasibility of achieving the entity's operational objectives.
     c. make recommendations for improving performance.
     d. report on the entity's success in maximizing profits.

_____ 10. Which of the following types of organizations receive funds directly from a federal agency?

     a. Subrecipient.
     b. Primary recipient.
     c. Prime funding agency.
     d. Ordinary recipient.

_____ 11. Which of the following is **not** a specific requirement for which auditors must best compliance for all major programs?

     a. Activities allowed or unallowed.
     b. Cash management.
     c. Program recidivism.
     d. Subrecipient monitoring.

_____ 12. *Government Auditing Standards* are developed by:

     a. the General Accounting Office.
     b. the AICPA.
     c. the Institute of Internal Auditors.
     d. the Governmental Auditing Standards Board.

EXERCISES

1.   Match the term in the first column with the related term or description in the second column.

	Term		Term or Description
___	1. General Accounting Office	a.	Substantive tests
___	2. Single audit	b.	Opinions on major federal assistance programs
___	3. Subrecipient	c.	Noncompliance
___	4. Compliance test	d.	Efficiency and effectiveness.
___	5. Specific requirements	e.	Pass–through funds
___	6. Operational audit	f.	*Government Auditing Standards*

2.   Describe the requirements of each of following types of audits.

a.   An audit in accordance with *Government Auditing Standards*.

b.   An audit in accordance with the Single Audit Act of 1984.

ANSWERS TO QUESTIONS AND SOLUTIONS TO EXERCISES

CHAPTER 1

TRUE OR FALSE

1.	F	6.	F	11.	T	16.	F
2.	F	7.	T	12.	F	17.	F
3.	T	8.	F	13.	F	18.	T
4.	F	9.	T	14.	F	19.	F
5.	T	10.	T	15.	F	20.	T

COMPLETION STATEMENTS

1. independence
2. attest
3. compilations; reviews
4. management
5. Securities and Exchange Commission; General Accounting Office
6. Public Company Accounting Oversight Board; peer reviews
7. proprietorships; corporations; limited liability companies (partnerships)
8. managers; senior auditors; staff assistants
9. continuing education
10. effectiveness; efficiency; management

MULTIPLE CHOICE

1.	a	4.	b	7.	b	10.	c
2.	c	5.	a	8.	a	11.	b
3.	c	6.	b	9.	d	12.	d

SOLUTIONS TO EXERCISES

1. SASs; Interpretations of generally accepted auditing standards
    Internal Revenue Service; Compliance audits
    Internal auditor; Operational audits
    Attest function; Providing credibility
    Audited financial statements; Dependable financial information
    Quality control; Peer review
    SEC; Protection of investors
    Accounting services by CPAs; Compilation of financial statements
    Consideration of internal control; Guide to the amount of testing and sampling
    Independence; Essential element for the attest function

2. a. 5
    b. 3
    c. 4
    d. 2
    e. 8
    f. 6
    g. 1
    h. 7

CHAPTER 2

TRUE OR FALSE

1.	F	6.	F	11.	F	16.	F
2.	T	7.	F	12.	T	17.	F
3.	F	8.	T	13.	T	18.	F
4.	T	9.	F	14.	T	19.	F
5.	T	10.	F	15.	T	20.	T

COMPLETION STATEMENTS

1. introductory; scope; opinion
2. Statements on Auditing Standards
3. generally accepted accounting principles
4. general standards; standards of field work; reporting standards
5. field work
6. the balance sheet; the statement of income; the statement of cash flows; the statement of retained earnings
7. authoritative body
8. quality control
9. assertion
10. International Auditing Practices; International Federation of Accountants

MULTIPLE CHOICE

1.	a	4.	a	7.	b	10.	d
2.	a	5.	c	8.	a	11.	d
3.	d	6.	b	9.	b	12.	c

SOLUTIONS TO EXERCISES

1.
1.	d	3.	e	5.	c
2.	b	4.	a	6.	f

2. a. **Objective:** To assure that professional staff maintain independence in all required circumstances , perform all professional services with integrity, and maintain objectivity in discharging professional responsibilities.

  Policy: An investigation is made to determine the firm's independence before accepting a new audit client.

  b. **Objective:** To assure that (1) those hired possess appropriate characteristics to perform competently, (2) work is assigned to those with appropriate technical training and proficiency, (3) personnel participate in appropriate continuing education and other professional development activities, and (4) personnel selected for advancement have necessary qualifications.

  Policy: Prospective employees are interviewed by both the personnel partner and a technical partner in the area in which they will work.

  c. **Objective:** Work performed meets applicable professional standards, regulatory requirements, and the firm's standards of quality.

  Policy: Working papers are reviewed by the manager, and any deficiencies are discussed with the preparer.

3. Case A   G2   Case D   FW2
    Case B   FW1   Case E   G3 FW2 FW3
    Case C   R4   Case F   G1 G3

CHAPTER 3

True or False

1.	T	6.	T	11.	T	16.	T
2.	T	7.	F	12.	T	17.	T
3.	F	8.	F	13.	T	18.	F
4.	T	9.	F	14.	F	19.	F
5.	F	10.	T	15.	F	20.	F

COMPLETION STATEMENTS

1. Principles; Rules
2. in fact; appear
3. direct financial interest; indirect
4. spouse; dependent
5. contingent
6. advisory; decision maker
7. Financial Accounting Standards Board; Governmental Accounting Standards Board
8. discreditable
9. false, misleading; deceptive
10. admonishment; suspension; expulsion

MULTIPLE CHOICE

1.	a	4.	c	7.	d	10.	a	13	c
2.	b	5.	b	8.	c	11.	b	14	b
3.	c	6.	d	9.	b	12.	d		

SOLUTIONS TO EXERCISES

1.   a. Yes
     b. No
     c. No
     d. Yes
     e. Yes

2.

a.	A		e.	J
b.	E		f.	D
c.	G		g.	G
d.	C		h.	F

CHAPTER 4

TRUE OR FALSE

1.	T	6.	T	11.	T	16.	F
2.	T	7.	F	12.	F	17.	F
3.	F	8.	T	13.	F	18.	F
4.	T	9.	T	14.	T	19.	T
5.	F	10.	F	15.	T	20.	F

COMPLETION STATEMENTS

1. proximate cause
2. common law
3. constructive fraud
4. relied; duly diligent
5. registration statement
6. BarChris
7. engagement letter
8. unaudited financial statements
9. review
10. 1136 Tenants' Corporation

MULTIPLE CHOICE

1.	d	4.	b	7.	a	10.	c
2.	c	5.	d	8.	b	11.	a
3.	d	6.	b	9.	b	12.	c

SOLUTIONS TO EXERCISES

1. a. Privity—the relationship between parties to a contract.
    b. Third–party beneficiary—a party who have been identified as directly benefiting from the contracted services and, thus, become in privity with the auditors and their clients.
    c. Fraud—intentional misrepresentation by one party that results in damages to another party.
    d. Negligence—failure to exercise due professional care.
    e. Gross negligence—failure to exercise even slight care.
    f. Foreseen third party—a limited class of users that is known to use the auditors' report.

2. a. A   d. B
    b. C   e. B
    c. A

CHAPTER 5

TRUE OR FALSE

1.	T	6.	F	11.	F	16.	T	21.	T
2.	T	7.	T	12.	F	17.	F	22.	T
3.	F	8.	F	13.	T	18.	F	23.	F
4.	F	9.	F	14.	F	19.	F	24.	F
5.	T	10.	T	15.	F	20.	F		

COMPLETION STATEMENTS

1. sufficient
2. inversely
3. valid; relevant
4. internal control; audit procedures
5. analytical procedures
6. confirmation
7. competence; assumptions
8. representation letter
9. standards of field work
10. working trial balance
11. lead schedules
12. permanent file
13. adjusting entries
14. changes
15. tick marks

MULTIPLE CHOICE

1.	a	4.	b	7.	b	10.	d	13.	d	16.	b		
2.	b	5.	c	8.	b	11.	a	14.	b	17.	a		
3.	d	6.	c	9.	a	12.	a	15.	c				

SOLUTIONS TO EXERCISES

1.
1.	g	5.	f
2.	d	6.	c
3.	b	7.	e
4.	a		

2.   a.   Analytical procedures are evaluations of financial information made by study of expected relationships between financial and nonfinancial data.

   b.   In planning analytical procedures can:

      (1)   provide a better understanding of the client's business, and
      (2)   identify balances that are more likely to contain material misstatements.

3.
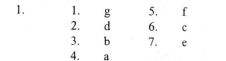

1	PF	4	PF	7	CF	10	PF
2	CF	5	PF	8	CF		
3	PF	6	CF	9	PF		

CHAPTER 6

TRUE OR FALSE

1.	F	6.	T	11.	F	16.	T
2.	T	7.	T	12.	F	17.	T
3.	T	8.	T	13.	T	18.	F
4.	T	9.	F	14.	T	19.	T
5.	T	10.	F	15.	F	20.	F

COMPLETION STATEMENTS

1. audit committee; employees; officers
2. fraudulent financial reporting; misappropriation of assets.
3. inherent risk; control risk; detection risk
4. audit plan; audit program; time budget
5. tests of controls; substantive procedures (tests)
6. interim date; risk
7. direct confirmation; vouching
8. substantive; evidence
9. representations; management
10. cutoff

MULTIPLE CHOICE

1.	b	4.	a	7.	c	10.	d	13.	b	16.	a
2.	d	5.	a	8.	c	11.	d	14.	b		
3.	c	6.	a	9.	d	12.	c	15.	d		

SOLUTIONS TO EXERCISES

1.   a. B
    b. D
    c. E
    d. A

2.   a. A, B, D
    b. A, C, D
    c. F
    d. A, B, D
    e. E

CHAPTER 7

TRUE OR FALSE

1.	F	6.	F	11.	T	16.	T
2.	F	7.	T	12.	T	17.	F
3.	T	8.	F	13.	F	18.	F
4.	T	9.	F	14.	F	19.	F
5.	F	10.	F	15.	T	20.	F

COMPLETION STATEMENTS

1. control environment; risk assessment; accounting information and communication system; control activities; monitoring
2. bribes; internal control
3. incompatible duties
4. general controls; application controls
5. collusion
6. control environment
7. fidelity bonds
8. internal control questionnaire
9. sampling; observation; inquiry
10. audit committee; board of directors

MULTIPLE CHOICE

1.	d	4.	c	7.	b	10.	a	13.	d
2.	b	5.	a	8.	b	11.	c	14.	d
3.	d	6.	c	9.	c	12	d		

SOLUTIONS TO EXERCISES

1. Characteristics of a company's control environment (only four required):

    a. integrity and ethical values
    b. commitment to competence
    c. board of directors or audit committee
    d. management philosophy and operating style
    e. organizational structure
    f. human resource policies and procedures
    g. assignment of authority and responsibility

2. a. Internal control questionnaire—a series of inquiries about the internal control structure; no answers generally indicate weaknesses.
    b. Internal control flowchart—a diagram symbolic representation of a system or series of procedures.
    c. Walk-through of the system—tracing one or more transactions through a system to verify the understanding of the system.
    d. Management letter—a letter to management from the auditors communicating suggestions for improvements in the client's internal control structure.

CHAPTER 8

TRUE OR FALSE

1.	F	6.	T	11.	F	16.	F
2.	T	7.	F	12.	T	17.	F
3.	F	8.	F	13.	T	18.	F
4.	F	9.	T	14.	T	19.	T
5.	F	10.	F	15.	F	20.	T

COMPLETION STATEMENTS

1. system; application
2. programmed; manual
3. librarian; computer operator
4. operations manual; instructions
5. message acknowledgment; echo check
6. validity test; input validation
7. hard disk drives
8. computer assisted audit
9. generalized audit software
10. service auditors; user auditors

MULTIPLE CHOICE

1.	c	4.	d	7.	a	10.	c	13.	a
2.	b	5.	a	8.	c	11.	d		
3.	a	6.	c	9.	d	12.	c		

SOLUTIONS TO EXERCISES

1.
    (1) g
    (2) e
    (3) a
    (4) b
    (5) f
    (6) c
    (7) h
    (8) d

2.   a. Hash total—a program control that helps ensure the accuracy of transaction processing. It is a total of one field of a batch of transactions that has no meaning other than as an internal control.

     b. Validity test—the test of a code (e.g., account or personnel) number against a master file of valid numbers.

     c. System software—software that controls the computer system and the processing of application programs.

     d. Echo check—a signal that is sent back to the central processing unit from a peripheral device confirming the performance of a function.

     e. Microcomputers—smaller computers that have less capacity and slower processing speed than main frame computers.

CHAPTER 9

TRUE OR FALSE

1.	T	6.	F	11.	F	16.	T
2.	F	7.	T	12.	F	17.	T
3.	F	8.	F	13.	F	18.	F
4.	F	9.	F	14.	T	19.	T
5.	T	10.	T	15.	F	20.	T

COMPLETION STATEMENTS

1. sampling error; population
2. nonstatistical
3. sampling with replacement
4. stratification; strata
5. risk of assessing control risk too low
6. risk of assessing control risk too low; deviation rate
7. allowance for sampling risk
8. standard deviation; increase
9. attribute sampling; substantive tests
10. analytical; details

MULTIPLE CHOICE

1.	d	4.	a	7.	a	10.	b	13.	a	16.	c	19.	b
2.	a	5.	b	8.	a	11.	d	14.	b	17.	a	20.	c
3.	b	6.	a	9.	b	12.	c	15.	a	18.	c		

SOLUTIONS TO EXERCISES

1.
   a. C
   b. A
   c. D
   d. B

2.
   a. Audit sampling—involves applying an audit procedure to less than 100 percent of a population to evaluate some characteristic of the population.
   b. Sampling risk—the risk that the auditors will come to a different conclusion from the sample than they would have come to had they examined the entire population.
   c. Nonsampling risk—the risk that the auditors will make an erroneous conclusion for any reason other than sampling (e.g., performing the wrong type of procedure).
   d. Risk of assessing control risk too low—the risk that the auditors will conclude that control risk is lower than it actually is.

CHAPTER 10

TRUE OR FALSE

1.	F	6.	T	11.	F	16.	F
2.	T	7.	F	12.	T	17.	T
3.	T	8.	F	13.	T	18.	F
4.	T	9.	T	14.	F	19.	F
5.	F	10.	T	15.	F	20.	F

COMPLETION STATEMENTS

1. cashier
2. mail room
3. prepared; signed
4. Confirm Account Balance Information with Financial Institutions; balance
5. cutoff bank statement
6. compensating balance
7. safe deposit box; joint
8. company
9. liquid assets
10. dividend records

MULTIPLE CHOICE

1.	d	4.	b	7.	b	10.	a
2.	b	5.	d	8.	a	11.	a
3.	b	6.	b	9.	d	12.	d

SOLUTIONS TO EXERCISES

1.
   - (1) b
   - (2) c
   - (3) a
   - (4) d
   - (5) e

2.
   - a. Prevents reusing the documents for support for other disbursements.
   - b. Prevents abstraction of cash receipts by personnel maintaining the records.
   - c. Prevents abstraction of cash receipts by cashier.
   - d. Prevents altering of checks.

CHAPTER 11

TRUE OR FALSE

1.	F	6.	F	11.	F	16.	T
2.	F	7.	F	12.	F	17.	F
3.	F	8.	T	13.	T	18.	F
4.	T	9.	F	14.	F	19.	F
5.	F	10.	T	15.	F	20.	T

COMPLETION STATEMENTS

1. credit department
2. bill of lading
3. collection agency
4. billing department
5. aged trial balance
6. shipping document
7. positive; negative
8. positive; second request
9. collections
10. related party receivables

MULTIPLE CHOICE

1.	b	4.	b	7.	c	10.	c
2.	a	5.	a	8.	d	11.	c
3.	d	6.	c	9.	d	12.	a

SOLUTIONS TO EXERCISES

1. (1) d
   (2) c
   (3) a
   (4) b

2. a. Helps insure that all shipments are billed to customers.
   b. Helps prevent conflict of objectives: maximizing sales versus collecting accounts.
   c. Prevents employees from taking collections of accounts that have been written-off.

CHAPTER 12

TRUE OR FALSE

1.	T	6.	T	11.	T	16.	T
2.	F	7.	T	12.	T	17.	F
3.	T	8.	F	13.	F	18.	T
4.	F	9.	T	14.	T	19.	F
5.	F	10.	F	15.	F	20.	T

COMPLETION STATEMENTS

1. planning; instructions
2. existence; rights
3. test counts; inventory listing
4. confirmed
5. pricing
6. net realizable value
7. receiving documents; cutoff
8. obsolescence
9. balance sheet
10. purchase orders

MULTIPLE CHOICE

1.	d	4.	d	7.	b	10.	a
2.	a	5.	d	8.	b	11.	a
3.	a	6.	c	9.	a	12.	a

SOLUTIONS TO EXERCISES

1. In planning the physical inventory, the client should consider (only four required):

   a. selecting the best date or dates
   b. suspending production
   c. segregating obsolete and defective goods
   d. establishing control over the counting process through the use of tags or sheets
   e. achieving proper cutoff of sales and purchase transactions
   f. arranging for the services of specialists

2. a. (1) Listing test counts in the working papers for later comparison to the final inventory listing.
      (2) Obtaining information on tag or sheet numbers used during the physical inventory for later comparison to final inventory listing.

   b. (1) Price testing of inventory by reference to current purchase invoices.

   c. (1) Examining receiving documents for goods received around year end.

   d. (1) Testing the clerical accuracy of the final inventory listing.

CHAPTER 13

TRUE OR FALSE

1.	T	6.	F	11.	F	16.	T
2.	F	7.	T	12.	F	17.	T
3.	T	8.	F	13.	F	18.	F
4.	F	9.	F	14.	F	19.	T
5.	F	10.	F	15.	T	20.	T

COMPLETION STATEMENTS

1. cutoff; net income
2. subsidiary ledger
3. revenue
4. retirement work order
5. repairs and maintenance
6. working papers
7. acquisition; retirements
8. ownership; property tax
9. goodwill; forty
10. capital lease

MULTIPLE CHOICE

1.	d	4.	a	7.	b	10.	c
2.	b	5.	d	8.	d		
3.	d	6.	c	9.	d		

SOLUTIONS TO EXERCISES

1. (1) e
    (2) a
    (3) c
    (4) d
    (5) b

2. a. A system of work orders is designed to help insure that all retirements of plant assets are approved and appropriately recorded.

    b. A subsidiary ledger of plant and equipment is designed to assure that proper control over individual plant and equipment is maintained.

    c. Handling all purchases of plant and equipment through the normal purchasing procedures allows these purchases go through all the authorization and approval processes that other purchases go through.

CHAPTER 14

TRUE OR FALSE

1.	T	6.	T	11.	F	16.	F
2.	F	7.	F	12.	F	17.	F
3.	T	8.	T	13.	T	18.	T
4.	F	9.	T	14.	F	19.	F
5.	F	10.	T	15.	F	20.	T

COMPLETION STATEMENTS

1. understatement; overstatement
2. completeness
3. confirmation
4. zero
5. material; adjusting journal entry
6. receiving report
7. related parties
8. representations
9. accrued liabilities
10. completeness; balance sheet

MULTIPLE CHOICE

1.	c	4.	a	7.	b	10.	a
2.	d	5.	a	8.	c	11.	a
3.	a	6.	c	9.	c	12.	a

SOLUTIONS TO EXERCISES

1.   (1) d
    (2) e
    (3) c
    (4) b
    (5) a

2.   a. (1) understatement of liabilities—$3,000
        (2) understatement of cost of goods sold—$3,000 overstatement of net income before taxes—$3,000

    b. (1) no effect
        (2) no effect

    c. (1) understatement of assets and liabilities—$8,000
        (2) no effect

    d. (1) understatement of liabilities—$1,000
        (2) understatement of expenses—$1,000 overstatement of net income before taxes—$1,000

CHAPTER 15

TRUE OR FALSE

1.	T	6.	T	11.	F	16.	T
2.	F	7.	F	12.	F	17.	T
3.	F	8.	F	13.	F	18.	T
4.	T	9.	F	14.	T	19.	F
5.	F	10.	F	15.	F	20.	F

COMPLETION STATEMENTS

1. indenture; trust indenture
2. current liability; waiver
3. intent; ability
4. premium; discount
5. dividend paying agent
6. registrar
7. issued; outstanding; registrar; transfer agent
8. net income; dividends
9. vouching; debt agreements; compliance
10. bylaws; board of directors

MULTIPLE CHOICE

1.	c	4.	c	7.	c	10.	d
2.	a	5.	a	8.	a		
3.	a	6.	a	9.	a		

SOLUTIONS TO EXERCISES

1. a. Indenture--the formal document creating bonded indebtedness.

    b. Bond trustee--represents the interests of the bondholders and monitors compliance with the covenants of the bond indenture.

    c. Stock registrar--to help ensure that the corporation does not over-issue its stock.

    d. Stock transfer agent--an independent party that handles transfers of stock between stockholders.

2. Answer (three required)

    a. Determine the date and amounts of dividends authorized.
    b. Verify the amounts paid
    c. Determine the amount of any preferred dividends in arrears.
    d. Review the treatment of unclaimed dividend

CHAPTER 16

TRUE OR FALSE

1.	T	6.	T	11.	T	16.	F	21.	T
2.	T	7.	F	12.	F	17.	T	22.	T
3.	T	8.	T	13.	T	18.	T	23.	T
4.	F	9.	F	14.	F	19.	F	24.	F
5.	F	10.	F	15.	T	20.	T		

COMPLETION STATEMENTS

1. asset; liability
2. misstatement
3. personnel
4. paymaster
5. disclosure checklist
6. representation letter
7. last day of field work
8. known; projected; other estimated
9. adjust; qualified; adverse
10. read; inconsistencies
11. subsequent event
12. proforma

MULTIPLE CHOICE

1.	c	4.	a	7.	c	10.	d	13.	a
2.	d	5.	c	8.	d	11.	b		
3.	d	6.	d	9.	a	12.	c		

SOLUTIONS TO EXERCISES

1.   a.   Depreciation; repairs and maintenance expenses; gains and losses on the sale of fixed assets
   b.   Interest expense; amortization of discount or premium; gain or loss on retirement of long–term debt
   c.   Cost of goods sold
   d.   Uncollectible account expense; sales

2.   a.   Obtain lawyer's letter
   b.   Obtain the letter of representations
   c.   Perform other procedures to identify subsequent events
   d.   Perform overall review using analytical procedures
   e.   Complete the search for unrecorded liabilities
   f.   Review the working papers

3.
(1)	ND	(4)	ND
(2)	A	(5)	D
(3)	D	(6)	D

CHAPTER 17

TRUE OR FALSE

1.	T	6.	F	11.	F	16.	F
2.	F	7.	T	12.	T	17.	F
3.	F	8.	T	13.	T	18.	T
4.	F	9.	F	14.	F	19.	F
5.	T	10.	F	15.	T	20.	T

COMPLETION STATEMENTS

1. firm; partner
2. opinion
3. unqualified
4. unqualified; explanatory paragraph
5. except for; adverse
6. amount; nature
7. qualified; adverse
8. disclaimer of opinion
9. explanatory paragraph
10. update

MULTIPLE CHOICE

1.	b	4.	b	7.	b	10.	a
2.	b	5.	b	8.	b	11.	a
3.	c	6.	b	9.	c	12.	d

SOLUTIONS TO EXERCISES

1. a B ; D
    b. C; C
    c. C; C
    d. B; E

2. a. No; Yes
    b. Yes; Yes
    c. No; Yes
    d. No; Yes
    e. No; Yes

CHAPTER 18

TRUE OR FALSE

1.	F	6.	F	11.	T	16.	T
2.	T	7.	T	12.	F	17.	F
3.	T	8.	F	13.	F	18.	F
4.	F	9.	T	14.	T	19.	T
5.	T	10.	T	15.	T	20.	F

COMPLETION STATEMENTS

1. special report
2. Auditing Standards Board; compilation; Accounting and Review Services Committee
3. inquiries; analytical
4. review; compilation
5. accountants
6. compliance; audit
7. underwriters; reasonable investigation
8. read; misstatements.
9. financial condition; completeness
10. generally accepted accounting principles; accounting principles

MULTIPLE CHOICE

1.	b	4.	d	7.	d	10.	d
2.	a	5.	c	8	d	11.	c
3.	a	6.	a	9.	a	12.	c

SOLUTIONS TO EXERCISES

1.
a.	1, 2	g.	3
b.	3, 4	h.	X
c.	4	i.	3
d.	X	j.	1
e.	4	k.	X
f.	3, 4	l.	2

2.
   a. reviewed
   b. Statements on Standards for Accounting and Review Services issued by the American Institute of Certified Public Accountants
   c. representation of the management
   d. inquiries
   e. analytical procedures
   f. less in scope
   g. opinion
   h. do not express such an opinion
   i. not aware of any material

CHAPTER 19

TRUE OR FALSE

1.	T	6.	T	11.	T	16.	F
2.	T	7.	F	12.	F	17.	F
3.	T	8.	T	13.	F	18.	T
4.	F	9.	T	14.	F	19.	T
5.	F	10.	F	15.	T	20.	T

COMPLETION STATEMENTS

1. subject matter; assertion; the subject matter
2. assertion; subject matter
3. objective; consistent measurements
4. quantitative; qualitative (nonquantitative)
5. qualified; adverse; materiality
6. examinations; reviews; agreed-upon procedures.
7. management; control criteria
8. financial forecast
9. elements; rules; financial amounts; reasonable basis; disclosures
10. Trust Services; WebTrust; SysTrust

MULTIPLE CHOICE

1.	b	4.	a	7.	c	10.	d
2.	a	5.	a	8.	a		
3.	b	6.	c	9.	a		

SOLUTIONS TO EXERCISES

1.

	Assurance Services that are Attestation Services	Other Assurance Services
Are forms of engagements are limited to examinations and reviews?	No (also includes agreed-upon procedures)	No (intended to be more flexible)
Must report form must be written?	Yes	No
Is independence required?	Yes	Yes
Is conclusion only on reliability of information?	Yes	No

2.   a.   express an opinion
   b.   attestation standards
   c.   examination
   d.   reasonable basis for our opinion
   e.   In our opinion
   f.   in all material respects

CHAPTER 20

TRUE OR FALSE

1.	F	6.	F	11.	F	16.	F
2.	F	7.	F	12.	F	17.	F
3.	T	8.	T	13.	T	18.	T
4.	T	9.	F	14.	F	19.	T
5.	T	10.	F	15.	T	20.	F

COMPLETION STATEMENTS

1.   independent; operations
2.   Foreign Corrupt Practices Act
3.   Institute of Internal Auditors
4.   efficiency; effectiveness; economy
5.   preliminary survey
6.   exit conference
7.   direct; material
8.   compliance with laws and regulations; internal control
9.   Single Audit Act
10. material instances of noncompliance

MULTIPLE CHOICE

1.	b	4.	a	7.	a	10.	b
2.	a	5.	c	8.	b	11.	c.
3.	c	6.	d	9.	c	12.	a

SOLUTIONS TO EXERCISES

1. (1) f   (4) a
   (2) b   (5) c
   (3) e   (6) d

2. a.   An audit in accordance with *Government Auditing Standards* includes:
   (1)   An audit in accordance with generally accepted auditing standards, including an opinion on the financial statements.
   (2)   A combined report on compliance with laws and regulations and on the organization's internal control.

   b.   An audit in accordance with the Single Audit Act includes:
   (1)   The requirements of an audit in accordance with *Government Auditing Standards*.
   (2)   A report on the schedule of financial assistance received.
   (3)   A report on compliance with the requirements applicable to major federal programs.
   (4)   A report on internal control used in administering federal assistance programs.